A LILY AMONG THORNS

THE MOHAWK REPATRIATION OF
KÁTERI TEKAHKWÍ:THA

DARREN BONAPARTE

AHKWESÁHSNE MOHAWK TERRITORY
2009

For information about permissions, or to inquire about bulk purchases of this book, address all correspondence to either of the following mailing addresses or via the internet:

The Wampum Chronicles
c/o The Mohawk Territory of Akwesasne
P. O. Box 459, Akwesasne QC Canada H0M 1A0
P. O. Box 1026 Akwesasne NY USA 13655
Phone: 613-575-9985
E-mail: wampumchronicles@hotmail.com
Website: www.wampumchronicles.com

First published 2009 by The Wampum Chronicles.
First Printing 2009.

Library of Congress Control Number: 2008910520

ISBN: 1-4392-1791-2

ACKNOWLEDGEMENTS

I would like to extend my gratitude to a number of individuals who assisted me in making this book a reality. First, I would like to thank R. *Kakwirakeron* Montour for taking on the monumental task of creating the beautiful pen and ink illustrations that appear throughout this volume. They exceeded all of my expectations.

I would also like to thank those whose photographs eventually became the illustrations that appear in this book: Kim Terrance, *Teioswathe* Cook, *Kahawinetha* Thompson, Kathy Jock, Kiera Thompson, Bobby Padlayat, Al White, Gary Sundown, Nancy Bomberry, Tom Clair and Brant Davis. Some of these were posed specifically for this book while others were taken from other projects I've been involved in over the years. I regret that we were not able to use all of the models for illustrations, but I hope they at least had fun being draped in heavy wool blankets for the afternoon! Brant went above and beyond the call of the duty by accompanying me on a research trip to Albany, and never complaining when the car broke down on the highway and we were forced to wait for an hour or so for a tow truck. Thanks also to Molly Scofield and her colleagues at the New York State Museum for their assistance in accessing the archaeological collections once we finally arrived.

Niawen-kowa to Cathy Rice, Deacon Ron Boyer, and Albert and Elaine Lazare who assisted me during my research visits to the Kateri Center and the St. François Xavier Church in Kahnawà:ke. Thanks also to Thomas *Teyowisonte* Deer and my anonymous language consultants for their assistance in standardizing and translating the many Kanien'keha words that appear in this book. I'd also like to thank my friend Brian Rice for allowing me to quote from an unpublished manuscript he wrote.

Special thanks to Professor Laurence M. Hauptman for reviewing the manuscript and offering many helpful comments; to Diego Paoletti for sharing his own research into the original French documents; and to Charles Tibble, the New York City photographer who not only agreed to let me use his photograph of the Káteri statue at St. Patrick's Cathedral, but went back to take more! Thanks also to Gisele Poirier for bringing her desktop publishing skills and talents to this book and my previous one.

Finally, I would like to thank my family for their patience and support throughout the writing of this book. My mother, who has been an advocate and follower of Káteri for many years, inspired me to write this biography. This book is dedicated to her.

Darren Bonaparte

TABLE OF CONTENTS

Introduction 9

1. Spirit Meets Girl 13
2. The Serpents of Silver and Gold 17
3. Sighting of the First Europeans 23
4. Jacques Cartier at Hochelaga 27
5. Samuel de Champlain at Ticonderoga 36
6. Treachery and Treaty with New Netherland 45
7. Keepers of the Eastern Door 53
8. People of the Longhouse 62
9. The Devil's Nephews 71
10. Village of the Turtle Clan 80
11. Councils with the Dutch, 1657-1660 85
12. Early Childhood of Tekahkwí:tha 93
13. 1666: The Year of the Beast 101
14. A Mohawk Apocalypse 111
15. A Layer of Ash 119
16. Return of the Black Robes 125
17. Baptism by Fire 133
18. A Lily Among Thorns 141
19. Journey to the Village of Prayer 149
20. The New Kahnawà:ke 155
21. Divine Fire 163
22. Wari Teres Tekaien'kwénhtha 172
23. "I Will Not Marry." 181
24. The Great Penances 187
25. Bride of Christ 195
26. A Bed of Thorns 205
27. "I Will Love You in Heaven ..." 213
28. Apparitions and Miracles 225
29. Life After Káteri 233
30. A Prophecy Fulfilled 239
31. Genevieve of Canada 251
32. The Mohawk Repatriation of Káteri Tekahkwí:tha 259

References 275
Bibliography 290
Appendix 295

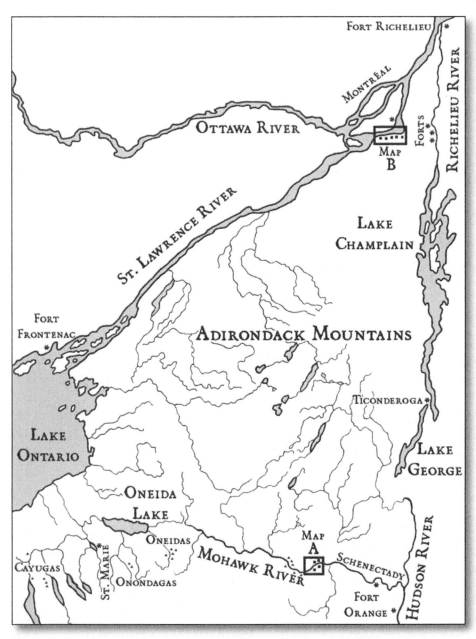

Map of locations mentioned in *A Lily Among Thorns*. Small triangles designate the location of Iroquois villages at various points in the life of Káteri Tekahkwí:tha. Maps by the author.

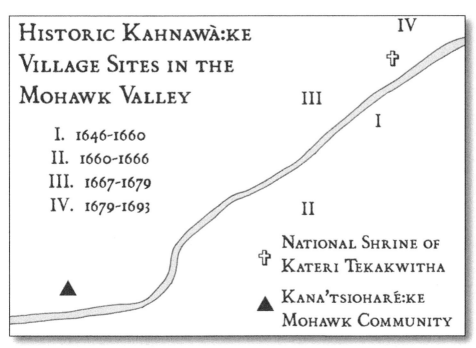

Historic Kahnawà:ke Village Sites in the Mohawk Valley

I. 1646–1660
II. 1660–1666
III. 1667–1679
IV. 1679–1693

✝ National Shrine of Kateri Tekakwitha

▲ Kana'tsioharé:ke Mohawk Community

Map A

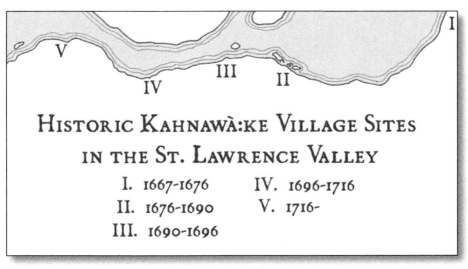

Historic Kahnawà:ke Village Sites in the St. Lawrence Valley

I. 1667–1676   IV. 1696–1716
II. 1676–1690   V. 1716–
III. 1690–1696

Map B

As the lily among thorns,
so is my love among the daughters.

The Song of Solomon 2:2

INTRODUCTION

Iroquois annalists periodize their history by the achievements of three prophets. Native theory speaks first of a time of Sapling, who brought cultural benefits to the people after the formation of the earth. The second period is that of Deganawi:dah, the Peacemaker, who founded the League of the Longhouse, or Iroquois League, and initiated the period of confederacy. The third period comprises the time since Handsome Lake, the Seneca Prophet—the nineteenth and twentieth centuries.

Dr. William N. Fenton[1]

With the above quote, the most learned scholar of Iroquoian studies demonstrated the "western Iroquois" bias that has dominated the literature on the Iroquois for generations.

To the Mohawks of the St. Lawrence River, the third prophet doesn't apply. We left the Mohawk Valley in the mid 1600's, long before Handsome Lake, or *Skaniatarí:io*, had his visions. Recitals of Handsome Lake's code, also known as *Kariwí:io*, did not occur in the communities of *Kahnawà:ke*, *Kanehsatà:ke*, and *Ahkwesáhsne* until the early part of the 20th century, and today not all traditional Mohawks accept Skaniatarí:io's teachings.

Scholars have in the past dismissed us as "praying Indians" who abandoned our ancestral traditions in favor of Christianity. Even Seneca scholar Arthur C. Parker wrote us off as all but assimilated in his 1913 *The Code of Handsome Lake, the Seneca Prophet:*

> There is no record of Handsome Lake visiting Tuscarora, Oneida, or St. Regis. The result is that these reservations contain only Indians who are nominally Christian. The Oneidas are virtually citizens, the Tuscarora as capable of being so as any community of whites, and the St. Regis progressive enough not only to use all their own lands but to rent from the whites. Their "Indianess" is largely gone. They have no Indian customs though they are affected by Indian folk-thought and exist as Indian communities, governing themselves and receiving annuities. Their material culture is now largely that of the whites about them and they are Indians only because

they dwell in an Indian reservation, possess Indian blood and speak an Iroquois dialect.[2]

One would think that Parker would have been able to recognize *some* degree of cultural persistence where others saw only assimilation. It is an unfortunate habit of some natives to disparage the "Indianess" of other tribes, and it may have been that Parker was guilty of a little of that himself in his time. The result of this characterization, appearing as it does in one of the most widely read books on the subject, *Parker on the Iroquois*, was an unfortunate gap in the anthropological literature that scholars have only lately begun to fill.

Recent scholarship has begun to recognize that the culture of the Mohawks of the St. Lawrence River Valley didn't magically disappear at baptism, but simply took on a new dimension. In fact, we used our knowledge of Iroquois diplomacy to forge a new peace with our former enemies, the Abenaki, Algonquin, and Huron. The alliance we created was known in our language as *Tsiá:ta Nihononhwentsá:ke*.[3] Colonials knew it as the Seven Nations of Canada.

Dr. Fenton's model of Iroquois cultural epochs can still be applied to us if we recognize that our third epoch began a century or so earlier than the one begun by Handsome Lake. Ours began with a prophet of sorts, a Mohawk mystic who has been largely ignored by Iroquoianists over the years—another victim of the assimilation myth that hangs over our people. The visions and miracles associated with this Mohawk mystic gave the people of the Seven Fires something more than just a political connection, but a spiritual one as well. Would it have worked any other way?

This "third prophet" was none other than *Kateri Tekahkwí:tha*, the "Lily of the Mohawks"—the 17th century woman who is one miracle away from being canonized as a saint by the Roman Catholic Church. In a way that has nothing at all to do with Christianity, her story completes a cosmological trilogy begun with the Iroquois creation story and its sequel, the epic of confederation. That we have all somehow missed this third manifestation of Iroquois mythic symbolism is a testament to the persuasive skills of the Jesuit fathers, who convinced us all that she could only be a symbol in *their* cultural world.

I present here a reconstruction of the life of the Mohawk maiden based on several biographies written by the Jesuit priests who knew her, contemporary historical documentation about the 17th century, current archaeological information about the places where she lived, and a few notable secondary accounts that have been published over the years. I set out to write about her life not from the usual devotional perspective, but from a "Longhouse" point of view, placing her story within the greater context of our cultural history. For far too long, her story has been burdened by the "between two worlds" cliché that paints Europeans and Indians as totally alien cultures from two different planets, whereas the real story was one of connections made and commonalities recognized. The Jesuits did not help matters any by painting the New World in stark black and white, with the Indians firmly under the sway of the devil until saved by Christian teachings. This has turned many a Mohawk off from the story of Káteri Tekahkwí:tha and the critical events of the 17th century. I have attempted to correct this situation by reading between the lines of the Jesuit biographies, searching other sources for what they left out, and keeping a healthy sense of skepticism about their portrayal of the Mohawks who rejected their teachings.

It is one of the greatest ironies of our history that the most famous Mohawk of all time was a woman who, by way of her vow of celibacy, wasn't an ancestor to any of us. Today the tendency among her people is to return to the traditional ways of the Longhouse, which is the opposite of what Káteri did by embracing Christianity. The story of her life may seem irrelevant to modern Mohawk sensibilities, but when you dig a little deeper you quickly realize that she has a great deal to teach us. The sources tell us that Káteri was noted for her skills as a traditional artisan, making everything from bark baskets, corn pounders, canoes, burden straps, beadwork, and even wampum belts. She also witnessed some of the most pivotal events in our history, such as the burning of our villages at the hands of a French army when she was just ten years old.

As a nation that has labored to repatriate cultural artifacts from museums around the world, the time has come for us to reclaim the memory of the Mohawk woman behind the porcelain icon. We can begin this process by confronting the documentation I have assembled in this book, because they reveal the truth about what really took place at the Indian missions. The people that wrote these documents never imagined that we would ever read them, so consider this a rare opportunity to see what was added to our "file."

It's the least we can do for our little sister.

1

SPIRIT MEETS GIRL

Our creation story tells us that the entire world was once covered with water as far as the eye could see—if there were an eye to see it. One day, the creatures of this endless sea looked up to see a pregnant woman falling from the sky. This "Sky Woman" was named *Iottsítsen*, or "Mature Flowers," and she came from a place we call *Karonhià:ke*, or "Sky World." A flock of birds caught her on their wings and gently lowered her to the shell of a sea turtle, which had risen from the primordial depths to provide her with a place to land. A muskrat dove to the bottom of the sea and brought up some of the soil in his paw. Iottsítsen walked about and sprinkled this soil on the shell of the turtle, causing it to grow. This was the origin of the continent of North America, which we call "Great Turtle Island" to this day.

Iottsítsen soon gave birth to a daughter. She named her *Tekaweráhkwa*, which means "Gusts of Wind."

> As years passed, the woman and her daughter did their best to adapt to their new surroundings. One night, after her daughter had developed to maturity, she was visited by a spirit of the "west wind."
>
> As the daughter gazed upon the visitor, she felt uneasy, but a strange feeling overcame her, and she fainted into a peaceful sleep. Later, her mother came by to awaken her and found two crossed arrows on her stomach. One was sharp, and the other was blunt. She realized what had happened, that her daughter had become pregnant. She realized also that her daughter was going to have twins.[4]

When it was time for them to be born, one was born the natural way, but the other grew impatient and cut his way out through his mother's side, killing her. The impatient one became known as *Tawískaron*, or "Flint," because he had rough skin and a sharp ridge on his head. The other was known as *Okwirá:se*, or "Sapling," and he looked more like his mother and grandmother.

Iottsítsen buried her daughter, and from her head grew corn, beans, and squash—the "Three Sisters." From her heart grew sacred tobacco, the smoke of which carries our words of thanksgiving to the Creator. From her feet grew strawberries and plants that we use as medicines. Some say we call the earth "our mother" because of Tekaweráhkwa.

To make a long story short—which we really shouldn't do—Iottsítsen's grandsons grew up and began to create many of the things that we see on earth today. When Okwirá:se made something, Tawískaron would put his little twist on it. When Okwirá:se created a rose, Tawískaron put thorns on it. When Okwirá:se created a river, Tawískaron would add the rapids.

One of the things Okwirá:se made were human beings, little replicas of himself. They were taught that they had special duties to take care of the living creatures, and to give thanks for everything above, around and below them.[5]

These creatures began to multiply, and as time went by, they divided themselves into separate nations and began to quarrel among themselves. They began to make war upon each other and forgot their original teachings. This was Tawískaron's contribution to the human beings.

One day a woman named *Kahentókta,* or "End of the Field," decided that all of the wickedness made her village an unfit place to raise her daughter, *Kahentéhso'k,* or "She Walks Ahead." She took her daughter into the woods and built a home for them away from the troubles.

Kahentéhso'k grew to maturity without ever knowing a man, just like Iotsitsisen's daughter. And just like Tekaweráhkwa, a powerful spirit came to her in the middle of the night and caused a baby to form inside her womb:

> In the course of time, notwithstanding, she showed signs of conception and her mother was very much aggrieved. The mother, therefore, spoke to her daughter and said: "I am going to ask you a question and I want you to tell me the truth. What has happened to you and how is it that you are going to bear a child?" Then the daughter replied and said, "Mother I will tell you the truth, I do not know how I became with child."[6]

Kahentókta did not believe her daughter and began to mistreat her, convinced that her daughter had lied to her about the pregnancy.

It so happened that as the time approached when the daughter would deliver the child, that the mother dreamed that she
saw a man whom she did not know, and that he said that he
appeared as a messenger to her on account of her troubled
mind, caused by the condition of her daughter who had in so
mysterious manner conceived a child.

"I am here to deliver you a message and now I will ask you
to cease your grieving and trouble of mind, and the ill-treat-
ment of your daughter from day to day because it is indeed a
fact that your daughter does not know how she became with
child. I will tell you what happened. It is the wish of the
Creator that she should bear a child, and when you will see the
male child you shall call him Dekanahwideh. The reason you
shall give him that name is because this child will reveal to
men-beings ... the Good Tidings of Peace and Power from
Heaven, and the Great Peace shall rule and govern on earth,
and I will charge you that you and your daughter should be
kind to him because he has an important mission to perform
in the world, and when he grows up to be a man do not
prevent him from leaving home."[7]

The child was born soon after, and just as the spirit commanded, he
was named *Tekanawí:ta*—"In Two Currents." He grew up faster than
normal boys, and would often disappear into the woods for great lengths
of time to carve a canoe out of stone. This would be a sign to all men
that he had been sent by the Creator. When the stone canoe was
finished, he pushed it into the water, climbed aboard, and set out on his
mission to bring peace to the warring nations.

With the assistance of *Aionwà:tha*, an Onondaga chief, Tekanawí:ta
united the Mohawk, Oneida, Onondaga, Cayuga, and Seneca into a
powerful confederacy, bound together by the *Kaianere'kó:wa*, or the
"Great Law of Peace, Power and Righteousness." We came to be known
as the *Rotinonhsión:ni*—"the People of the Longhouse"—not just because
we lived in a bark longhouse, or *Kanonhsión:ni*, but because we were to
be considered as one family.[8]

In acknowledgement of the important role women played in the
creation of our world, the Rotinonhsión:ni adhered to a matrilineal clan
structure. All rights and privileges descended from the mother's line.

This was purely logical, as it was always known who the mother of a child was, even if its paternity was in question. In days of old, it was the women who controlled the village and the fields, while the men took care of hunting, fishing, warfare, and diplomacy. It was the women who determined which of the men would be chiefs. This was also logical, as it was the women who knew which of the children were hard workers and generous of spirit, having raised them in the village while the men were rambling about. Not only did the women choose who spoke for them, they told them what to say.

When Europeans came to Great Turtle Island, they were astonished to find a society that gave women such a powerful voice. In their culture, all rights and privileges came down through the father's line. They did have one thing in common with the Rotinonhsón:ni, however: they revered a woman who had given birth to a child without having ever been with a man. As they sat down and listened to our ancestors recount our stories, they were surprised to learn that we were already familiar with the concept of a virgin birth. Thus, an important connection was made. They had an "in."

In less time than it takes for a child to grow up and then grow old, the newcomers were able to get many of our people to embrace a new epic myth. The mystical union of a virgin woman and a powerful spirit, so central to our cosmological thinking, was our bridge from one belief system to the next. Could our ancestors have seen Sky Woman's daughter, the Peacemaker's mother, and the Virgin Mary as a kind of feminine "Holy Trinity?" If this was the case, was Christianity as alien to our ancestors as many would have us believe?

2

THE SERPENTS OF
SILVER AND GOLD

The People of the Longhouse come together on a semi-annual basis to recite the epic stories of our cultural history. Told in our traditional languages, they take several days to tell properly. The Peacemaker legend, in fact, takes the better part of a week to tell in its entirety. The storyteller goes to great lengths to describe the things that happen in each nation the Peacemaker visits. There is a part of the story that is usually left out of the telling, however.

According to a Mohawk version of the story, the Peacemaker had one last teaching to impart to the Five Nations before he left them. It was prophecy of what was to befall the Five Nations in the Peacemaker's absence.

I first heard the story from Mohawk elder *Sakokwenonkwas* (Tom Porter) many years ago. To my knowledge, it was first published in 1980 in *7 Generations: A History of the Kanienkehaka*, a Mohawk history book written by David Blanchard for the Kahnawà:ke Survival School. Doug George-Kanentiio published another version in his book, *Iroquois Culture & Commentary*, in 2000. Since none of the Golden Age Iroquoianists like Lewis Henry Morgan, Arthur Parker, and J. N. B. Hewitt mentioned it, it is considered somewhat apocryphal, or of dubious origin—if it is even considered at all.

Here is how Blanchard tells the story:

> The story is told that a long time ago, before the time that Europeans arrived in the Americas, two hunters went out over the Great Water to look for a new hunting territory. Game was scarce in Kanienkeh, and they hoped to find more food beyond the horizon in the east.
>
> These two hunters set out in their canoe for a richer game. After they had gone out beyond the horizon's edge, they noticed a glowing in the distance. They quickened their paddling and came upon a very strange sight. There in the water were two

small serpents, one gold and one silver. These serpents were glowing and turned the sky into wonderful colors.

The two hunters were amazed at the beauty of the serpents. They did not want to leave them in the water for fear they would drown or else be eaten by a large fish. They knew if they brought these serpents back to their own nation, the people would admire the serpents and call the two hunters men of great skill and daring. They paddled up close to the serpents and scooped them up into their canoe.

Before the two hunters returned to their village, the people could see them approaching from the great light that glowed from the serpents. When the hunters reached their homes with their prize, the people were impressed by the catch. Everybody crowded around the serpents to watch the beautiful light that they gave off.

The people kept the serpents in an extra canoe. They were fed daily, and soon began to eat twenty four hours a day. They grew too large for the canoe, and had to be moved to a stockade especially built for that purpose. At first the serpents were fed mosquitoes, flies and other insects. As they grew larger they ate small animals like rabbits, raccoons and muskrats. Soon they grew so large that they needed to be fed deer and finally moose.

One day the serpents grew so large that they managed to escape from their stockade pen. They attacked the children and swallowed quite a few of them whole. The people were in terrible circumstances. They could see the children squirming around in the bellies of the huge gold and silver serpents.

They attacked these serpents with clubs, with arrows and with spears, but to no avail. The serpents continued to ravage through the village, killing more and more of the people and swallowing more of the children. Finally they left the village and headed for the woods.

The people fought amongst themselves as to what to do. They couldn't agree as to what was the best way to stop the serpents. They fought until it became too late and the serpents disappeared. The gold serpent went south, and the silver one headed north.

These serpents left trails wherever they went. They cut through mountains and blocked up the rivers. They killed all of the animals wherever they went, not always stopping to eat the meat. When the serpents approached a mountain, instead of going around it or over the top, they burrowed through the middle. The serpents left trails of filth and destruction wherever they went. They poisoned the waters, killed the forests, and made the earth an ugly and barren place.

One day a hunter from the land of the Kanienkehaka happened to see the golden serpent. It had grown to be the size of a mountain, and it had turned around, and was heading for the Mohawk country once again. Similarly word came down from the north that the silver serpent had grown and it too was heading for the land of the Kanienkehaka. One day, the two serpents could be seen from the original village from whence they had come three hundred years earlier.

Again the people argued and argued. They could not agree as to the best way to kill the serpents off. The people remembered the legends of the serpents, and how they had eaten the children of their ancestors, and they fled to the mountains.

Once in the mountains the people were told by the Creator that the day would come when a small boy would show them the way to kill the two serpents. The boy would make a bow from willow. He would string the bow with a string made from the hair of the clan mothers. An arrow would be made of a straight sapling and tipped with the white flint of the Kanienkehaka. With this arrow and this bow, the people were told, the Kanienkehaka would protect themselves from the two serpents of the United States and Canada.[9]

Kanentiio takes the story one step further and tells us,

When the serpents appeared, the surviving Mohawk people gathered together around the boy as he pulled back on the bow and let the arrows fly. His aim was good, his heart strong. The arrows pierced the hides of the gigantic beasts, killing them.

Mohawk elders say the story has been handed down over the generations as a warning to the Iroquois about the great

suffering they would endure at the hands of the Europeans. It is believed the gold serpent is the United States of America and the silver one is Canada.[10]

I would go one step further and say that the serpents were the Dutch and the French, the first colonial superpowers our people encountered. Eventually the English took the place of the Dutch, the Americans took the place of the French, and, finally, Canada took the place of the English. It matters little which one was silver and which was gold; the effect was the same. One cannot look at the massive highways crisscrossing the land, the tunnels bored through mountains, the dammed rivers and polluted lakes, and not see evidence that this land has been nearly destroyed by giant serpents.

The more cynical among us might look upon this as "prophecy after the fact," a prediction only revealed after the events have already taken place, bolstered by its similarity to other oral traditions. It is oddly similar to a Seneca creation legend published by George Abrams in *The Seneca People* (1976):

> After the Creator caused the original Seneca to be formed in the interior of the Great Hill, they emerged from a hole in the top and built their first village on it. They found that they were entirely encircled by a huge snake whose insatiable appetite and poisonous breath killed all those who attempted to escape ... It swallowed all members of the small tribe except two children ... By means of an oracle, the Creator later instructed the two surviving children to make a willow bow and arrow tipped with a special poison with which to kill the serpent. Bravely the orphan children approached the snake and shot the arrow under the scales. Immediately the snake began to thrash violently about, uncoiling from around the hill, and as he vomited the skulls of the dead Seneca, these rolled down the side of the hill into the lake and immediately petrified. They can be seen at the bottom of the lake in the form of large, round stones. As the snake convulsed in its death throes, it rolled down the hillside uprooting trees in its path and creating a cleft in the hillside ... The Seneca Indians sprang from these two heroic orphans.[11]

Some may find that the similarity of the Mohawk serpent prophecy to this Seneca creation myth may undermine its credibility as bona fide Mohawk oral tradition, but it nevertheless has value to us today as an expression of our understanding of the colonization of North America. Considering the centuries of trauma our people have experienced in the age of European invasion, it is understandable that our allegory for it would throw any sense of subtlety out the window. Nor is it any wonder that our only salvation would be a return to the "old ways," represented in the story by the willow bow strung with the hair of clan mothers and arrows of made of sapling and flint.

If the story of the serpents is how we describe European contact today, how did we describe it as it happened? To answer that question, we must delve into a collection of documents written not in parchment and ink, but woven into belts with purple and white beads made from clamshells. I call these archives *The Wampum Chronicles*.

3

SIGHTING OF THE FIRST EUROPEANS

Imagine yourself walking along a beach in New England, the ocean surf rolling in and out, leaving thousands of different shells on the sandy shore. One of these shells, long abandoned by the clam that created it, has a beautiful purple swirl in its hard, white interior. This is the shell of a quahog (*Mercenaria mercenaria*), also known as a hard shell.

Long ago, the Algonquian peoples of the region fashioned these shells into tubular beads commonly known as *wampum*.[12] Dutch colonists referred to it as *seawan* or *sewant*, while the French called it *porcelain*. In addition to using it for personal adornment, the coastal tribes traded it with the European colonists who came ashore on these same beaches. It was also traded with tribes and nations further inland, and was sometimes referred to as "Indian money" because of its commerciality. Wampum has become one of the most enduring symbols of the colonial era in North America.

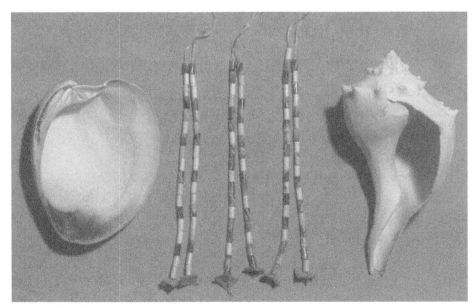

Quahog shell, condolence strings, & whelk shell.
Photo by the author.

The *Kanien'kehá:ka*, or "People of the Land of Flint"—more commonly known as the Mohawk—are the easternmost nation of the Iroquois Confederacy. We were one of those interior nations who received wampum in trade. Our word for wampum is *onehkórha*, and it was far from just a type of currency to us.[13] Strung together as *kanáhsa*, or woven into a belt, or *kaión:ni*—"A River Made by the Hand of Man"—wampum became the *lingua franca* of intertribal diplomacy.[14] Ray Fadden, or *Tehanetorens*, described our use of it in his *Wampum Belts of the Iroquois*:

> Wampum strings served as credentials or certificates of authority. No Iroquois chief would listen to a message or pay attention to a report until he received official information through a runner who carried the proper wampum string or belt. Wampum guaranteed a message or a promise. Treaties meant nothing unless they were accompanied by wampum.[15]

Wampum belts were preserved as historical archives of our political dealings, the symbols woven into them serving as a mnemonic device for the recall of complex oral traditions. If properly cared for, wampum would last forever. If regularly recited, so too would the message that went with it.

Among the many wampum belts that preserve our oral traditions is one that we know as *Sighting of the First Europeans*. This white belt has a number of purple diagonal lines arrayed in groups of three. It depicts the

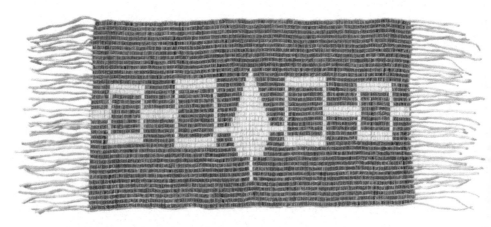

Aionwà:tha wampum belt, representing the Five Nations of the Iroquois Confederacy. Reproduction and photo by the author.

arrival of European colonists to North America in a weakened state, numerically outnumbered by the natives they found, unable to subsist in an alien environment, and in dire need of native support. No particular European nation is identified in this story, but many assume that this is a reference to the English pilgrims and their desperate need for a turkey dinner. Of course, the pilgrims did not encounter the Iroquois, who lived much deeper in the interior, so if the belt is indeed about our first encounter with Europeans, it must depict some other nation, either the Dutch or the French.

Here is what the New York State Museum published about the belt in 1931:

> The third belt in this collection is 28 inches long and 13 beads in width, or 3½ inches. It is woven on buckskin thongs with a white background bearing four groups of three purple beaded diagonal lines. It was made by the Iroquois to commemorate "the first coming of the people with pale faces." It is not known whether this refers to the first sight of Spaniards, French or Dutch. John Buck, who was an Onondaga chief and once wampum keeper, remarked that diagonal stripes across a belt were symbols of agreement that the tribe giving the belt would help the Six Nations in war. These were props, or supports, for the Long House; the symbol of the confederacy. In this sense the diagonal lines may be considered to signify the willingness of support to the whites by the Indians.[16]

Most of the books about the history of the Iroquois published in recent years tend to identify our first Europeans as the French—the

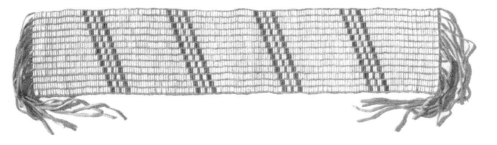

Wampum belt commemorating the sighting of the first Europeans. Reproduction and photo by the author.

Onserón:ni, or "They Make Hatchets"—but exactly when this encounter occurred is still a question that, in my mind, has not yet been resolved.[17] In the late 1800's, it was believed that our first encounter took place in the early 16th century, while more recent scholarship puts that date in the early 17th, some seven decades later.

Historical documentation, linguistics, and archaeological evidence are locked in combat with modern politics to determine whether our first European was a man named Jack or Sam. We will attempt to navigate these contested waterways about "first contact." We will also discuss other wampum belts that pertain to the early days of colonization.

If you're still imagining yourself on that New England beach with sand between your toes, feel free to linger a few moments longer before joining me on this expedition. I'll wait.

4

JACQUES CARTIER
AT HOCHELAGA

Canadian children are taught in school that their nation bears an Indian name, *kaná:ta* being an Iroquoian word for village. They also learn that this name came about during the second voyage of French explorer Jacques Cartier, when he visited a village named *Hochelaga*, said to be somewhere on the island of Montreal.

As it happens, kaná:ta is the root of the word *Kanata:kon*, the Mohawk name for the historic village of St. Regis in Ahkwesáhsne. It is only fitting to mention this fact because there is a major disconnect in the minds of many mainstream scholars between the Mohawks of today and the people Jacques Cartier encountered in 1535.

A century ago, it was believed that the Mohawks and the *Hochelagans* were one and the same. Modern archaeologists, however, have come to the conclusion that the people of the St. Lawrence were a completely separate tribe. Naturally, this doesn't sit very well with some of the Mohawks, especially those who live on the shores of *Kania'tarowá:nen*— "The Great River" —and still feel a strong ancestral connection to the land on which we live.

Cartier's journal is often cited by those who see similarities between his Hochelaga and the historic Mohawk villages visited by Jesuits in the 17th century. This is most evident in his description of the village itself:

> And in the middle of these fields is situated and stands the village of Hochelaga, near and adjacent to a mountain, the slopes of which are fertile and are cultivated, and from the top of which one can see for a long distance. We named this mountain "Mount Royal." The village is circular and is completely enclosed by a wooden palisade in three tiers like a pyramid. The top one is built crosswise, the middle one perpendicular and the lowest one of strips of wood placed lengthwise. The whole is well joined and lashed together after their manner, and is some two lances in height. There is only one gate and

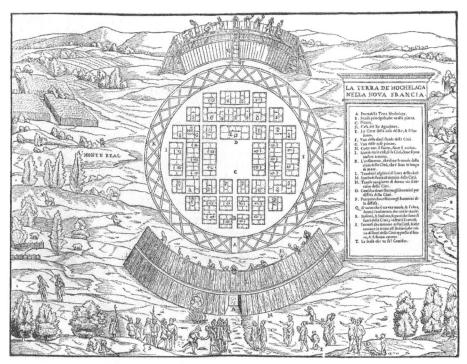

Diagram of Hochelaga.

entrance to this village, and that can be barred up. Over this gate and in many places about the enclosure are species of galleries with ladders for mounting to them, which galleries are provided with rocks and stones for defense and protection of the place. There are some fifty houses in this village, each about fifty or more paces in length, and twelve or fifteen in width, built completely of wood and covered in and bordered up with large pieces of bark and rind of trees, as broad as a table, which are well and cunningly lashed after their manner. And inside these houses are many rooms and chambers; and in the middle is a large space without a floor, where they light their fire and live together in common.[18]

While it would certainly compare favorably to a description of a Mohawk (or any other Iroquois) village, it also has a lot in common with those of the Huron, the other leading contender in the Hochelagan identity fight. Scholars argued about which of these it was for generations until it was finally agreed that the Hochelagans were a completely

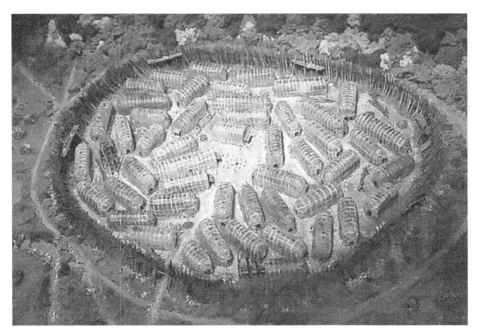

Hochelaga longhouses and palisades, as envisioned by the Canadian Museum of Civilization. Digital art by the author.

separate group within the Iroquoian family, dubbing them first the "Laurentian Iroquois," but eventually settling on "St. Lawrence Iroquoians," so as not to confuse them with the Iroquois that everyone knows and loves today.

The Hochelagan question may have been resolved among archaeologists, but beyond the hallowed halls of academia, the fight was far from over, as the staff of one museum would eventually find out.

In 2006, Pointe-à-Callière, the Montréal Museum of Archaeology and History, opened an exhibit about the St. Lawrence Iroquoians who greeted Cartier. The museum, built on the archaeological remains of one of the earliest structures of the French settlement, overlooks the St. Lawrence River that brought Cartier into the region, and is probably not far from the actual location of Hochelaga, still buried somewhere beneath the streets of Montréal.[19]

In the media coverage of the event, exhibition project manager Louise Pothier emphasized that the St. Lawrence Iroquoians, who had seemingly vanished by the time Samuel Champlain came through the area in 1603, were not to be confused with the more well-known Iroquois Confederacy:

Pothier says the most important lesson of the exhibition is the distinction between Iroquoian and Iroquois.

"The Iroquoians were distinct from the Iroquois confederacy," she says.

"Iroquois is a linguistic family. They shared a language but not necessarily the same dialect. They were closely connected, like cousins. But we can recognize the St. Lawrence Iroquoians as a specific group."

Another distinction is pottery. A trademark artifact of the St. Lawrence Iroquoians is a wide-mouth earthen pot that usually lacked glaze or colour. "One popular design was the reed punctuation motif which had small circles with geometric designs," Pothier says.[20]

Further up the St. Lawrence, on the opposite shore, lies the Mohawk community of Kahnawà:ke, where the historical position put forward by the museum about the identity of these "Hochelagans" encountered by Cartier was flatly rejected.

Mohawks like former chief Billy Two Rivers contend that Hochelaga was a Mohawk village, a position archaeologists agreed with in the late 19th century and early 20th century, but have since abandoned.[21] Citing oral traditions as well as similarities between the vocabularies recorded by Cartier and the modern Mohawk language, these *Kahnawa'kehró:non* made their disagreement known both through the news media and on the internet. As one Mohawk woman said, "We complained to the guide that we had not disappeared, that he was not staring at ghosts, that this whole exhibit was misleading and that we are definitely still here. In other words, we were unconvinced by the story of our death."[22]

St. Lawrence Iroquoian pottery reproduction by Roger Sosakete Perkins.
Photo by the author.

Some of the more vocal Mohawks perceived a political agenda behind the positions taken by the museum's experts, suggesting that this was part of an overall strategy to undermine Mohawk claims not only to our aboriginal territories, but to the reserve lands we now inhabit. Others recalled specific stories handed down in the oral tradition about the Cartier encounters, but left open the possibility that while the Hochelagans might not have been Mohawk *per se,* remnants of the post-Cartier dispersal ended up being absorbed by us over time, thus leaving us with the theoretical notion that at least *some* of our ancestors were Hochelagans.

I tend to agree with this more nuanced view of history, having studied the work of archaeologists, linguists, and historians who sought to follow the trail of the Hochelagans and found traces of them among the Huron, Abenaki, and Iroquois. My understanding was that late 19th century scholars identified the Hochelagans as Mohawks because Mohawk archaeology was in its infancy and hadn't yet established a much earlier presence in the Mohawk Valley. At the same time, however, I noticed that some of the non-native scholars cited in the latest debate were leaving out the information that remnants of the Hochelagans had ended up among the Iroquois, and were more or less denying that we had *any* ancestral claim to the homelands of the St. Lawrence Iroquoians.

Teyowisonte (Thomas Deer) is an employee of *Kanien'kehaka Onkwawén:na Raotitiohkwa,* Kahnawà:ke's cultural center. His encounter with the museum's experts illustrate that the cultural divide is even wider than the mighty St. Lawrence:

> The people from Pointe A'Calliere visited us here at the KOR Cultural Center in Kahnawake a few months while they were preparing for the exhibit. They had wanted us to contribute to the physical exhibit in some way. The meeting immediately turned into a mild argument over the St. Lawrence Iroquois versus Mohawks debate.
>
> My primary inquiry to their archeologist was how did they determine that this specific group of people were not Mohawks. My question was genuine and was not addressed in a hostile or belittling fashion. I truly wanted to understand and appreciate their rationale without my bias.
>
> It was explained to me that the archaeological survey of

certain sites in comparison to those found in the Mohawk Valley suggested a different rate of development in terms of their material culture. For example, the pottery in the St. Lawrence river valley evolved in technology at a different rate than it did in the Mohawk Valley.

I didn't doubt their assessment on how technology and material culture evolved differently geographically, but I didn't understand how that difference would determine a distinction in one group's citizenship. She didn't follow me.

I told her for example, while technology and material culture evolve differently geographically between New York City and Des Moines, Iowa; wouldn't both people in those areas remain Americans? She gave me a blank look. So I said by that rationale, couldn't the St. Lawrence river valley inhabitants be Mohawk, seeing as their isolation in the north would force their material culture and technology to evolve at a different rate than in the Mohawk Valley?

She then accused me of being an ethnocentric, stating that the pottery remains tell a different story. Mind you, I genuinely wanted to engage in a good discussion on the subject, but she wasn't having any of it.

I also told her of Kahnawake's oral history concerning the three villages that were here at the time of Cartier and how after a dispute with neighboring Algonquins we were forced to flee to Vermont and the Mohawk Valley, which seemed to explain our "disappearance" at the exact time it supposedly occurred. She said that while oral tradition is beautiful, they needed to use more scientific means of proof.

Then we confronted her on Cartier's journal ... which contains a glossary of the Hochelagan language; which surprisingly matches the Mohawk language. And I'm not drawing general matches as we could between let's say Mohawk and Oneida or even Mohawk and Seneca which are particularly different; these were Mohawk words.

Again, she dispelled that evidence, basically saying that language can transcend nationality. If anything, I'd say that language identifies one's nationality more accurately than technology or material culture.

....

In the end we were asked if we would contribute to their exhibit. We explained that we couldn't be a part of anything if it means we concede to their theory that Mohawks are immigrants to this area. It ended there.[23]

The idea that there is some sinister political motivation behind the museum's negating of a Mohawk identity for the Hochelagans, which some might dismiss as paranoia, appears to be confirmed by the stubbornness of museum officials to even consider this possibility.

Scholars would do well to keep an open mind when consulting modern-day Mohawks. There is a wealth of knowledge to be found in linguistics and oral traditions, as Brian Rice, a Kahnawà:ke Mohawk with a doctorate in traditional knowledge education, discovered when he probed the "mystery" of the St. Lawrence Iroquoians:

It was Mohawk traditionalist Charley Patton of Kahnawake who helped clarify the meaning of Hochelaga years ago. He believed that Hochelaga came from the word *Otsiraga* which he translated as council fire or people of the council fire from *otsire* – fire and *aga* – people. Among the Five Nations Iroquois, the Onondaga held the national council fire at *Kanata Kowa* village while each of the four other nations held the council fire of their respected nations.

Charley thought that Hochelaga may have been pronounced wrong as it would have sounded like *Otsiraga*. This may not have been the case. Mohawk educator Barry Montour explained to me while we were both at McGill University, that when the Jesuits first put down the Mohawk language into a written form, they replaced the L sounding letters with R sounding letters. This might have eventually resulted in a dialetic change in speakers of the language. In old Mohawk it would have made Otsiraga to have originally sounded as *Otsilaga*.[24]

Rice went on to consider the Mohawk name for the island of Montréal, sometimes given as *Tiotiake* and *Tsotiahke*.

They say within a language one can find references to the

culture and history of a people. This brings us to the name given to Montreal by the Mohawk of Kahnawake: Tsotiahke 'where the people split apart.' There are only three possibilities in Mohawk history that can possibly account for the name. The first I will mention occurred in 1723 when Mohawks were forced to move to the north end of Montreal and then the Lake of Two Mountains from Mountain Royal. The second is during the 1750's when some Mohawks moved upriver and settled in Akwesasne. Neither of these moves can truly account for the name given Tsotiahke. For one thing most Mohawks didn't live on Mount Royal during the two periods mentioned, they lived at Kahnawake; therefore, neither could account for the name being given for the location at Montreal. The name Tsotiahke for Montreal is remembered most specifically today by Mohawks from Kahnawake. Therefore, the final possibility which I hold to be the right one is that there was a prior dispersal of Mohawks and possibly other Five Nations people that occurred at a previous date that was significant enough that the name has remained to this day within the oral traditions of the Mohawks of Kahnawake. That would be the dispersal that occurred as a result of their battles with the Algonquins and their allies the Huron. Some Huron traditions say they were defeated at the hands of the Algonquin and then allied with them at a later date. As we have seen and know from history, by the seventeenth century both groups became adversaries of the Five Nations Iroquois and by 1650 would pay the price for doing so.[25]

He also examines the archaeological evidence that scholars rely on so heavily, highlighting the variances in scholarly opinion:

Some Anthropologists have based their theory that the St. Lawrence Iroquoians could not have been any of the Five Nations Iroquois because each has a very distinct type of pottery. Professor Gagne who taught an Anthropology course at McGill University in 1992 informed me that the rims of the St. Lawrence Iroquoians are much larger than any of the Five Nations Iroquois found in New York State and they are made better. Therefore, I decided to go to the source and ask an expert who worked on Mohawk archeological sites if this was true. In 1992 a group of us traveled to Fort Plain and visited a Mohawk site with archeologist Dean Snow. Dean Snow had worked on several Mohawk sites, the most prominent being Otstungo. He said that there was little difference between Mohawk pottery and St. Lawrence Iroquoian pottery. He noted that the rims are the same with the main difference being that the St. Lawrence Iroquoians punctured their pottery with a piece of reed leaving it in as a form of decoration. In fact, it was probably more than simply decoration. During a course I took at Kahnawake around the same time, we fired pottery. Some of our pottery cracked right away. I learned later that you need something to hold the clay together and in the case of the St. Lawrence Iroquoians it was probably reed. Snow also said that this particular type of pottery appeared at Mohawk sites in the 16th century the same time as the recorded dispersal of the St. Lawrence Iroquoians between the arrival of Cartier and Champlain.[26]

Ultimately, Rice supports the notion that the St. Lawrence Iroquoians were a separate group that eventually merged with not only the Mohawks, but other Iroquoian and Algonquian tribes. He gathered oral traditions from a variety of sources that tracked the movements of the St. Lawrence Iroquoians after their alleged disappearance, painting a more complete picture of this event than the stark pronouncements coming out of the museum placard-writers. Although the St. Lawrence Iroquoians may not have had been Mohawk *per se*, Teyowisonte and his comrades were justified in staking an ancestral claim to Hochelaga.

When it comes to this particular debate, there may be ideological extremes on both sides of the river, but Rice's scholarship suggests that the more likely scenario paddles quietly in the middle, unnoticed by those entrenched on each shore. As we continue on our own journey through history, we will do well to navigate in a like manner.[27]

5

SAMUEL DE CHAMPLAIN
AT TICONDEROGA

If mainstream scholars don't agree that our first encounter with Europeans was with Jacques Cartier at Hochelaga, where and when do they say our first encounter occurred?

To answer that question we must travel on a different waterway, one that is known in Mohawk as *Kania'taraká:ronte,* which one historian interpreted as "lake that is the gate to the country."[28] It is more commonly known by the name was given to it by the first Frenchman to "discover" it, Samuel de Champlain, who named it after himself.

Champlain came upon the North American scene to find New France's Indian allies already poised for war against the Iroquois. In 1603, a French delegation, accompanied by two Indians who had been taken to France years before, was welcomed to a celebratory feast with 80 to 100 of these allies at Point aux Allouettes, which in Champlain's time was known as St. Matthew's Point:

> One of the savages whom we had taken with us began to make an address, speaking of the cordial reception the king had given them, and the good treatment they had received in France, and saying they were assured that his Majesty was favorably disposed towards them, and was desirous of peopling their country, and of making peace with their enemies, the Iroquois, or of sending forces to conquer them.[29]

We can presume that their hosts were more interested in conquering the Iroquois from the following passage:

> They were having this celebration in honor of the victory they had obtained over the Iroquois, several hundred of whom they had killed, whose heads they had cut off and had with them to contribute to the pomp of their festivity. Three nations had engaged in the war, the Etechemins, Algonquins, and

Montagnais. These, to the number of a thousand, proceeded to make war upon the Iroquois, whom they encountered at the mouth of the river of the Iroquois, and of whom they killed a hundred. They carry on war only by surprising their enemies; for they would not dare to do so otherwise, and fear too much the Iroquois, who are more numerous than the Montagnais, Etechemins, and Algonquins.[30]

The "river of the Iroquois" mentioned in Champlain's journal was today's Richelieu, the river that links Lake Champlain to the St. Lawrence below Montréal. This was the route by which the Iroquois attacked from the south. (In later years, the upper St. Lawrence would carry this name.) In the summer of 1609, Champlain joined his Montagnais, Huron and Algonquin allies on an expedition to make war upon them via this water route.

Champlain's journal is the first European description of Lake Champlain. Of particular note was its lack of human habitation:

> The next day we entered the lake, which is of great extent, say eighty or a hundred leagues long, where I saw four fine islands, ten, twelve, and fifteen leagues long, which were formerly inhabited by the savages, like the River of the Iroquois; but they have been abandoned since the wars of the savages with one another prevail.[31]

As they traveled southward to do battle with their Iroquois, he described the mountains he saw to the east in what is now Vermont:

> Continuing our course over this lake on the western side, I noticed, while observing the country, some very high mountains on the eastern side, on the top of which there was snow. I made inquiry of the savages whether these localities were inhabited, when they told me that the Iroquois dwelt there, and that there were beautiful valleys in these places, with plains productive in grain, such as I had eaten in this country, together with many kinds of fruit without limit.[32]

Today scholars refute the notion that the Iroquois once inhabited the land that Champlain's allies pointed to on the Vermont side of the lake, even though we laid claim to it at various points in history, going so far as to make representations to that effect in the Vermont legislature in the 19th century. (In case you're wondering, it's unlikely that our ancestors got the idea from reading Champlain's account!)

> They said also that the lake extended near mountains, some twenty-five leagues distant from us, as I judge. I saw, on the south, other mountains, no less high than the first, but without any snow. The savages told me that these mountains were thickly settled, and that it was there we were to find their enemies; but that it was necessary to pass a fall in order to go there (which I afterwards saw), when we should enter another lake, nine or ten leagues long. After reaching the end of the lake, we should have to go, they said, two leagues by land, and pass through a river flowing into the sea on the Norumbegue coast, near that of Florida, whither it took them only two days to go by canoe, as I have since ascertained from some prisoners we captured, who gave me minute information in regard to all they had personal knowledge of, through some Algonquin interpreters, who understood the Iroquois language.[33]

The "other mountains" to the south were probably not as "thickly settled" as the Indians claimed. Scholars concede, however, that they were more accurate in their description of the route that would eventually lead them from Lake Champlain to Lake George and then on to the Hudson River and the Atlantic Ocean—providing, of course, that they managed to get past the Iroquois who controlled the area. We continue with Champlain's journal:

> Now, as we began to approach within two or three days' journey of the abode of their enemies, we advanced only at night, resting during the day. But they did not fail to practise constantly their accustomed superstitions, in order to ascertain what was to be the result of their undertaking; and they often asked me if I had had a dream, and seen their enemies, to which I replied in the negative. Yet I did not cease to encourage them, and inspire in them hope. When night came, we set

out on the journey until the next day, when we withdrew into the interior of the forest, and spent the rest of the day there. About ten or eleven o'clock, after taking a little walk about our encampment, I retired. While sleeping, I dreamed that I saw our enemies, the Iroquois, drowning in the lake near a mountain, within sight. When I expressed a wish to help them, our allies, the savages, told me we must let them all die, and that they were of no importance. When I awoke, they did not fail to ask me, as usual, if I had had a dream. I told them that I had, in fact, had a dream. This, upon being related, gave them so much confidence that they did not doubt any longer that good was to happen to them.[34]

It would not be long before the combatants met:

> When it was evening, we embarked in our canoes to continue our course; and, as we advanced very quietly and without making any noise, we met on the 29th of the month the Iroquois, about ten o'clock at evening, at the extremity of a cape which extends into the lake on the western bank. They had come to fight. We both began to utter loud cries, all getting their arms in readiness. We withdrew out on the water, and the Iroquois went on shore, where they drew up all their canoes close to each other and began to fell trees with poor axes, which they acquire in war sometimes, using also others of stone. Thus they barricaded themselves very well.[35]

Champlain and his forces remained on the lake with their canoes lashed together, watching the Iroquois prepare for battle. Eventually, Champlain's Indian allies went forward to make an appointment with the enemy:

> When they were armed and in array, they despatched two canoes by themselves to the enemy to inquire if they wished to fight, to which the latter replied that they wanted nothing else; but they said that, at present, there was not much light, and that it would be necessary to wait for daylight, so as to be able to recognize each other; and that, as soon as the sun rose,

they would offer us battle. This was agreed to by our side. Meanwhile, the entire night was spent in dancing and singing, on both sides, with endless insults and other talk; as, how little courage we had, how feeble a resistance we would make against their arms, and that, when day came, we should realize it to our ruin.[36]

At daybreak, Champlain's forces prepared for battle. He and his two French companions had so far gone unnoticed by the Iroquois, so they kept a "low profile" as they prepared:

We arranged our arms in the best manner possible, being, however, separated, each in one of the canoes of the savage Montagnais. After arming ourselves with light armor, we each took an arquebuse, and went on shore. I saw the enemy go out of their barricade, nearly two hundred in number, stout and rugged in appearance. They came at a slow pace towards us, with a dignity and assurance which greatly amused me, having three chiefs at their head. Our men also advanced in the same order, telling me that those who had three large plumes were the chiefs, and that they had only these three, and that they could be distinguished by these plumes, which were much larger than those of their companions, and that I should do what I could to kill them.[37]

Due to language difficulties, Champlain was unable to take command of his Indians, so he consented to serving as their secret weapon:

As soon as we had landed, they began to run for some two hundred paces towards their enemies, who stood firmly, not having as yet noticed my companions, who went into the woods with some savages. Our men began to call me with loud cries; and, in order to give me a passage-way, they opened in two parts, and put me at their head, where I marched some twenty paces in advance of the rest, until I was within about thirty paces of the enemy, who at once noticed me, and, halting, gazed at me, as I did also at them. When I saw them making a move to fire at us, I rested my musket against my cheek, and aimed directly at one of the three chiefs. With the same shot, two fell to the ground; and one of their men was so wounded that he died some time after. I had loaded my musket with four balls. When our side saw this shot so favorable for them, they began to raise such loud cries that one could not have heard it thunder. Meanwhile, the arrows flew on both sides. The Iroquois were greatly astonished that two men had been so quickly killed, although they were equipped with armor woven from cotton thread, and with wood which was proof against their arrows. This caused great alarm among them. As I was loading again, one of my companions fired a shot from the woods, which astonished them anew to such a degree that, seeing their chiefs dead, they lost courage, and took to flight, abandoning their camp and fort, and fleeing into the woods, whither I pursued them, killing still more of them. Our savages also killed several of them, and took ten or twelve prisoners. The remainder escaped with the wounded. Fifteen or sixteen were wounded on our side with arrow-shots; but they were soon healed.

After gaining the victory, our men amused themselves by taking a great quantity of Indian corn and some meal from their enemies, also their armor, which they had left behind that they might run better. After feasting sumptuously, dancing and singing, we returned three hours after, with the prisoners.[38]

As did many of his fellow historians, Francis Parkman read quite a bit into this event:

Thus did New France rush into collision with the redoubted warriors of the Five Nations. Here was the beginning, and in some measure doubtless the cause, of a long suite of murderous conflicts, bearing havoc and flame to generations yet unborn. Champlain had invaded the tiger's den; and now, in smothered fury, the patient savage would lie biding his day of blood.[39]

Leave it to the "Dean of Iroquoian Studies," William Fenton, to burst the notion that this clash turned our ancestors into the vengeance-

Fanciful depiction of Champlain's encounter with "Iroquois" warriors in the vicinity of Ticonderoga on Lake Champlain.

seeking psychopaths of the New World: "Nineteenth-century historians to the contrary, this incident did not precipitate a hundred years of Mohawk vengeance against New France: the Iroquois wars had economic causes rooted in the fur trade."[40]

Scholar Matthew Dennis, whose *Cultivating a Landscape of Peace: Iroquois-European Encounters in Seventeenth-Century America* (1993) was noted for being perceptive and sympathetic to the Iroquois, saw in this event a type of pageantry, the subtleties of which were apparently lost on Champlain: "We can see this battle—the first encounter between Frenchman and Iroquois—as a performance of traditional, aboriginal blood feud. But it was also a failure, for not all of the actors knew their roles."[41]

It wouldn't be long before the Iroquois abandoned their wooden armor and battles-by-appointment in favor of ambushes and "skulking." Nor would it be very long before they had access to European firearms. While it is probably best not to overemphasize the importance of the clash with Champlain, it was definitely pivotal in that it marked an end to the "pageantry" of aboriginal warfare. That is, if it was indeed the Iroquois that Champlain and his friends encountered.

As we have seen from the Parkman, Fenton, and Dennis quotations, scholars have always accepted the tribal identity of these ill-fated

Indians as Iroquois, just as Champlain's allies said—or at least, as he claimed they said. (For some reason, their account of the encounter doesn't seem to have survived the canoe trip.) They also take the identification one step further and assume that they were Mohawks, the closest of the Five Nations to Lake Champlain.

Why do scholars put such faith in this identification, and are they justified in doing so?

In the Cartier case, scholars had ample archaeological evidence to work with, but Champlain's "Mohawk" group was just camped out somewhere on the lakeshore near Ticonderoga. Lacking distinctive pottery sherds to compare, scholars have had to rely on the existing literature, namely Champlain's journal, to make what is ultimately a very circumstantial case.

Mohawk orators were noted for recalling specific events many generations later. Yet there is no mention of this event in any of the treaty councils that were recorded in the years that followed. The first time it was acknowledged, more than two centuries later, was in the 1816 journal of Major John Norton, or *Teyoninhokawaren*, a half-Scot, half-Cherokee adopted by the Mohawks:

> The first knowledge which the Five Nations acquired of the French, was by their hostility. Elated by the possession of more destructive Implements of War, the Latter had readily become the Allies of the Algonquin and Weandot, and joined them in an expedition against the former, their ancient enemies. The Five Nations, on the first encounter, were defeated,—which the French attributed to their own prowess, and the efficacy of their fire Arms.[42]

"The substance of the narrative," Norton's editors tell us in a footnote, "was well-known. There is no evidence to suggest that Norton had derived his information directly from Champlain's accounts of these events of 1608-1609."[43]

The Mohawk identification of Champlain's enemies is so uncritically accepted that even our own people repeat it as fact.[44] It has been suggested that Champlain's description of the enemy chiefs having "three large plumes" in their headdress was evidence that they were Mohawks, as the Mohawk traditional headgear, the *kastówa*, is distinguished by three eagle fathers standing up. Unfortunately, there is no evidence that this particular array of feathers is really that old; it is not described in the documentation nor depicted in the historic art of this era. It may very well be that the three feathers array was inspired by the Champlain account!

There is also a wampum belt in the collection of New York State which has for years been called the *Champlain Wampum Belt*. It is a purple belt with five white hexagons arrayed at intervals and four small white rows at each end. It measures 39½ inches long and is seven rows wide. Although it has been labeled as representing Champlain's 1609 incursion into the country of the Iroquois, there is only one oral tradition cited by the museum, given by Daniel and Thomas La Fort at Onondaga Castle in 1898, but it mentions nothing about Champlain:

> Represents a Sorrow Meeting of the Five Nations. If a misfortune happen: If little boys and girls were taken and one killed—to consider what should be done for remedy that misfortune—a tooth for a tooth, an eye for an eye. This is a Hiawatha belt. This belt is used when meeting of that kind is called.[45]

In the end, it doesn't matter if those were Mohawks at the business end of Champlain's weaponry or some other Iroquoian nation: this "first encounter" with Europeans was violent and destructive, a harbinger of dark times yet to come.

"Champlain" Wampum Belt, formerly held by New York State Museum, now in the possession of the Onondaga Nation of the Haudenosaunee Confederacy. Digital Reproduction by the author.

6

TREACHERY AND TREATY WITH NEW NETHERLAND

In comparison to the violence of our first encounters with the French, the Rotinonhsión:ni view our initial contact with the Dutch colonists of New Netherland—the *Ron'sharón:ni,* or "They are Knife Makers"—in a much more favorable light.[46] We point to two important wampum belts that memorialize this relationship, suggesting that this was a model for other nations to follow in their dealings with us. But there was a dark side to our initial dealings with the Dutch which we tend to overlook, and at least one act of violence so unspeakably brutal that it's no wonder we don't speak of it today!

Four centuries ago, English explorer Henry Hudson made his way up the Hudson River on the *Halve Maen* (Half Moon) for the Dutch East Indian Company. This led to the establishment of a Dutch fur trading post, Fort Nassau, near what is now Albany, New York, in 1614. Not far from this location was the place where the Mohawk River—*Teionontatátie,* "The River that Flows through the Mountains"—empties into the Hudson.[47] It wasn't long before our ancestors made contact with the colonists and entered into trade.

In 1691, a delegation of Rotinonhsión:ni leaders told the governor of New York,

> We have been informed by our Forefathers that in former times a Ship arrived here in this Country which was matter of great admiration to us, especially our desire was to know what was within her Belly. In that Ship were Christians, amongst the rest one Jaques with whom we made a Covenant of friendship, which covenant hath since been tied together with a chaine and always ever since kept inviolable by the Brethren and us.[48]

Historians have wondered if this is a reference to French explorer Jacques Cartier on the St. Lawrence or one of the early Dutch colonists.

William M. Beauchamp, writing in 1905, thought this was a reference to Dutch colonist "Captain Jacobs," who arrived in New Netherland in 1623. George T. Hunt, writing in 1940, was convinced that it referred to Cartier, so much so that he left off the last part of the quote that mentions the "chaine" representing the "Covenant of friendship," which would almost certainly be a reference to a treaty metaphor that was first employed in dealings with the Dutch.[49]

Historical materials from the colony of New Netherland suggest that the Jacques referred to was Jacques Eelkens, whose name is sometimes given as Elckins and other variants. The Mohawk tradition emphasizes the harmonious relationship our ancestors had with Jacques and his countrymen, but this was unduly charitable in light of the violence and treachery of some of these early dealings.

In 1634, Bastiaen Jansz Crol, the former director of New Netherland, was interrogated about events that had occurred in Eelkens' time. After being questioned about his own involvement with Fort Orange and Fort Amsterdam, he was asked about an incident that took place between the Dutch and the Mohawks around 1622.[50] It is from the transcripts of his interrogation that we extract the following:

> Whether, when residing at Fort Orange, he did not hear from the chiefs of the *Maquaas* that there had formerly traded with them a certain *Hans Jorisz Hontom,* who had first for skipper *Jacob Eelkens,* whom he later employed as his supercargo.
> Yes.
> Whether a misunderstanding did not arise between himself and *Hontom,* who had taken prisoner one of the chiefs.
> Yes.
> Whether, although the ransom was paid by the chief's subjects, *Hontom,* in spite of his promise, did not emasculate the chief, hang the severed member on the stay and so killed the *Sackima.*
> Yes.[51]

Later on in the interrogation, Crol told of the aftermath of this butchery:

> Whether he, when he was at Fort Orange, was not present, when *Saggodryochta,* head chief of the Maquaas, came, and

seeing *Hontom*, at once packed up his skins and rising up, said, "That man is a scoundrel, I will not trade with him."

Yes.

Whether soon afterwards, the Company's yacht *de Bever* was not burned by the savages near Fort Orange.

Yes.

Whether the tribe of the *Macquaas*, shortly before he left Fort Orange did not tell him, as he understood their language, that they would kill the said *Hans Jorissen Hontom* the first time they should find him alone, and whether he had not warned *Hontom* about this.

Yes.

What answer Hontom made thereto.

"That the *Macquaas* might do their best," or something to that effect.

Whether, on the 20th July, 1633, as he, *Crol*, lay ready to sail for the fatherland, a *Mahican* savage, named *Dickop*, did not come bringing the tidings to the island *Manhates*, that all the cattle in the neighborhood of Fort Orange had been killed.

Yes.[52]

The Mohawks of old apparently let bygones be bygones, just as they did with Champlain's shooting of three chiefs at Ticonderoga, because they never seemed to bring up Hontom's treacherous murder of their chief in subsequent treaty councils. Indeed, oral traditions about the early Dutch encounters are generally positive, linked as it is to the "covenant chain" wampum belt metaphor, as described by Onondaga chief *Canassatego* in a council with Maryland and Virginia officials 1744:

It is true that above One hundred Years ago the Dutch came here in a Ship and brought with them several Goods, such as Awls, Knives, Hatchets, Guns, and many other particulars, which they gave Us, and when they had taught us how to use their things, and we saw what sort of People they were, we were so well pleased with them that we tyed their Ship to the Bushes on the Shoar, and afterwards liking them still better the longer they stayed with Us, and thinking the Bushes to slender, we removed the Rope and tyed it to the Trees, and as

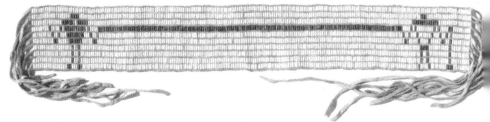

Friendship Belt. Reproduction and photo by the author.

the Trees were lyable to be blown down by high Winds, or to decay of themselves, We, from the affection We bore them, again removed the Rope, and tyed it to a Strong and big Rock (Here the Interpreter said they mean the Oneida Country), and not content with this, for its further Security We removed the Rope to the Big-Mountain (Here the Interpreter says they mean the Onondaga Country), and there we tyed it very fast and rowled Wampum about it, and to make it still more Secure we stood upon the Wampum, and sat down upon it to defend it, to prevent any hurt coming to it, and did our Best endeavours that it might remain uninjured forever During all this Time; the Newcomers, the Dutch, acknowledged Our Rights to the Lands, and solicited us from time to time to grant them Parts of Our Country, and to enter into League and Covenant with Us, and to become one People with Us.[53]

There are several wampum belts that depict this legendary *Covenant Chain of Peace and Friendship*. They depict two or more human figures holding hands, squares or rectangles joined by a solid bar, or a combination of these symbols. In *Kanien'kéha*, we would call this kind of belt *Tehonatenetshawá:ko*, which translates literally as "They are Holding Each Other's Arms."[54] This relationship was inherited by Great Britain when they took over the Dutch colony of New Netherland and renamed it New York, whereupon the covenant became a chain of silver:

After this the English came into the Country, and, as we were told, became one People with the Dutch; about two years after the Arrival of the English, an English Governor came to Albany, and finding what great friendship subsisted between

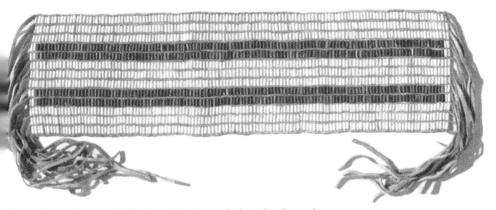

Two Row Wampum Belt. Reproduction and photo by the author.

us and the Dutch, he approved it mightily, and desired to make as Strong a league and to be upon as good Terms with us as the Dutch were, with whom he was united, and to become one People with Us, and by his further care in looking what had passed between us he found that the Rope which tyed the Ship to the Great mountain was only fastened with Wampum, which was liable to break and rot, and to perish in a course of years, he therefore told us that he would give us a silver Chain, which would be much stronger and last for Ever. This we accepted, and fastened the Ship with it, and it has lasted ever since.[55]

As further evidence that we tend to forgive and forget when it is probably not in our best interests to do so, modern Rotinonhsión:ni no longer emphasize the evolving Covenant Chain metaphor when speaking about our relationship with New Netherland, stressing instead *Tékeni Teiohá:te*—the *Two Row Wampum Belt*—that defined the non-interference pact between the confederacy and the colonists.[56]

Generally speaking, the "Two Row" is a white belt with two parallel rows of purple. Several of these belts exist, which is strong evidence for its political importance. The tradition associated with this belt comes down to us from the late Onondaga Pine Tree Chief Huron Miller and the late Cayuga Chief Jake Thomas. In their telling, the "whiteman" first explains the symbol of the Covenant Chain to the Indian, and then asks what the Indian will use as his symbol:

The whiteman said, "What symbol will you go by?" The Onkwehonwe replied, "When the Creator made Mother Earth, man was created to walk upon the Earth to enjoy all nature's fruits, saying that no one will claim Mother Earth except by the rising faces which are to be born. We will go by these symbols:

As long as the sun shines upon this earth, as long as the water still flows, and as long as the grass grows green at a certain time of the year, that is how long our agreement will stand. Now we have symbolized this agreement and it shall be binding forever, as long as Mother Earth is still in motion. We have finished and we understand what we have confirmed and this is what our generation should know and learn not to forget."

The whiteman said, "I confirm what you have said and this we shall always remember. What we do about or own way of belief, we shall both respect having our own rights and power." The Onkwehonwe replied, "I have a canoe and you have a vessel with sails and this is what we shall do. I will put in my canoe my beliefs and laws. In your vessel you shall put your beliefs and your laws. All my people will be in my canoe, your people in your vessel. We shall put these boats in the water and they shall always be parallel, as long as there is Mother Earth, this will be everlasting."

The whiteman said, "What will happen if your people will like to go into my vessel?" The Onkwehonwe replied, "If this happens, then they will have to be guided by my canoe." Now the whiteman fully understands the agreement.

The whiteman said, "What will happen if any of our people may someday want to have one foot in each of the boats that are parallel?" The Onkwehonwe replied, "If this so happens that my people may wish to have their feet in each of the two boats, there will be a high wind and the boats will separate and the person that has his feet in each of the boats shall fall between the two boats, and there is no living soul who will be able to bring them back to the right way given by the Creator but one—the Creator himself."

The Onkwehonwe called the wampum belt "Guswhenta." One of the two paths signifies the whiteman's laws and beliefs, and the other signifies the laws and beliefs of the Onkwehonwe. The white background signifies purity, good minds and peace, and they should not interfere with one another's views.

The whiteman said, "I understand. I confirm what you have said, that this will be everlasting as long as there is Mother Earth. We have confirmed this and our generation to come will never forget what we have agreed. Now it is understood that we shall never interfere with one another's belief or laws for generations to come."[57]

Although the ship and canoe tradition has become enshrined as "gospel" among modern Rotinonhsión:ni today, it is doubtful that the early Dutch colonists, who were more concerned about entering into a peaceful trade alliance with a people whose language they could barely understand, would have contemplated changing how their new Indian allies governed themselves. There is no mention of this "parallel vessels" metaphor in any of the early documentation.[58] In fact, it does not seem to emerge as a "tradition" until well into the late 19th century, when the Canadian government attempted to change the way the Indians were governed by passing the *Indian Act* legislation. Specifically, it was invoked by the "Iroquois of St. Regis" in a petition to the Queen in 1892:

Madam, concerning the question referred to by all our treaties from the time of discovery to the time of the last treaty - 1st. That the English have made an illustration that they shall abide in their vessel - 2nd - That the Indians of the Iroquois remain in our Birchbark Canoe; 3rd- That the English shall make no compulsory laws for the Indians, but the treaties are to be unmolested forever.[59]

While this quote affirms the spirit of non-interference that our elders have always attributed to the Two Row, the mention of the English and not the Dutch places the ship and canoe motif well after the earliest days of European contact. Moreover, it ascribes an English origin to the metaphor, which blows the rest of the oral tradition completely out of the water, so to speak. Could it in fact be an old seafarer's tradition modified for Indian diplomacy?

Undoubtedly our ancestors recognized that the Europeans had different ways of conducting their political and religious affairs, and they may well have foreseen the day when a non-interference pact might become necessary. Religious and political interference *did* take place, as the rest of our historical journey will demonstrate. The changes that resulted were something that no treaty or wampum belt, no matter how solemnly adhered to, could have possibly prevented. Had these events been predicted by a prophet, as has been suggested, he might better have kept his mouth shut, lest he be considered mad by all who heard him speak!

7

KEEPERS OF THE EASTERN DOOR

The European invasion of *Kanonhsionnì:ke*—Iroquois Country—had begun.

Not with a great army moving like a tide across our land, decimating everything in its path, but with explorers and traders venturing slowly but surely up rivers and across lakes, followed closely by missionaries, tradesmen, and farmers. The decimation came later, passed first in the breath of a spoken word of greeting, then in a handshake of friendship. Before any of our ancestors realized what was happening, the world had changed around them. While their eyes were diverted elsewhere, the lakes and streams had risen over their banks and were about to submerge them completely.

In the early part of the 17th century, the Dutch colony of New Netherland entered into a trading relationship with the Mohawks. By doing so, they opened a literal doorway to an extensive trading alliance. If the most powerful Indian confederacy of the northeast woodlands took for its symbol a bark longhouse, then the Mohawks were the "Keepers of the Eastern Door," or *Na'kónhke Rontehnhohanónhnha*. We were anxious to be a part of the trade that so many other Indian nations were already enjoying with the competitors of the Dutch. By forging ties to New Netherland, the Five Nations gained a powerful ally against New France, who countered by entering into short-lived peace treaties with the Iroquois starting in 1624.[60] This was the beginning of the Iroquois policy of playing one European power off the other, something our leaders attempt to do even today with the United States and Canada! Apparently the Dutch weren't above this same kind of tactic because they assisted the Mahican Indians near Fort Orange in a war against the Mohawks. The Mohawks won this war in 1628 and resumed trade with the Dutch.[61]

The French sought to establish peaceful trade with the Iroquois again in 1633, prompting the Dutch to send emissaries into Mohawk and Oneida territory in 1634. Harmen Meyendertsz van den Bogaert described the easternmost Mohawk village, which stood on the top of a hill:

There were only 36 houses, row on row in the manner of streets, so that we easily could pass through. These houses are constructed and covered with the bark of trees, and are mostly flat above. Some are 100, 90, or 80 steps long; 22 or 23 feet high. There were also some interior doors made of split planks furnished with iron hinges. In some houses we also saw iron-work: iron chains, bolts, harrow teeth, iron hoops, spikes, which they steal when they are away from here. Most of the people were out hunting for bear and deer. These houses were full of grain that they call ONESTI and we corn; indeed, some held 300 or 400 skipples. They make boats and barrels of tree-bark and sew with it. We ate here many baked and boiled pumpkins which they call ANONSIRA. None of the chiefs was at home, except for the most principal one called ADRI-OCHTE, who was living one quarter mile from the fort in a small cabin because many of the Indians here in the castle had died of smallpox.[62]

This was the first documented case of an epidemic striking the Mohawks. It would not be the last.

The Dutch delegation continued westward, visiting villages with 16, 32, 9, 14, and 55 houses. Eventually they reached an Oneida village with two rows of palisades and 66 houses. Their lack of presents resulted in a chillier reception:

In the afternoon, one of the councillors came to ask me what we were doing in his country and what we brought him for gifts. I said that we brought him nothing, but that we just came for a visit. However, he said that we were worth nothing because we brought him no gifts. Then he told how the French had traded with them here with six men and had given them good gifts; for they had traded in the aforementioned river last August of this year with six men. We saw there good timber axes, French shirts, coats, and razors. And this councilor derided us as scoundrels, and said that we were worthless because we gave them so little for their furs. They said that the French gave them six hands of sewant for one beaver and all sorts of other things in addition.[63]

The next day, a chief and another man returned from a visit with the "French Indians." Apparently, diplomatic efforts were under way:

> The Indians here told us that in that high country that we had seen near the lake there lived people with horns. They also said that many beavers were caught there; however, they dared not travel so far because of the French Indians. For this reason, therefore, they would make peace.[64]

They were shown evidence of these diplomatic overtures in the form of a wampum belt the following day:

> In the evening the Indians hung up a belt of sewant and some other strung sewant that the chief had brought back from the French Indians as a token of peace that the French Indians were free to come among them, and they sang HO SCHENE JO HO HO SCHENE I ATSIEHOENE ATSIEHOENE. Whereupon all the Indians shouted three times NETHO NETHO NETHO, and then hung another belt, singing KATON KATON KATON KATON. Then they shouted in a loud voice H_ H_ H_. After long deliberation they concluded the peace for four years, and then each went to his house.[65]

Peace with the "French Indians" was to be short lived, because the Senecas, the "Keepers of the Western Door," were soon launching attacks upon the Huron Confederacy, bringing back more than one hundred prisoners after one battle alone. The Mohawks and the other Iroquois began raiding the St. Lawrence River valley around this time. In 1642, the Seneca destroyed an *Arendaronon* village in Huronia. This was also the year that Jesuit Father Isaac Jogues, along with two French companions and a number of Hurons, were captured and tortured by Mohawks. In the summer of the following year, the Mohawks attacked a flotilla of Huron canoes as they approached Montréal.[66] Jogues escaped from captivity with the help of sympathetic Dutch merchants in November. The Mohawks made peace with the French in 1645. Jogues returned to Mohawk country as an envoy of the French the next year, but he and a companion were killed, apparently because the Mohawks blamed Jogues for the misfortunes that had befallen them since his escape:

Sickness having fallen upon their bodies after his departure, as we have learned from the Savage prisoners who have escaped, and the worms having perhaps damaged their corn, as the letter of the Dutch testifies,—these poor blind creatures have believed that the Father had left the Demon among them, and that all our discourses and all our instructions aimed only to exterminate them.[67]

The Mohawks were not alone in suspecting that the Jesuits were the source of deadly contagion. The Hurons also suspected this, as a French nun, Marie de l'Incarnation, wrote in 1640:

One of the oldest and most prominent women of this [Huron] nation harangued an assembly in this way: "It is the Black Robes that make us die by their spells. Hearken to me, I am proving by arguments you will know to be true. They lodged in a certain village where everyone was well. As soon as they were established there, everyone was dead except for three or four persons. They went everywhere and the same thing happened. They visited the cabins in other villages and only those they did not enter were free of mortality and sickness…. If they are not promptly put to death, they will finally ruin the country so that neither great nor small will remain."[68]

Were the Jesuits aware that their very presence among people with no immunity to European diseases was the cause of these "provident" epidemics? The following quote, taken from the *Jesuit Relations* of 1673-1674, suggests that they saw these outbreaks not as a tragedy but an opportunity:

Were we not convinced by experience that it is dangerous to administer baptism to little children who are not sick, we would baptize a very large number of them, with their parents' consent; but we do not venture to risk administering the sacrament, lest they might, later on, profane it by the infidelity in which they usually live when they grow older. Therefore we baptize only the children of Christians and of catechumens, and all who are in danger of death. I count twenty-seven who were baptized this year,—six of whom received baptism with the usual rites, the others without the rites; and they all died, with the exception of three. This is the most certain fruit that we gather in this country, where it is desirable that the children should die before obtaining the use of their reason.[69]

Even with the pitiful state of 17th century medical science, it is hard to believe that the Jesuits, the most educated people of their time, were unaware that they were firebrands igniting a forest of humanity. Our ancestors certainly knew it. Yet the writings of the Jesuits suggest it was just some bizarre coincidence that everywhere they went, pestilence was soon to follow.

The death of Father Jogues—another incident that will haunt us until the end of time—broke the tenuous peace between the Five Nations and New France and her Indian allies, and the "Iroquois Wars" resumed. The Jesuits documented these conflicts in their *Relations*. They cast the Iroquois as the villains of this great wilderness drama, as we see in the writing of Father Jerome Lalemont in 1659-1660:

That was at the time when the Dutch took possession of these regions and conceived a fondness for the beavers of the natives, some thirty years ago; and in order to secure them in greater number they furnished those people with firearms, with which it was easy for them to conquer their conquerors, whom they put to rout, and filled with terror at the mere sound of their guns. And that is what has rendered them formidable everywhere, and victorious over all the Nations with whom they have been at war; it has also put into their heads that idea of sovereign sway to which they aspire, mere barbarians although they are, with an ambition so lofty that they think and say that their own destruction cannot occur without bringing in its train the downfall of the whole earth.

But what is more astonishing is, that they actually hold dominion for five hundred leagues around, although their numbers are very small; for, of the five Nations constituting the Iroquois, the Agnieronnons [Mohawks] do not exceed five hundred men able to bear arms, who occupy three or four wretched Villages.

The Onneioutheronnons [Oneidas] have not a hundred warriors; the Onnontagehronnons [Onondagas] and Oiogoenhronons [Cayugas] have three hundred each, and the Sonontwaehronons [Senecas], who are the farthest removed from us and the most populous, have not more than a thousand combatants. If any one should compute the number of pure-blooded Iroquois, he would have difficulty in finding more than twelve hundred of them in all the five Nations, since these are, for the most part, only aggregations of different tribes whom they have conquered,—as the Hurons; the Tionnontatehronnons, otherwise called the Tobacco Nation; the Atiwendaronk, called the Neutrals when they were still independent; the Riquehronnons, who are the Cat Nation; the Ontwagannhas, or fire Nation; the Trakwaehronnons, and others,—who, utter Foreigners although they are, form without doubt the largest and best part of the Iroquois.

It is therefore a marvel that so few people work such great havoc and render themselves so redoubtable to so large a number of tribes, who, on all sides, bow before this conqueror.[70]

Historians at one time likened the Five Nations to an empire, but today they shy away from such grandiose terminology. We did have one thing in common with other empires, however: we were destined to fall!

Even before our dispersal of the Petuns, Neutrals, and Eries in the 1650's, Iroquois unity had begun to unravel, with individual nations making peace or waging war according to their own interests. In 1647, the Onondagas grew weary of war and sent an embassy of three Onondaga chiefs and 15 Huron captives to Huronia. In January of 1648, the Huron sent a delegation of their own to Onondaga with one of the Onondaga ambassadors. En route, they were attacked by a combined force of Seneca and Mohawk warriors. The Onondaga was spared and two Hurons managed to escape. The Jesuits describe what happened when news of this attack reached the two Onondaga ambassadors who were still among the Huron:

At the beginning of the month of April, Scandaouati, the Onnontaeronnon Ambassador who had remained here as hostage, disappeared, and our Hurons thought that he had escaped; but after some days his Corpse was found in the middle of a wood, not far from the Village where he resided. The poor man had killed himself by cutting his throat with a knife, after having prepared a sort of bed made of fir-branches, on which he was found stretched out.

At this spectacle, his companion was sent for, that he might witness all that had occurred and see that the Hurons had had nothing to do with the murder. "In fact," he said to them, "I suspected that he would do such a deed; what caused his despair is the shame that he felt at seeing the Sonnontoueronnons and the Annieronnons come and massacre your people on your very frontiers. For, although they are your enemies, they are our allies; and they ought to have shown us this much respect that, as we had come here on an embassy, they should have waited to strike an evil blow until after our return, when our lives would have been safe. He has considered it too great a contempt for his person, and that shame has caused him to sink into desperate thoughts. And, doubtless, that is what he meant to say to our third companion, who has gone back with your Ambassadors, when, on his departure, he told him to notify those of our Nation that if, during these negotiations for peace and while he was here, any evil blow were struck, the shame of it would cause his death. He added that he was not a dead dog, to be abandoned; and that he well deserved that the eyes of the whole earth should be fixed on him, and that it should remain quiet while his life would be in danger." Such is the extent to which our Savages pique themselves upon a point of honor.[71]

In 1654, when Jesuit Father Simon Le Moyne went directly to Onondaga to establish a mission, two Mohawk delegates went to Quebec to express their disappointment that the French had not obeyed confederacy protocol by going to the Mohawks first:

The Anniehronnon Captain made his complaints on the subject with cleverness and intelligence. "Ought not one," said he, "to enter a house by the door, and not by the chimney or roof of the cabin, unless he be a thief, and wish to take the inmates by surprise? We, the five Iroquois Nations, compose but one cabin; we maintain but one fire; and we have, from time immemorial, dwelt under one and the same roof." In fact, from the earliest times, these five Iroquois Nations have been called in their own language, which is Huron, *Hotinnonchiendi*,—that is, "the completed Cabin," as if to express that they constituted but one family. "Well, then," he continued, "will you not enter the cabin by the door, which is at the ground floor of the house? It is with us Anniehronnons, that you should begin; whereas you, by beginning with the Onnontaehronnons, try to enter by the roof and through the chimney. Have you no fear that the smoke may blind you, our fire not being extinguished, and that you may fall from the top to the bottom, having nothing solid on which to plant your feet?"[72]

It had only been a half century since European colonists first came knocking on the eastern door of the Longhouse, and already the great structure was starting to break apart. It was as if a great wind was blowing bark sheaths loose from the walls, compromising the effectiveness of its centuries-old design. In the decades to follow, factionalism and strife would make their way into the individual nations, villages, clans and families of the Rotinonhsón:ni.

8

PEOPLE OF THE LONGHOUSE

Let us consider for a moment the engineering marvel of the northeast woodlands, the bark longhouse that was known in Mohawk as *Kanonhsión:ni,* or "Extended House."

There is ample historical documentation about the dwellings and the villages of the Iroquoians encountered by Cartier, Champlain, and Jesuit missionaries. They suggest a consistency in construction from nation to nation, with only minor differences. There have been many attempts to reconstruct them over the years with varying degrees of success. One of the more recent attempts is found at the Drouler's Archaeological Site in Saint-Anicet, Quebec. The debate about how they were constructed has become a sub-genre within the Iroquoian literature.

Adriean Cornelissen van der Donck, a Dutch colonist, left us a fairly detailed description of not only of the longhouses, but the palisaded "castles" where they were found. We presume he described what he saw among the Mohawks, the Iroquoian nation closest to New Netherland. Here is what he recorded in 1653:

> Their houses are mostly of one and the same shape, without any special embellishment or remarkable design. When building a house, large or small,—for sometimes they build them as long as some hundred feet, though never more than twenty feet wide—they stick long, thin, peeled hickory poles in the ground, as wide apart and as long in a row as the house is to be. The poles are then bent over and fastened one to another, so that it looks like a wagon or arbor as are put in gardens. Next, strips like split laths are laid across these poles from one end to the other. On large houses the strips below are laid rather close together than on the roofs, and upwards in proportion until they are a foot or so apart. This is then well covered all over with very tough bark. For durability everything is peeled, so that no worms can get in it. Then they go out and get the bark

Longhouse recreation at Drouler's Archaeological Site. Photo by the author.

of ash, elm, and chestnut trees; if it is late in summer, rather than peel those, though they need the bark, they take yew trees that grow near the waterside, whose bark yields easily even when the others are dry. With such pieces of bark about a fathom square, the smooth side turned inward, they cover the entire wooden frame, [the members of which are] up to a foot apart near the top, as has been stated, and tie the bark down securely where needed. If there is a hole or tear in the bark they know how to plug it up, and against shrinking, they let the [sheets of] bark overlap one another. In sum, they arrange it so that their houses repel rain and wind, and are also fairly warm, but they know nothing about fitting them out with rooms, salons, halls, closets, or cabinets. From one end of the house to the other along the center they kindle fires, and the area left open, which is also in the middle, serves as chimney to release the smoke. Often there are sixteen or eighteen families in a house, fewer or more according as the houses are large or small. The door is in the middle, and the people on either side. Everyone knows his space and how far his place extends. If they have room for pot and kettle and whatever else they have, and

Interior of longhouse. Photo by the author.

a place to sleep, they desire no more. This means that often a hundred or a hundred and fifty and more lodge in one house. Such is the arrangement of a house as they commonly are found everywhere, unless they are out hunting or fishing, then they merely put up a makeshift.[73]

Bark longhouses were far from the crude structures that European descriptions seem to imply. The people who inhabited the woodlands were skilled in making canoes and baskets made from bark and employed the same skills and techniques in creating their homes. These structures were able to sustain not only their own weight but the addition of a heavy snow load each winter.

Van der Donck described the defensive fortifications, or palisades, that surrounded the longhouses:

> In the villages and castles they always do solid and good work. As sites for their castles they tend to prefer, if possible, a high or steep hill near water or a riverside, which is difficult to climb up and often accessible on one side only. They always take care also that it is flat and even on top. This they enclose with a very heavy wooden stockade constructed in a peculiar interlocking diamond pattern. First they lay a heavy tree along the ground, sometimes with a lighter one on top, as wide and as broad as they intend to make the foundation. Then they set

heavy oak palisades diagonally in the ground on both sides, which form a cross at the upper end where they are notched to fit tighter together. Next another tree is laid in there to make a very solid work. The palisades stand two deep, sufficiently strong to protect them from a surprise attack or sudden raid by their enemies, but they do not as yet have any knowledge of properly equipping such a work with curtains, bastions, and flanking walls.[74]

There were other types of dwellings less fortified:

They also build some small forts here and there on the level and low land near their plantations to shelter their wives and children from any assault, in case they have enemies so nearby that they could be fallen upon by small parties. They think highly of their forts and castles built in that fashion, but these actually are of little consequence, and cause them more harm than good in war with the Christians. In such a castle they often put twenty or thirty houses, up to a hundred feet and some even longer, like those measured by our people at up to 180 paces. Seeing that they manage with so little space in these castles, as related above, they cram such a multitude of people inside that it is unbelievable and leaves one amazed when he sees them come out. Besides these castles they have other settlements that lie in the open in the manner of villages. Most of them have the woods on one side and their corn fields on the other. They also have settlements at some places near waterways where they are accustomed to do much fishing every year, and at the same time do some planting, but those places they leave toward winter and go to live in the castles or in the deep woods where it is warm and firewood is close at hand. There as well no wind can trouble them, and they have good opportunity for hunting, by which they nourish themselves in place of fishing. They seldom abandon their secure castles and large settlements completely; otherwise they find it very easy to pack up and move. They seldom remain long in one place, but follow the season and time of the year. That is, in the summer, when the fishing is good, they move to the

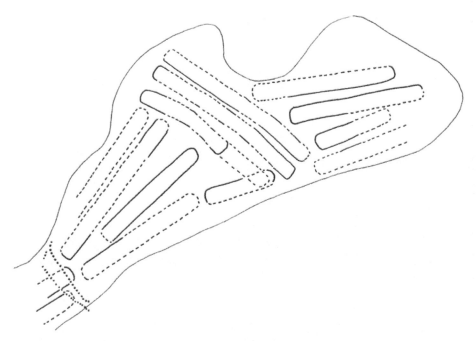

Garoga Archaeological Site, showing excavated longhouses in solid lines and projected longhouse outlines in dashes. Circa 1525-1580. Sketch by the author.

watersides and rivers; in the autumn and winter, when meat is
best, they seek the woods.[75]

The 17th century was the beginning of the end of the classic bark longhouse. Before Europeans came onto the scene, longhouses were built
according to the topography of the land and were extended with addi-
tions as daughters grew up and started their own families. A good
example of this would be the Garoga site, which had longhouses more
than 200 feet long and was located at the top of a steep, high hill, the
longhouses arrayed in a way that flowed naturally with the contours of
the land, perhaps to minimize wind resistance on the structures.

By the last decades of the 17th century, less than a generation after
Adriean Cornelissen van der Donck described them, Mohawk longhouses were seldom more than about 130 feet long. They were arrayed
in neat little rows within a very geometrical stockade pattern, as is evi-
denced at the Caughnawaga site in Fonda, New York. This was purely
for defensive purposes, as a number of attacks by native and non-native
foes occurred in the mid- to late-1600's that made the old "extended
lodge" model increasingly untenable. For that matter, even this compact

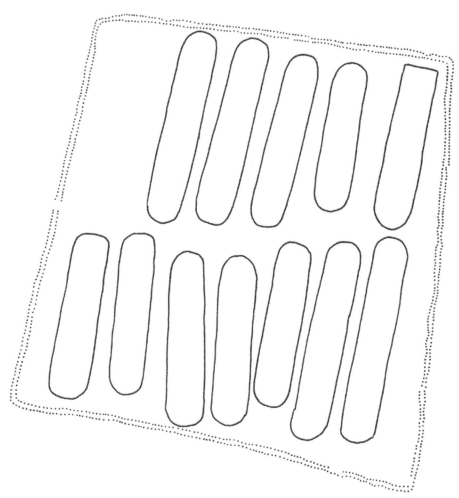

Caughnawaga Archaeological Site. Circa 1679-1683. Sketch by the author.

village model proved to be ineffective as the close proximity of the long-houses to one another made it easy for enemies to burn the entire castle to the ground. This happened at the Caughnawaga site in 1693.

It is usually assumed that by the 18th century, bark longhouses were gone completely, replaced by European-styled houses that were in many cases of higher quality than those of surrounding colonists. Archaeologist Wayne Lenig informs us that the bark longhouse did survive for a while longer, albeit in a somewhat abbreviated form:

Some writers have intimated that the classic bark longhouse was totally replaced by single family frame and log structures in the Mohawk homeland by 1725, and that I would absolutely disagree with. The "short house," as it sometimes called, may have signaled the locally dwindling population and size of family units, but it was clad with bark and built on the same plan as the earlier longhouses. There is good historical evidence that at least some of these structures ("short houses") were still in use in the 3rd quarter of the 18th century. Of course at the same time many Mohawk families, like the Brants, owned far more substantial frame houses—so the late 18th century was a time of transition in the Mohawk Valley.[76]

One of these "short longhouses" was excavated at a site west of Seneca Lake that dates to the 1720's. The two-family dwelling measuring 7.5 by 5.3 meters (24.6 by 17.4 feet) was described by archaeologist Kurt A. Jordan:

> This structure clearly has an Iroquoian floorplan with four weight-bearing interior support posts, meaning that it likely contained a central hearth and two sleeping platforms. Based on the presence of a significant number of iron nails, the use of large and square posts in exterior walls, and the decreased frequency of wall posts as compared to earlier structures, I have interpreted the short longhouse as an "intercultural" dwelling. Its Seneca builders used European tools and hardware in the service of traditional Iroquoian architectural principles, and also likely substituted rigid log or plank siding in the place of bark.[77]

Archaeologist Dean R. Snow informs us that the Onondagas were also living in these kinds of structures by the 1740's. John Bartram described the existence of a single longhouse at Onondaga in 1743 that was used as a place for lodging guests, while the typical Onondaga family resided in smaller dwellings with either gabled or rounded roofs. There is evidence that a similar architecture was evolving at the Kahnawà:ke community near Montréal in this same time period. In the Mohawk Valley, the 18th century villages consisted of scattered log cabins and frame houses with a British fort nearby for protection.[78]

In modern times, the "longhouse" is a just a long log cabin or frame house where ceremonies and socials are held. However, there is a growing interest in the old bark longhouse concept, perhaps due to modern reconstructions at historic sites and museums. Although these are admittedly based on conjectural interpretations of historic documentation and archaeological research, walking through them evokes something very powerful within us, a sense that our ancestors were able to use our natural resources to create something far more impressive than has previously been recognized. We also see how our dwellings reinforced the strength of the extended family by keeping everyone beneath one roof where they could interact and work in concert. Such a living arrangement was perfectly suited for a matrilineal society such as ours where work activities were gender-specific and bound to a seasonal schedule.

In more than just name, the old bark longhouse is at the very heart of our identity, even if today's longhouse is just a structure that we hold our ceremonies in, and not a place where we dwell. It leaves one to wonder if our modern society, broken up into "nuclear" divisions and single-family homes for so long, could ever return to the "extended lodge" way of life and all that comes with it. One could not live in such close confines without a "Great Law of Peace" to govern our interactions. This friendly spirit would have to extend to all of our neighbors, just as it did in days of old. If we have learned anything from our teachings, it's that people who live in bark longhouses should not throw burning spears.[79]

9

THE DEVIL'S NEPHEWS

By now the reader has noticed that we are already several chapters into this book and our subject has not yet made an appearance. There's a perfectly good reason for this. Most biographies of Káteri Tekahkwí:tha begin by painting a quaint picture of a child of nature waiting for the Jesuits to show up. They rarely address the historical and cultural background of the story, and when they do it is usually in passing. The authors of these books are basically telling the story of a religious awakening, so they see no need to describe the darkness of the slumber leading up to it.

From my perspective, you simply can't tell this story properly without an extensive background, because the background *is* the story.

As later chapters will reveal, the Jesuits who knew her personally portrayed Káteri Tekahkwí:tha as someone who had Christian virtues long before she knew anything about Christianity, as if she had been a Christian all along. Yet when you read their words, they describe a child going about her life like anyone else, participating in work and recreational activities the same as other Mohawk girls. In fact, they say that she was a particularly gifted artisan with a deft touch. As much as they try to convey that she was somehow alien to it, she was a part of her culture, and a valued one at that.

Some of the more superficial biographies tend to portray the arrival of Jesuits as a watershed moment not only in her life, but for the Mohawks in general. They come bearing a blazing torch that either attracts the Mohawks to it or drives them further into the shadows.

The reality is, Mohawks were no strangers to Christianity and its teachings, having been in contact with missionaries and laymen colonists for generations by the time our subject met her first Jesuit. They had plenty of time to think about this new religion and debate its fine points. Before Káteri Tekahkwí:tha was even born, they had generally made up their minds that it wasn't for them, and they chose to express this rejection in a way that was both respectful and sarcastic at the same time.

In the preceding chapter we encountered Adriean Cornelissen van der Donck's description of Iroquois longhouses and villages in the middle of the 17th century. His 1653 manuscript, written three years before Káteri's birth, contains a wide range of observations, including the clothing our ancestors wore; the food they ate; their manner of hunting, fishing, and planting; their marriage customs; the way they mourned their dead; and their religious beliefs. Let us consider what he said about this last topic:

> They are all heathens, have no particular religion or devotion, and no known idols or images they venerate, let alone worship. When swearing an oath they take as witness the sun, regarding as all seeing. They have great affection for the moon, as governing all growth, yet do not worship or pay homage to it. The other planets they know by name, and through that knowledge and from other signs they are fairly weather-wise. To pray and celebrate holy days, or anything like it, is not known among them. They do know something of God, as we shall remark later, and are in great fear of the devil, for he harms and torments them much. When they have been out fishing or hunting they customarily throw a portion of the catch in the fire and say without ceremony, there, devil, eat you that.[80]

The Indians had an ironic way of looking at Christianity that posed a challenge to both the Dutch and the French:

> They appreciate hearing about God and our religion, and during our services and prayers they keep very quiet and seem to pay attention, but in reality they have no notion of these matters. They live without religion and inner or outward devotions; even superstition and idolatry are unknown to them and they follow the dictates of nature alone. For that reason some suppose that they may all the easier be led to the knowledge and fear of God. Only one of the Indian nations has a word for Sunday, which they call *Kintowen*. The oldest among them say that in early times a greater knowledge and fear of God existed, but, they say, because we are unable to read and write and the people are becoming more wicked, the Sunday has fallen into disuse and oblivion. When talking earnestly with them about this, they show some signs of regret, but none of emotion.

When one berates them, individually or generally, for some wicked act or speech on the ground that it incurs the wrath of God in heaven, they reply, we do not know that God or where he is and have never seen him; if you know and fear him, as you say you do, how come there are so many whores, thieves, drunkards, and other evildoers among you; surely that God of yours will punish you severely, since He warned you of it. He never warned us, and left us in ignorance, therefore we do not deserve such punishment. Very seldom do they adopt our religion, nor have any particular official measures been resorted to or applied to induce them to do so. When their children are still young it happens that our people take them into the home as servants, and as opportunities arise give them some slight religious instruction, but when they grow to be young men and women, and begin to mix with other Indians, they soon forget what they never learnt thoroughly, and revert to Indian ways and manners. The Jesuits in Canada have made an effort and led many to the Roman Catholic religion, but because they have no inner inclination towards it or were not properly taught the principles and have regard to appearances only, they easily lapse from the faith and actually mock it.[81]

He then relates an anecdote about an old Indian chief who was instructed in Christianity, but walked away from the faith when the Christian God was put to the test—and apparently failed!

Thus it happened when a certain merchant who still resides amongst us went up to trade with the Indians in the year 1639 and got into a discussion on religion with a chief who spoke French well, which the merchant also understood. After they had downed five or six glasses of wine the chief said, I myself had so far been instructed in religion by your people that I frequently said mass among the Indians; once upon a time the place in which the altar stood accidentally caught fire and the people rushed forward to quench it, but I checked them, saying, the God standing there is almighty and will shortly make the fire go out by itself; then we waited expectantly, but the fire burned steadily on until it had consumed everything, including even your almighty God and all the fine objects around him. Ever since I have disliked religion and esteemed the sun and the moon much more and better than all your gods, for they (the sun and the moon) warm the earth and make the crops grow, and your God cannot save himself from fire.[82]

Van der Donck noted that the Indians' view of the afterlife gave him hope that they might one day accept Christianity:

It is cause for great wonder and powerful evidence against all unbelieving free-thinkers that these people who are so barbaric and wild, as has been shown, nevertheless are able to distinguish between body and soul, and believe, as in fact they do, the one to be perishable and the other immortal. The soul, they say, is that which animates and rules the body, and from which springs all the virtues and vices. When separated from the body at death the soul travels to a region to the southward so equable one never needs protective covering against the cold, yet not so hot as to be uncomfortable. That is the destination of the souls who were good and virtuous in this life, and where they enjoy everything in abundance, for all things needed are in infinite supply without requiring, any labour. Those who in this life were wicked and evil will be in another place differing completely in condition and qualities from the first, nor will they enjoy anything like the contentment of the virtuous. Whether the body will at some time be reunited with the soul, I have never been able to ascertain from them. I have spoken with Christians who thought to have heard them say so, but I cannot affirm it. When they hear voices or sounds coming from the woods in the dead of night that we reckon were made by a wild animal, they say in consternation, what you hear calling there are the souls of the wicked persons who are doomed to wander about and haunt woods and wilderness in the night and at unseasonable times. For fear of them the Indians will not go anywhere at night, unless in a group when they must; otherwise they always take a torch. They are frightened of evil spirits who, they believe, remain intent on hurting and terrifying them. They confess and believe also that the soul comes from, and is given by, God. That is what one may on occasion learn from them when talking in a serious vein with the old and wise; more perhaps could be gotten from them if one knew their language thoroughly. Among the common people or the youngsters one never hears those matters spoken of, but one can nevertheless see the righteousness of God who through the universal light of mankind's nature has made these people understand, recognize, and surmise that the reward for doing good and evil awaits men after this life.[83]

While there were strong similarities between the Indian beliefs and Christian teachings, some of what the Indians believed was bewildering to van der Donck:

Although the original natives of New Netherlands are heathen and unbelievers, they all know and confess that there is a God in heaven, eternal and almighty. Since God is in the highest degree good and merciful, they aver, and unwilling to hurt or punish any human being He does not concern Himself at all with the ordinary affairs of the world. The devil takes advantage of the scope thus given him, and all that happens to man here below, they believe, the devil disposes, guides, and governs at will. God, or the supreme chief, who dwells in heaven is no doubt much greater and higher than the devil and also has dominion over him, but declines to become involved in all those troubles. When we respond to this by saying that the devil is evil, cunning, and wicked, they frankly admit that to be true and also that he takes great pleasure in directing all matters in as baneful a way as he can. They further maintain that every misfortune, scourge, calamity, and infirmity is inflicted on them by the devil. They express by the general appellation of devil all accidents and illnesses they suffer, for example, in case of internal disorder they say there is a devil within my body, and if something ails them in an arm, leg, foot, hand, shoulder, or the head they say, pointing to the affected part, there is a devil inside. Since the devil is so malicious and merciless towards them they have no choice but to fear and yet keep on friendly terms with him and sometimes throw him a morsel into the fire to please him, as stated above. When we refute those absurdities easily we do so by saying to them that God is omniscient and omnipotent; knows the nature of devils exactly, quietly observes their doings; and will not permit a puffed-up and faithless servant to tyrannize man, who is the most glorious creature of all and made in God's image, provided he duly puts his trust in God and does not forsake His commandments in favor of evil. To that they respond with a weird and fantastic argument: You Dutch say so, and seen superficially it may seem to be as you maintain, but you do not understand the matter aright. This God, who is supremely good, almighty, and beneficent, Lord of all heaven and earth and all its host, is not alone up there in heaven without any company or diversion, but has with him a goddess or woman who is the fairest the eye has ever seen or can see. With this goddess or beauty He passes and forgets the time, being deeply attached to her, and meanwhile the devil lords it on earth and does whatever he wishes. That conviction is firmly inculcated in them and no matter how far one pursues the argument and reasons with them, whatever abominable absurdities they resort to, and whether one checkmates them in debate, in the end they return to the view, like the dog that licks up its own vomit, that the devil must be served because he has power to harm them.[84]

Van der Donck's observations are reminiscent of what Dutch minister Johannes Megapolensis recorded about the Mohawks in 1644:

They have also naturally a high opinion of themselves; they say, *Ihy Othkon,* ("I am the Devil") by which they mean that they are superior folks. In order to praise themselves and their people, whenever we tell them they are very expert at catching deer, or doing this and that, they say, *Tkoschs ko, aguweechon Kajingahaga kouaane Jountuckcha Othkon;* that is, "Really all the Mohawks are very cunning devils."

...

They are entire strangers to all religion, but they have a Tharonhijouaagon, (whom they also otherwise call Athzoockkuatoriaho,) that is, a Genius, whom they esteem in the place of God; but they do not serve him or make offerings to him. They worship and present offerings to the Devil, whom they call *Otskon,* or *Aireskuoni.* If they have any bad luck in war, they catch a bear, which they cut in pieces, and roast, and that they offer up to their Aireskuoni, saying in substance, the following words: "Oh! great and mighty Aireskuoni, we confess that we have offended against thee, inasmuch as we have not killed and eaten our captive enemies;—forgive us this. We promise that we will kill and eat all the captives we shall hereafter take as certainly as we have killed, and now eat this bear." Also when the weather is very hot, and there comes a cooling breeze, they cry out directly, *Asorunusi, asorunusi, Otskon aworouhsi reinnuha;* that is, "I thank thee, I thank thee, devil, I thank thee, little uncle!" If they are sick, or have a pain or soreness anywhere in their limbs, and I ask them what ails them they say that the Devil sits in their body, or in the sore places, and bites them there; so that they attribute to the Devil at once the accidents which befall them; they have otherwise no religion.[85]

When the Indians spoke of God and the Devil, they were usually referring to characters of our own mythology, and not necessarily those from the colonists' Holy Scripture. Sapling and Flint were brothers, so it makes sense that they would infer a family relationship between the various entities—and between the entities and themselves—as they did by referring to "Otskon" as "little uncle."

When we pray they laugh at us. Some of them despise it entirely; and some, when we tell them what we do when we pray, stand astonished. When we deliver a sermon, sometimes ten or twelve of them, more or less, will attend, each having a long tobacco pipe, made by himself, in his mouth, and will stand awhile and look, and afterwards ask me what I am doing and what I want, that I stand there alone and make so many words, while none of the rest may speak. I tell them that I am admonishing the Christians, that they must not steal, nor commit lewdness, nor get drunk, nor commit murder, and that they too ought not to do these things; and that I intend in process of time to preach the same to them and come to them in their own country and castles (about three days' journey from here, further inland), when I am acquainted with their language. Then they say I do well to teach the Christians; but immediately add, *Diatennon jawij Assirioni, hagiouisk,* that is, "Why do so many Christians do these things?"[86]

The sardonic Mohawks were not the only Iroquois to reject the precepts of Christianity. In 1657, about a year after Káteri Tekahkwí:tha was born, a French colonist named Pierre-Esprit Radisson was part of an expedition to the Mission of Sainte-Marie-de-Gannentaa (Onondaga). Radisson shared a canoe with a young Onondaga man with whom he did not get along very well. While paddling on Lake Ontario, the two were overtaken by a fierce storm, which resulted in an impromptu diatribe against Christian beliefs by Radisson's rain-soaked companion:

Instantly comes a shower of rain with a storm of wind that was able to perish us by reason of the great quantity of water that came into our boat. The lake began to vapor and make a show of his Neptune's sheep. Seeing we went backwards rather than forwards, we thought ourselves utterly lost. The rogue that was with me said, "See thy God that thou sayest he is above. Will you make me believe now that he is good, as the black-coats [the father Jesuits] say? They do lie, and you see the contrary; for first you see that the sun burns us often, the rain wets us, the wind makes us have shipwreck, the thundering, the lightnings burns and kills, and all come from above, and you say that it's good to be there. For my part I will not go there. Contrary they say that the reprobates and guilty go down & burn. They are mistaken; all is good here. Do not you see the earth that nourishes all living creatures, the water the fishes, and the yews, and that corn and all other seasonable fruits for our food, which are not so contrary to us as that from above?" As he said so he cursed vehemently after his own manner. He took his instruments & showed them to the heavens, saying, "I will not be above; here will [I] stay on earth, where all my friends are, and not with the French, that are to be burned above with torments."[87]

Although their canoe took on a dangerous level of water, Radisson and his companion were finally able to overcome the storm and complete their journey to Onondaga territory. Radisson eventually published an account of his adventures, preserving forever that moment on Lake Ontario when a haughty Onondaga warrior raised his paddle and chastised a raging tempest.

10

VILLAGE OF THE
TURTLE CLAN

A lthough Rotinonhsión:ni society is divided into numerous animal clans, there are three that are common to each nation—the turtle, bear and wolf. Historically, the Mohawk and Oneida had only these three clans. The turtles, bears, and wolves among the Mohawk controlled separate villages laid out from east to west, respectively. There were members of other clans at each of these villages, since you could not marry someone of your own clan, but it was generally understood by European visitors that Mohawk villages were associated with specific totems. This had largely faded away by the 18th century due to various disruptions, migrations, and consolidations of populations, but in the 17th century, Mohawk villages were still affiliated with the three clans. Of special interest to us are the turtle clan villages located east of the modern-day settlement of Kana'tsioharé:ke. This area was the home Káteri Tekahkwí:tha.

Modern-day followers of Káteri inevitably make a pilgrimage to her two shrines in the Mohawk Valley of New York State. One is located at Auriesville and the other at Fonda, two small towns south and north of the Mohawk River, respectively. They are said to be the site of two villages where she lived at different points in her life. The Auriesville site is notable for the presence of a massive, coliseum-like church, the National Shrine of the North American Martyrs. This is a memorial to the Jesuit missionaries who gave their lives for the faith in the 17th century. The National Shrine of Blessed Káteri Tekahkwí:tha at Fonda is noted for the presence of the Caughnawaga archaeological site, identified as the place where Káteri lived before moving north to the St. Lawrence River. The location of the palisades and longhouses are marked by metal pegs, which gives you an idea of the size and layout of a late-17th century Mohawk village. There is also a museum with countless artifacts acquired from the survey conducted on the site in the 1950's by Father Thomas Grassmann, author of *The Mohawk Indians and Their Valley* (1969).[88]

On any given day, one is likely to find the faithful followers of Káteri Tekahkwí:tha at either of these shrines, happily following in the footsteps of the Lily of the Mohawks. The problem is, she never actually lived there, and probably never even set foot at either location. The places where she really lived are miles away, completely unmarked, and known only to professional archaeologists, local residents, and the occasional pothunter.

The misidentification of the Káteri shrines as actual villages where she lived is due to the lack of sophisticated archaeological knowledge at the time these memorials were constructed. Today we know the real site locations because of the presence of glass trade beads and other artifacts which can help pinpoint the timeframe of village occupation. Because so much time, money, and publicity had been invested in the shrines by the time this knowledge became available, nobody was in a big hurry to correct this historical error for the general public. Perhaps this is just as well, because the true sites remain somewhat protected from the casual pothunter, although the more serious of that ilk have probably scoured the archaeological reports by now and figured out where to look!

Káteri Tekahkwí:tha lived in four different villages throughout her life. Three were in the Mohawk Valley, and the forth was on the St. Lawrence in Canada. Archaeologists refer to the village where she was born as the Printup site, but 17th century colonists called it *Ossernenon, Osserrïon, Asserue, Gandaouage,* and *Kaghnuwage.*

Dean Snow documented the known Mohawk village sites in his *Mohawk Valley Archaeology: The Sites* (1995), and its companion piece, *The Collections.*[89] This is an exhaustive survey of the published literature; the only thing missing is any mention of archaeologists being chased through tunnels by giant, rolling rocks.

Snow describes the Printup site as being located in the town of Glen on a bluff overlooking the Mohawk River to the north and west.[90] He describes some of the artifacts that suggest the time of occupation:

> Many of the artifacts in the assemblage were available in earlier periods. However, the R mouth harps and Jesuit rings are crucial in showing that the initial date of the site was no earlier than 1646. The most frequently noted kaolin pipe heel marks bear the EB mark. Diamond fleur-de-lis kaolin pipes are also known for the site. The EB pipes first appeared at Fort Orange after 1644, and they are diagnostic of the A.D. 1646-

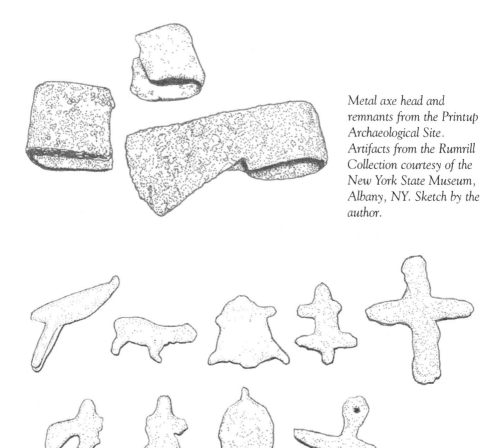

Metal axe head and remnants from the Printup Archaeological Site. Artifacts from the Rumrill Collection courtesy of the New York State Museum, Albany, NY. Sketch by the author.

Lead effigies from the Printup Archaeological Site. Artifacts from the Rumrill Collection courtesy of the New York State Museum, Albany, NY. Sketch by the author.

1666 period. Some of these have funnel bowls and EB marks stamped flush on their unheeled bases. The distinctive funnel bowl shape might have been made only for the North American Indian trade. McCashion puts their date of manufacture at A.D. 1655-1665. He suggested that the absence of funnel bowl types at Printup provides evidence that the site was abandoned by that time....

Round red beads, which come to dominate the assemblages by the end of A.D. 1646-1666 period, are also missing here. This too is evidence that the site was abandoned before the end of the period.

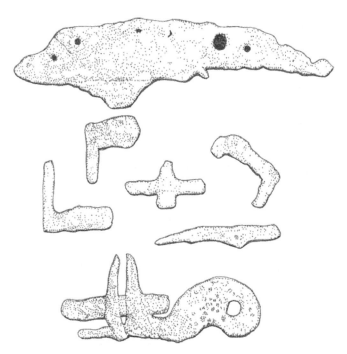

Metal gun parts from the Printup Archaeological Site. Artifacts from the Rumrill Collection courtesy of the New York State Museum, Albany, NY. Sketch by the author.

Many incised Jesuit rings have been found on the site, and these all point to an occupation in the 1650's. Jogues and his companions might have brought a few rings with them before 1646, but it is likely that most or all of them came in after 1655, when Jesuit missionaries were again allowed to be active in Mohawk villages...

Rumrill estimates that that the Printup site dated to the period A.D. 1647-1660. He infers that this community moved to the Freeman site around 1660, and he makes a strong case for that inference.

Mohawk chiefs asked for assistance in building a new castle in 1659. They called the new castle "Kaghnuwage," the first appearance of this place-name. Thus the Printup site was occupied during, but not throughout, the A.D. 1646-1666 period. Its span of occupation was probably A.D. 1646-1659.[91]

Snow cites the research of Donald A. Rumrill, who published the following information about the site in 1985:

A rather significant fact about Printup is the abundance of gun parts. Fortunately, the make up of the soil seems to somewhat preserve rather than to destroy iron. Pistol locks and right and left hand musket gunlocks are in evidence.

....

Converse to the substantial number of gun parts is the almost absolute dearth of native pottery. I know of only a very few fragments of Indian ceramics to come from this site.

....

At least 100 Jesuit rings and other religious artifacts have been found at this location to date. This by itself surely places the Printup village site within the dates of 1655 to 1678 and most probably in the earlier spans of 1655-56 and 1657-58....

Brass artifacts include kettle remnants, especially lugs whose styles were cast, rolled, folded corners, and clipped corners. Arrow points that are conical, triangular, round shouldered, bifurcated, shafted, single and double perforations, and imperforate, bangles, pendants, bracelets, and thimbles are other brass items.

....

There are several of us who have been surface hunting Printup for a good number of years and we all pretty much agree as to what the perimeters seem to be. Having measured these outlines, it appears to be a site of approximately 1.87 acres including three large midden areas. The fields have also been plowed most of these years and the Indian dirt at times is well pronounced. Keeping records and sharing information of where the artifacts have been found and at least four good interpretive estimates without any actual excavation, the probability is for seven or, at most, eight longhouses running west to east on an "L" shaped plot.[92]

The artifacts gathered by Rumrill and other archaeologists from the Printup site confirm that a major transition was taking place in the material culture of the Mohawk at this time. This became more pronounced in the villages that succeeded this one. One can only wonder what future archaeologists will say about us when they find the things we leave behind.

11

COUNCILS WITH THE DUTCH, 1657-1660

Archaeologist Dean Snow mentions in his summary of the Printup site that the Mohawk chiefs had asked the Dutch for assistance in constructing a new "castle" in 1659. In fact, there were a number of councils in which repairs and construction of palisades and castles was discussed starting in 1657. They are documented in *Minutes of the Court of Fort Orange and Beverwyck, 1657-1660*. They illustrate not only that a new castle was being created, but the precarious state of affairs not only with other Indians, but with the French and Dutch colonists.

The 16th of June Anno 1657, the sachems of the three castles of the Maquaes sent to Mr Lamontagne, vice-director, the chief named Sadiadego, who requested in the name of the said sachems that they might be heard the same day. Whereupon the vice-director convened the court.

At which meeting appeared the three sachems of the three Maquaes castles, who after the usual ceremonies made the following propositions:

First, they requested us as old friends that we should accommodate them with some horses to haul logs out of the woods to repair their castles and that we should protect their wives and children here in the village in case they should be involved in a war with the Sinnekes, offering on this proposition a string of seawan amounting to fl.16:12:-

Secondly, as all three castles belong to the same nation and they are bound to help each other in time of need, which can not well be done without warning each other of their distress, they ask that we should assist each of the castles with a cannon and that the same should be drawn by horses from here to the flatts (*de vlackte*), being 8 [Dutch] miles from here. Upon which proposition they offered another string of seawan, amounting to fl.16:9:-

Thirdly, [they state] that in passing through on their way to the Mahikanders they called upon us to renew the old friendship between us and them. Whereupon they offered a third string of seawan, amounting to fl.13:10:-[93]

Their appeal suggests instability in Mohawk Country. Five days later, the court replied as follows:

As to the first proposition, concerning the horses, the answer is that they have no horses of their own, but if they [the Indians] are willing to pay for them, they will try to persuade some people to accommodate them. As to lodging their women and children in case of war against the Sinnekens, they are ready to do so for the sake of their old friendship, but they hope that it will not be necessary.

As to the second proposition, about the request for the cannon, the answer is that the cannon do not belong to them, but to their superiors, who have given them to them for their defense, so that they can neither give them away nor loan them without their consent. They will write about it to the director general and await his reply.

As to the third proposition, about renewing the old friendship between us and them, the answer is that they are ready to maintain it and thank them for the favorable disposition which they show toward us.[94]

The "Sinnekes" or "Sinnekens" mentioned in these quotes refers not only to the Senecas, but to the Oneidas, Onondagas, and Cayugas. The Dutch lumped all of the non-Mohawk Iroquois together under this name. They may have misinterpreted the Mohawk comment that they were going to war *with* the so-called Sinnekens as meaning they were going to war *against* the Sinnekens, but things were so chaotic back then that they may have heard them right!

The Mohawks returned to Fort Orange on September 6th, 1659:

They say they have taken the path to treat with one another in friendship and thereupon give a string of seawan.

They say that they and other savages dislike to see their

nation drink so much brandy. Give thereupon two beavers.

They say that they have been here before and made an alliance. The Dutch, indeed, say we are brothers and are joined together with chains, but that lasts only as long as we have beavers. After that we are no longer thought of, but much will depend upon it when we shall need each other. They thereupon give two beavers.

They say, the alliance which was made in this country, who can break it? Let us always maintain this alliance which was once made. Give thereupon two beavers.

They say, we have to expect our enemies, the French, and if we drink ourselves drunk, we can not fight. They request therefore that we shall sell no brandy to them and bung up the casks. Give thereupon two beavers.[95]

The chiefs went on to request repairs for their guns, powder, and 50 or 60 men in case the enemy should come. They then asked the Dutch for assistance in having two of their men released from French captivity. There was also a renewed request for assistance with their construction efforts:

They say and request that we shall go there with 30 men and horses to cut and draw wood for their castles to repair them, for they are too lazy to work, and that the Dutch would carry the wood sleds into the country. Give thereupon a beaver coat and one beaver.[96]

Two days later the Dutch resolved to tell the Mohawks, "That there is no doubt of the brotherly union which many years ago was concluded between the Dutch and the Maquaes and that this shall always be maintained and held securely together by a chain." 50 guilders of wampum were given to them.[97] A week later they appointed a delegation to journey to the Mohawk villages "to enter into a further alliance with the said Maquaes, to thank them for their old and continued friendship shown to our nation and further to give them a fair and proper answer to their propositions ..." They gave the Mohawks a quantity of wampum, 75 pounds of powder, 100 pounds of lead, 15 axes and two beavers' worth of knives.[98]

On September 24th, 1659, the Dutch delegation traveled to the "first castle of the Maquaes called Kaghnuwage" for a council, carrying with them the above-mentioned trade goods. In their speech, they demonstrated how adept they had become at forest diplomacy:

> Brothers, we have come here only to renew our old friendship and brotherhood and you must tell it to your children; our children will always be able to know and remember it through the writings which we leave behind us; we die but they remain. From them they will always be able to see how we have lived in friendship with our brothers. Brothers, we have not been able to bring with us any cloth, for we could not get men to carry it. But friendship can not be bought for merchandise; our heart has always been good and is still so and if that is no good, one can not buy friendship, even if this whole land were full of goods and beavers. We give thereupon three bunches of seawan.
>
> Brothers, it is now sixteen years ago that we made our first treaty of friendship and brotherhood between you and all the Dutch, which we then joined together with an iron chain and which until now has not been broken either by us or our brothers and we have no fear that it will be broken by either side, so that we shall not speak of that any more, but shall all be and remain as if we had lain under one heart. We therefore give you now as a token of thankfulness that we are brothers two bunches of seawan.[99]

The speaker urged the Mohawks not to listen to any nation who would attempt to stir them up to make war against the Dutch, and they would do the same for the Mohawks. He then addressed several of the propositions made by the Mohawks two weeks before about having their guns repaired and banishing the sale of brandy. He presented them with the powder and lead, saying, "You must take good care of it so as to use it in case any enemies should attack you, when you can distribute it among the young men." He then addressed the fortifications the Mohawks were making:

> Brothers, we see that you are very busy cutting wood to build your fort. The brothers have asked us for horses to haul it out.

That is not feasible for horses, because the hills here are so high and steep, and the Dutch can not carry it out as they become sick merely from marching to this place, as you may see by looking at our people; how, then, could they in addition carry palisades? But as the brothers sometimes break their axes in cutting wood, we give the brothers these axes. Gave them 15 axes.[100]

He then urged them to forbid their people from killing the livestock of the Dutch, as had happened in the past even with the Mahicans and "Sinnekus," giving them two beaver's worth of knives. A messenger then arrived with a message that fighting had broken out between the Dutch and the Esopus Indians to the south:

We immediately communicated the news to the chiefs and the bystanders, who listened to it in great astonishment and said in reply that we had done very well in making it known so frankly and that they were very glad of it, and for this reason, if the Esopus or other river Indians should come to them with presents and asked them for assistance to fight with them against our people, they would kick them away with the foot and say to them: You beasts, you hogs, go away from here, we will have nothing to do with you.[101]

The Dutch then asked for the release of eight French prisoners, which they would then take back to their country. The Mohawks replied that they would have to deliberate about this: "They complain bitterly about the French, because the French do not keep the peace made with them, for whenever they are out hunting, they are attacked by the French savages, among whom are always concealed parties of Frenchmen, who meanwhile beat them."[102]

Apparently they got this kind of abuse from the Dutch as well, as the Mohawks told them on June 26, 1660:

They say, first, that the Dutch when they are in the woods to fetch Indians beat them severely with fists and drive them out of the woods and they therefore ask who of the three nations are to be the masters, the Maquas, the Sinnekus, or the Dutch?

They say that it might develop into the same trouble as between the Dutch and the Indians in the Esopus.

They request that no Dutchmen with horses or otherwise may be allowed to roam in the woods to fetch the Indians with beavers, because they maltreat them greatly and presently ten or twelve of them surround an Indian and drag him along, saying: "Come with me, so and so has no goods," thus interfering with one another, which they fear will end badly.

They ask us to forbid the Dutch to molest the Indians as theretofore by kicking, beating and assaulting them, in order that we many not break the old friendship which we have enjoyed for more than thirty years, and if it is not prevented they will go away and not be seen by us anymore. Whereupon they offered 7½ fathoms of seawan.[103]

The name of the village where this council took place, which the Dutch wrote as Kaghnuwage and the Jesuits as Gandaouage, would probably be rendered today as Kahnawà:ke, or "At the Rapids." This name carried over to its successor, which was being constructed two miles southwest of the Printup site, and then to two other villages on the north side of the Mohawk River. The name would eventually make its way to a series of villages on the St. Lawrence River, where it persists to this day.

12

EARLY CHILDHOOD
OF TEKAHKWÍ:THA

In the three centuries since she lived, there have been more than two hundred books written about Káteri Tekahkwí:tha, ranging in format from children's coloring books to full-length novels. They have been published around the world and in at least twenty different languages.[104] Most of these are loosely based on the writings of the Jesuit priests who knew her personally, Fathers Pierre Cholenec, Claude Chauchetière, and James de Lamberville. Of the three, Cholenec and Chauchetière were the most prolific, producing a number of biographies of varying lengths in the form of hagiography, or "sacred biography." Their writings were compiled and included in *The Positio of the Historical Section of the Sacred Congregation of Rites on the Introduction of the Cause for the Beatification and Canonization and on the Virtues of the Servant of God Katharine Tekakwitha, The Lily of the Mohawks*, which was submitted to the Vatican prior to her beatification by Pope Pius XII on January 3, 1943. Fordham University Press published it as a book in 1940.[105]

Although the translations of the original French have been criticized by some, I chose to quote extensively from the *Positio* in the chapters that follow, highlighting the more glaring errors we may find along the way as well as any important discrepancies between Chauchetière and Cholenec.[106] We begin with an extract from *The Life of Katharine Tegakoüita, First Iroquois Virgin* by Cholenec:

> Katharine Tegakoüita who today is so renowned in New France because of the extraordinary marvels which God has performed and continues to perform everywhere through her intercession, was born among the Iroquois in the year 1656, in the village of Agniers, called Gandaouage. Her mother, who was of the Algonquin nation, had been baptized and raised among the French in the city of Three Rivers. It was there she was captured by the Iroquois, who were then waging war with us, and who carried her off as a slave to their country. She lived

among them and soon after was married to an Indian of that nation, by whom she had two children, a boy and a girl, Katharine. It was told of this virtuous woman, as it has been said before her of the holy man Tobias, that she preserved her faith and the fear of God in her captivity, that she always prayed until her last breath, but that she had neither the time nor the consolation to inspire these praiseworthy sentiments in her two children, and that if she had the joy of bringing them into the world, she also had the sorrow of leaving it without seeing them baptized, which was her one desire.[107]

Thus we come to our first discrepancy: the English translation in the *Positio* states that the father of Káteri Tekahkwí:tha was an "Indian of that nation," but the French original states that he was "one of the chiefs of the village."[108] We can only speculate why the editor would choose to downplay his status.

Some have also drawn attention to the fact that the mother of Káteri was an Algonquin captive, which they presume diminished her status among the matrilineal Mohawk. They ignore the importance of the adoption ceremony, wherein an adopted person took the place of someone who had recently died, and was thereafter treated as if he or she had been that person all along. If captives of European descent were treated thus, then surely this would have applied to an Algonquin woman! Her children, therefore, would be considered Mohawk, and ould be members of the clan that had adopted their mother. Káteri's Algonquin heritage would not be an issue, because it simply did not exist.

An epidemic of smallpox broke out among the Iroquois and killed a great many. She also died from the disease, leaving her two children who were still very young and incapable of taking care of themselves. She prayed to Him who was their Creator, that He might also be their Father and take them under His divine protection. We see in the person of our Katharine that God heard so just a prayer; as for her brother, he died from the same sickness a little while after his mother. Katharine also caught this disease, but Our Lord, who had chosen her to be His bride, so that in her the marvels of His grace might shine forth, saved her from death. She remained very weak for the rest of her life; her eyes especially were so affected that she was not able to suffer broad daylight, but was obliged during her entire life to hide her face in her blanket when she left the cabin. Thus she is always portrayed unlike the other savages, who wear their blankets on the shoulders.

We have not been able to ascertain what became of her father; we only know that Katharine, being orphaned at the age of four, lived with her uncle, one of the most important seniors of the village. Her aunts, who took all the more care of her since they hoped to benefit by it in the future, succeeded in giving her a good formation.[109]

Father Chauchetière's account, *The Life of Good Katharine Tegakoüita, Now Called The Holy Savage,* elaborates on the effects Tekahkwí:tha suffered:

It was thought that she too would die at the age of four, because she had an attack of smallpox. This, in the course of time, obtained for her the blessing of virginity. Her face, which was formerly pretty, became ugly; she almost lost her eyesight, and her eyes were so hurt by this disease that she could not bear a strong light. This obliged her to remain wrapped in her blanket, and favored her wish to remain unknown. She often thanked Our Lord for this favor, calling her affliction a blessing, for if she had been pretty she would have been more sought by the young men, and so might have abandoned herself to sin as did the other girls in the country of the Iroquois.

This child never did anything that might be said to offend God, since from the age of six or seven she began to have a certain natural modesty, which is the guardian of chastity. Her good nature and the care her mother took of her while she was still living, that is until she was four or five years old, went far to make her grow in age and wisdom. Nevertheless, during her life she considered herself a great sinner, because it seemed as if she had a stain on her body, which she was very careful to hide.[110]

Tekahkwí:tha has been translated as "She Gropes Her Way," "She Bumps into Things," and "She Who Puts Things in Order." A more literal translation would be "She Moves Things Aside." Many assume that her name refers to her poor vision, but it may have been a traditional Mohawk name given to her before her affliction.[111]

Recent scholarship casts doubt upon the timeline presented by the Jesuit biographers. José António Brandão, whose *"Your fyre shall burn no more": Iroquois Policy toward New France and Its Native Allies to 1701* (1997) goes into considerable detail about the epidemics suffered by the Iroquois, has this to say about the traditional narratives of the Mohawk maiden's life:

> In 1660, the Mohawks were again struck by disease. The reference, however, is open to question. In the *Annales de l'Hôtel-Dieu de Québec* Catherine Tekawitha was said to have been orphaned at the age of four when both her parents' died of the smallpox that hit their Mohawk village. Since she was born in 1656, this would place the epidemic in 1660. The question is, how sure can we be of the record of her birth, and her age when her parents died? Indians did not issue birth certificates, and all the information about her life was gathered much later. If the record is off by one year that would place her parents' death in the clearly recorded epidemic of 1661-62.[112]

Brandão documents the catastrophic losses suffered by the Iroquois during the 17th century due to disease. He calculates that we lost more than a thousand souls in the early 1660's alone. While his questioning of the Jesuit's chronology only adjusts the smallpox outbreak by one or two years, it leads us to wonder if its occurrence did not encourage the Mohawks to step up their construction efforts. Archaeological and documentary sources are unclear about the transition from her first village to the next. (The same can't be said for the transition from the second village to the third, as we can ascertain the end of occupation of her second village to the very day!)

Father Chauchetière tells us what occurred in the life of Tekahkwí:tha at the second village:

> The natural inclination which girls have to appear attractive makes them put great value on bodily ornaments. For this

reason savage girls of seven or eight are foolish and very fond of beads. The mothers, who are even more foolish, spend a great deal of time dressing the hair of their daughters. They see to it that their ears are well pierced, and begin from the cradle to pierce them. They paint their faces and cover themselves with beads when they are going to dance.

The people to whose care Katharine was committed when her mother died, decided that she should marry early and therefore encouraged all these small vanities, but the little Tekakwitha, who was not yet a Christian and had not been baptized, had a natural indifference for such things. She was still a small tree without flowers or fruit, but the small wild olive-tree was growing so well that one day it would bear beautiful fruit. She was a heaven, covered by the darkness of paganism, but a heaven indeed, because she was very far removed from the corruption of the savages. She was gentle, patient, chaste, innocent, and behaved like a well-bred French child. This is the testimony given concerning her by those who knew her from the time she was a small child, and who have thus spoken to give in few words a beautiful panegyric of Katharine.

When someone asked her how she had lived among the Iroquois (during the time they had not seen her), that is, from the age of seven or eight years until the time that Providence conducted her to the mission, she answered that she had continued living during their absence as before. The person who asked her this question knew both Katharine and her mother, and was the same who became her mother and mistress at the Sault for two years. This good Christian, named Anastasia Tegonhatsihongo, said that from that time forward Katharine had no shortcomings.

Katharine's duties were to gather firewood with her aunt, to tend the fire when her mother ordered her, to get water when those in the lodge needed it. When she had nothing else to do, she amused herself with small jewels. I mean to say, she decorated herself, as other little girls of her age, simply to pass the time away. She put glass beads around her neck, glass bracelets on her arms, rings on her fingers, and ornaments in her ears. She made ribbons and bands such as the savages make from the skin of eels. These they color red and prepare very efficiently for hair-ribbons. She wore large and beautiful belts which were called glass necklaces. Twenty years later, when she performed harsh penances to chastise her body, she wept much for these acts, saying that she had loved her body more than she should have done.[113]

While the priests were more concerned about extolling the virtues of the young woman than providing anthropological data, they nevertheless provide us a glimpse of the cultural world in which she lived. They are rather blunt when it comes to describing the way a marriage was arranged for the young girl:

Katharine, who had a natural aversion to the pleasures of marriage, had no thought of marrying, and as the smallpox had spoiled her looks, the young men did not think of her. Her relatives, however, wished to see her established, and urged her to marry, whereas she did not wish to do so. In order to rid themselves of her, and because she was looked upon as an ill-favored slave who would become a burden on the cabin, they sent her from lodge to lodge. This caused some of the savages to say after her death that God had taken her because men did not want her.[114]

Tekahkwí:tha was skilled at making crafts. She also has the distinction of being the first weaver of wampum belts mentioned by name:

People who knew her from her childhood said that she was intelligent and skilful, especially with her hands, making such objects as the little savages make. If I can judge by the objects which I saw her make, I should say that she worked daintily in pigskin and deerskin. She made belts in which the savage women and girls carry wood, and those which the ancients used in negotiating the affairs of the nation, made of glass beads. Another occupation of the savage women is sewing, which they learned from their own slaves or from the Christian women from Europe. She was also skilful in making ribbons, as the savages do, from the skins of eels or from thick tree-bark. These she colored red with the glue from sturgeons which are plentiful among the Iroquois. She knew more than the Iroquois girls, for she made baskets and boxes and the buckets used for drawing water. Her skill, therefore, was such that she always had some occupation to fall back on. Sometimes she made an instrument for grinding Indian corn, sometimes she made matting from tree-bark, and sometimes she made poles for stacking corn. In addition to these occupations there were her daily tasks in the service of the others— grinding corn for soup and bread and serving the food in abundance. Although she was infirm, she was always the first to be at work. She spent some years before her Baptism performing these daily tasks of the life of the savage. She remained at home and did not go about, nor was she a gossip. She was neither lazy nor proud, a vice common to savage maidens. She paid no heed to her fancies nor to dreams. It has been said that from her childhood she did not care to assist at the dances or games and that on several occasions she had shown great prudence. But she was timid by nature, appearing only when it was necessary. She never showed the cruel spirit which savage women have; she could not bear to see anyone harmed, not even a slave, and she thought it a sin to see anyone burned.[115]

The reference to the "cruel spirit" of her fellow Mohawk females and other negative comments about Káteri's people become a common theme throughout the biographies, as later passages will reveal. The impression is created that Káteri was somehow "alien" to her people, a Christian long before she even know what such a thing was.

Chauchetière goes on to describe how her aunts arranged a marriage for her at eight years of age:

Among the Iroquois marriage is not only the contract and agreement of two people who intend to live together as long as they are congenial, but also called by the name of marriage are certain agreements which are no more than links of friendship, strengthened by giving in marriage a child who sometimes is still in the cradle. Thus they marry a little boy to a little girl. This was done when Katharine was still very small. When she was only eight years old she was given in marriage to a boy who was her own age. They were alike in disposition. The boy bothered no more about this marriage than the girl, so that it was only in name what Katharine's relatives pretended it to be.[116]

With this, the narrative brings us up to the middle of the 1660's. Although the village is relatively new, its occupation is nearing an end. Fathers Chauchetière and Cholenec rarely provide the historical context of their narratives, so they do not concern themselves with village movements. They gloss over the cataclysmic event that prompted the Mohawks to relocate from Tekahkwí:tha's second village to her third—and, ultimately, from our Mohawk homeland to the valley of the St. Lawrence River.

13

1666:
THE YEAR OF THE BEAST

In 1663, a massive earthquake shook the northeast and sent everyone into a state of ecstatic terror, especially in New France, where it was seen as judgment against the sins committed in the country:

> On the 3rd day of February of this year 1663 a woman Savage, but a very good and very excellent Christian, wakening in her cabin while all the others slept, heard a distinct and articulated voice that said to her, 'In two days, very astonishing and marvellous things will come to pass.' And the next day, while she was in the forest with her sister, cutting her daily provision of wood, she distinctly heard the same voice, which said, 'Tomorrow, between five and six o'clock in the evening, the earth will be shaken and will tremble in an astonishing way.'[117]

Not long after this, Mother Marie-Catherine de Saint-Augustin, disgusted with the sinful life she witnessed in New France, felt an "infallible conviction" that "God was ready to punish the country for the sins committed here, especially the contempt for the ordinances of the Church." Her description is biblical in its imagery: "Forthwith, and a little before the earthquake came to pass, she saw four furious and enraged demons at the four corners of Quebec, shaking the earth with such violence it was evident they wished to turn it right over."[118]

This cataclysm, which is talked about by seismologists to this day, was particularly frightening to the Indians of New France:

> The Savages, who were extremely frightened, said the trees had beaten them. Several among them said they were demons God was using to chastise them because of the excesses they had committed while drinking the brandy that the wicked French had given them. Some other less-instructed Savages, who had come to hunt in these regions, said it was the souls of

their ancestors, who wished to return to their former dwelling. Possessed by this error, they took their guns and shot into the air at what they said was a band of passing spirits.[119]

We do not know what the Rotinonhsión:ni thought of this earthquake. They were certainly close enough to have felt its effects, but they had other calamities to worry about at the time. First, there was the war with the Susquehannocks to the south. Then there was the war with the Sokokis of the Connecticut River in New England. They had also not seen the last of the Mahicans, their old foes in the Hudson Valley. On the political front, major changes had taken place on their eastern boundaries. In 1664, the colony of New Netherland passed from Dutch hands to English and became New York, prompting a new round of diplomacy with our ancestors. It was a boom time for wampum belt weavers and gunsmiths alike.

Relations with the French were especially tumultuous in the 1660's. A new governor, Baron du Bois d'Avaugour, was sent to Canada in 1661 "to plant Lilies over the ashes of the Iroquois," as one poetic Jesuit put it.[120] In the spring of 1664, an Iroquois embassy was sent to New France to make peace. The French were suspicious of their motives:

> Since war broke out between the Iroquois and ourselves, we have not yet seen on their part a more solemn Embassy— whether in point of the number and rank of the ambassadors, or the beauty and number of the presents—than that which they despatched last Spring.
>
> Upon investigating the causes of such an extraordinary event, it is not easy to hit on the true one. They proclaim that they wish to unite all the nations of the earth and to hurl the hatchet so far into the depths of the earth that it shall never again be seen in the future; that they wish to place an entirely new Sun in the Heavens, which shall never again be obscured by a single cloud; that they wish to level all the mountains, and remove all the falls from the rivers—in a word, that they wish peace. Moreover, as an evidence of the sincerity of their intentions, they declare that they are coming—women, and children, and old men—to deliver themselves into the hands of the French,—not so much in the way of hostages for their

good faith as to begin to make only one Earth and one Nation of themselves and us.

All these words are specious, but for more than five years we have known from our own experience that the Iroquois is of a crafty disposition, adroit, dissembling, and haughty; and that he will never descend so as to be the first to ask peace from us, unless he has a great scheme in his head, or is driven to it for some very pressing reason.

Some think that the Agniehronnons—the nation nearest to us and the most arrogant and cruel—ask us for peace because they are no longer in a condition to make war, being reduced to a very small number by famine, disease, and the losses that they have suffered in the last two or three years, on all sides whither they have directed their arms.[121]

The leader of this "notable embassy" was a particularly eloquent Onondaga:

In fact, a short time afterward, Captain Garakonti—who was the soul, as it were, of this enterprise—joined the Sonnontouaehronnons, together with those of his nation; and to this end he made a prodigious collection of porcelain, which is the gold of the country, in order to make us the most beautiful presents that had ever been given us. There were, among other gifts, a hundred collars, some of which were more than a foot in width.[122]

The French were cautiously optimistic about these peace proposals. Unfortunately, some Algonquins attacked this embassy while they were in transit, prompting the French to fear retaliation from the Iroquois:

Thus the grand project of this Embassy has vanished in smoke, and instead of the peace which it was bringing us, we have on our hands a more cruel war than before; for the Iroquois would cease to be Iroquois if they did not make every effort to avenge the deaths of those Ambassadors.[123]

The French were not content to sit back and wait for an Iroquois attack. They began to build forts on the Richelieu River and an island on Lake Champlain, and then launched an attack on the eastern door of the Longhouse in January of 1666. Led by Daniel de Rémy de Courcelle, the force consisted of 300 men from the Carignan-Salières Regiment and 200 colonists.

Cadwallader Colden describes their failure in *The History of the Five Indian Nations Depending on the Province of New-York in America* (1727/1747):

> The French Force being thus so considerably augmented, he resolved in the Winter to send out a Party against the Mohawks, which by the Cold, and their not knowing the use of Snow-Shoes, suffered very much, without doing any thing against the Enemy.
>
> This Party fell in with Schenectady, a small Town which Corlaer (a considerable Man among the Dutch) had then newly settled. When they appear'd near Schenectady they were almost kill'd with Cold and Hunger, and the Indians, who then were in that Village, had entirely finished their Ruin, if Corlaer, (in Compassion of fellow Christians) had not contriv'd their escape. He had a mighty Influence over the Indians, and it is from him that all the Governors of New-York are call'd Corlaer by the Indians to this Day, tho' he himself never was Governor. He perswaded the Indians that this was but a small Party of the French Army, come to amuse them, that the great Body was gone directly towards their Castles, and that it was necessary for them immediately to go in Defence of their Wives and Children: which they did. As soon as the Indians were gone, he sent to the French, and supply'd them with Provisions to carry them back.[124]

The lieutenant-general of France's North American possessions, Alexandre de Prouville, Marquis de Tracy, later wrote to the first English governor of New-York, Colonel Richard Nicholls, to explain why a French army had just invaded their colony:

> In answer to your letter of the 31st of August I shall tell you that Monsieur de Courcelle, Governor General of this country,

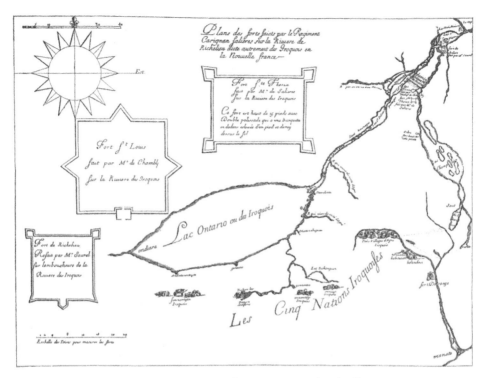

French map of 1666 showing route from Lake George to Mohawk villages.

signifying to me that he had a desire to make inroad upon the Maquaes, to put a stop to their barbarous insolences; I gave my consent to further design, that he might take with him so many officers and soldiers as he thought fit, either of his Majesty's companies, or those of the country. Whereupon he advanced within fifteen or twenty leagues of the villages of the Anniés. But fortunately for them his guides conducting him a wrong way. He did not meet with them, till he came near the village which you name in your letter, neither had he known there was any of them there, until he had surprised all the Indians that were in two small huts at some distance from that place. This truth is sufficiently convincing, to justify Monsieur de Courcelle, that he had no intention to infringe the peace that was then between us, for that he thought himself in the Maquaes land. The moderation which he used in the said huts (although the persons under his command were driven to the uttermost extremity, for want of provisions) hath sufficiently manifested the consideration we have always had for our allies (for until then we had no intelligence, that New Holland was under any other dominion than that of the States of the United Belgick Provinces) and understanding that he was upon the lands belonging to the Dutch, he took great care to hinder his companies from falling into the village, by which means he alone the Maquaes that were there saved themselves.[125]

Not long after this aborted invasion, French troops stationed at Fort Sainte-Anne on Lake Champlain were out hunting and were attacked by Mohawk warriors led by one *Agariata*. Several men were killed in this engagement, including an officer, de Chasy, the nephew of Monsieur de Tracy. Others were either wounded or taken prisoner.[126] On July 24, 1666, 300 men from the Carignan-Salières Regiment set out for Mohawk territory to exact revenge for this latest attack. En route, they encountered a peace delegation led by *Canaqueese,* also known as the "Flemish Bastard" due to his Dutch and Mohawk parentage. Canaqueese was returning French captives to Canada.[127]

This is how Jesuit Father Pierre-François-Xavier de Charlevoix tells the story in *Histoire et description générale de la Nouvelle France:*

> Mr. de Sorel, when on the point of falling upon a Mohawk town, met a troop of warriors headed by the Flemish Bastard. He was about to attack them, when the Mohawk chief, himself greatly inferior to the French, and with no means of escape, adopted the plan of advancing to Sorel and telling him, with a very confident air, that he was going to Quebec to treat of peace with Mr. de Tracy. Sorel believed him, and himself took him to the viceroy, who received him well. Another Mohawk chief arrived at Quebec a few days after, and gave himself out also as a deputy from his canton. No doubt was now entertained but that the Mohawks were really disposed to peace; but one day, when de Tracy had invited the two pretended deputies to his table, the conversation turning on the death of Mr. de Chasy, the Mohawk chief, raising his arm, exclaimed: "This is the arm that tomahawked that young officer." The indignation of all present may be imagined. The Viceroy told the insolent savage that he would never kill another, and had

him strangled on the spot by the executioner, in presence of the Flemish Bastard, whom he retained as a prisoner.[128]

And you thought your dinner parties were a bust. Mr. de Tracy clearly has you beat in that regard, if this version of events is true.[129]

The *Jesuit Relations* tell us that on August 30, "A council was held in our enclosure, at which representatives from all the five Iroquois nations were present. The two nations who dwell above gave a present of 52 porcelain collars."[130]

It was far too late for wampum: Monsieur de Tracy was determined to make war on the Mohawks.

> These Negotiations did not yet meet with all the success hoped for, and Monsieur de Tracy concluded that, to assure their satisfactory issue, it was necessary by force of arms to render the Agniehronnons still more tractable, as they were always the occasion of new obstacles to the public tranquillity. Despite his advanced age, he determined to conduct, in person, against those Barbarians an army, composed of six hundred soldiers drawn from all the Companies, six hundred settlers of the country, and a hundred Huron and Algonquin Savages.[131]

Even the French nun, Marie de l'Incarnation, seemed anxious to see the Mohawks annihilated:

> All this information has so roused the French that they are resolved to destroy these wretches themselves, with the help they are awaiting from France. They can no longer delay their destruction after so many acts of hostility and ruptures of the peace....
>
> After so many useless efforts and so much experience of the perfidy of these infidels, Monseigneur has completely changed his opinion and agrees with all the wise persons in the colony that these barbarians must be exterminated, if possible, or all the Christians and Christianity itself in Canada will perish. When there is no more Christianity or missionaries, what hope will there be for their salvation?[132]

On October 16, 1666, l'Incarnation described de Tracy's plan of attack in a letter to her son:

> He has departed to be present in person at the war against the Iroquois of New Holland [Mohawks], which is the nation that prevents the other nations from believing. He has done all he can to win them over with kindness, but they are brutes that would not let themselves be conquered by the charm that wins all those that have any remnant reason.
>
> According to calculations of the army's march, battle should have been joined in the first village these three days past. If God blesses this first effort, the other two villages will then be attacked. These barbarians have good forts, they have cannon, and they are valiant, and doubtless it will not be easy to vanquish them. But our French soldiers are so fervent they fear nothing, and there is nothing they do not do and undertake. They undertook to carry cannon on their backs over very difficult rapids and portages. They have even carried shallops, which is an unheard-of thing. It seems to all these soldiers that they are going to besiege paradise, and they hope to capture and enter it, because it is for the good of the Faith and religion that they are going to do battle.[133]

In a letter to one of her sisters written on November 2, 1666, l'Incarnation described the reactions of the Mohawk prisoners to the army setting out for their country:

> They weep like children at the knowledge that the French have gone to destroy their nation. What causes them even more vexation is that they are obliged to make a great many snowshoes to go against their own people—that is to say, they are making weapons to fight them. Although they are working against their will and are forced to obey, they are not otherwise molested, which makes them wonder at the goodness of the French. The Flemish Bastard, who is a famous Iroquois, is treated at Monsieur the Intendant's [Jean Talon's] table like a great lord; to honour him, Monsieur de Tracy gave him a fine suit of clothing for his use and promised him his life before he

set out with the army. He is not in irons like the others and he has freedom to walk about, but he is guarded by several soldiers who never leave him. He is treated with courtesy because, having captured a close kinsman of Monsieur de Tracy, along with a few other gentlemen, he did not ill-treat them but brought them back with complete goodwill.

When the army was drawn up ready to depart, Monsieur de Tracy had it pass before him and said to him, 'Now that we are going to your country, what do you say?'

Tears fell from the Flemish Bastard's eyes, 'Onontio—' (that is to say, 'great chief')—'I clearly see that we are lost, but our destruction will cost you dear. Our nation will be no more, but I warn you that many fine young men will remain behind, for ours will fight till the end. I beg you only to save my wife and children who are in such and such a place.'

Monsieur de Tracy promised to do so if they could be found and to bring his wife and all his family to him.

We do not yet know the outcome of this enterprise. God, who is the God of armies, knows. If he has fought for us, we have victory. May his very holy will be done, because in ordering of this will, he is glorified by our losses as much as by our prospering.[134]

In light of the nun's invocation of God, it is truly ironic that French success in this enterprise would endanger the life of a future Roman Catholic saint, who was at the time ten years old and living in the village that was first on their list of targets.

R. VAKUUM PELON
MONTOCK 08

14

A MOHAWK APOCALYPSE

After a challenging journey, de Tracy's army found themselves
running out of provisions and in danger of having to turn back.
Marie de l'Incarnation, hearing firsthand accounts of the mission when
the troops returned to Canada, relayed what she heard to her son in a
letter dated November 12, 1666:

> The army arrived close to the Iroquois on St Theresa's day,
> [15th October]. There was such untoward weather with rain,
> storms, and tempests that everyone almost despaired of being
> able to accomplish anything. Monsieur de Tracy nevertheless
> did not lose heart and had his troops march all night.
> Meanwhile the Iroquois did not know that a French army was
> coming to attack them and would undoubtedly have been
> taken by surprise had not some of their people, who during the
> march had met and been beaten by the Algonkins, warned the
> villages that they had encountered some Frenchmen and
> Algonkins, who were coming apparently to attack them. The
> alarm at once spread among them and, in order to put them-
> selves in a state of defence, they had the women and children
> flee. Our men advanced with beating drums, wishing to attack
> in force without any other ruses or skills than their courage
> and God's protection. The Iroquois, despite their resolution to
> defend themselves, were seized with such fright when they saw
> the French approaching in order and without fear that,
> without awaiting the attack, they abandoned their village and
> retired to another. Our men entered the village without resist-
> ance, pillaged it, and after setting it afire pursued the enemy to
> the village to which they had retired.[135]

This is echoed in the *Jesuit Relations*:

> However great the care taken to conduct this march with little
> noise, our men could not prevent some Iroquois, who had been

sent as far as thirty or forty leagues to reconnoiter our forces, from gaining a view, from the mountain-tops, of this little naval army, and hastening to the first village to give warning of its approach. Consequently, the alarm having then spread from hamlet to hamlet, our troops found them abandoned; while in the distance could be seen the Barbarians, loudly hooting on the mountains and discharging many wasted shots at our soldiers.[136]

From Marie de l'Incarnation:

Some Iroquois, who had climbed a mountain, seeing the army, which seemed to them more than four thousand men, cried to one of our Savages, 'Akaroe, we pity you and all the French. There are eight hundred of our men in the next village very well armed and resolved to fight well. Be assured, they will kill all the men you see.'

The other man replied, 'The French will go and I also.'

The barbarians spoke thus to pretend courage but in their hearts they were so frightened that, when they went to inform their leaders of what they had seen, he was no less terrified. He heard twenty drums making a great din and at the same time saw the French coming straight and resolute towards him. He did not wait for them but was the first to take flight; everyone followed him, so that the four villages were empty of people but so full of food, implements, and all sorts of appurtenances and furnishings that nothing was lacking. The French believed they would find only shacks, or shepherds' or beasts' huts, but all was found to be so fine and so pleasing that Monsieur de Tracy and all the members of his retinue were quite taken back. They saw timber cabins a hundred and twenty feet in length and broad in proportion, in each of which lived eight or nine families.[137]

From the *Jesuit Relations:*

Our Troops, halting at each of these villages, which they found empty of men but full of corn and provisions, only long enough to take necessary refreshment, were hopeful of meeting with a stout resistance in the last one, which they prepared to attack in regular form, since the Barbarians showed clearly enough by the great fire they were making there and by the fortifications they had constructed, their determination to offer there a vigorous defense. But our men were again disappointed in their hope; for scarcely had the enemy seen the advance-guard approaching, when they promptly took flight into the woods, whither the night prevented our forces from pursuing them. It was evident enough—from the triple palisade, twenty feet high, with which their place was surrounded; from the four bastions flanking it; from their prodigious hoard of provisions; and from the abundant supply of water they had provided, in bark receptacles, for extinguishing the fire when it should be necessary—that their first resolve had been quite different from that which the fear of our arms had made them suddenly adopt. There were found only some persons who had been prevented by their great age from leaving the village, two days before, with all the women and children; and also the mutilated bodies of two or three Savages of another nation, whom these people had, with their wonted rage, half burned over a slow fire. So our people were forced to content themselves, after erecting the Cross, saying Mass, and chanting the *Te Deum* on that spot, with setting fire to the palisades and cabins, and consuming the entire supply of Indian corn, beans, and other produce of the country, which was found there. Then they turned back to the other villages and wrought the same havoc there, as well as in all the outlying fields. As a result, those familiar with these Barbarians' mode of life have not a doubt that almost as many will die of hunger as would have perished by the weapons of our soldiers, had they dared await the latter's approach; and that all who remain will be forced by fear to accept such conditions of peace, and observe such a demeanor, as would have been secured from them with greater difficulty by more sanguinary victories.[138]

From Marie de l'Incarnation:

The first thing that was done was to sing *Te Deum*, to praise God for having himself overcome his enemies by fear. The four ecclesiastics that accompanied the army said holy Mass; after this the holy Cross and the arms of France were planted every-where, to take possession of all these regions for His Majesty. To provide bonfires they set fire to the four villages—all the cabins, all the forts, and all the cereals, both that which was stored and that which was still standing in the fields. The cabins and storehouses were so filled with food that it is deemed that there was enough to nourish all Canada for two years. All of it burned, after enough had been set aside to provide for the needs of the army.

The villages were but three or four leagues' distance one from another, and Monsieur de Tracy had been given to under-stand there were but two. But fortunately among our Algonkins there was a woman that had been a captive of the Iroquois in her youth and in another encounter rescued by the people of her nation. She told Monsieur de Courcelle, our Governor, that there were four, which made him continue farther with Monsieur le Chevalier de Chaumont. It was almost night when the third village was taken, so that it seemed impossible to go to the fourth, particularly for persons that did not know the ways or approaches.

However, the woman took a musket in one hand and Monsieur de Courcelle by the other, saying, 'Come. I am going to lead you straight to it.'

She did in fact lead them there without peril and, so as not to enter rashly, men were sent to spy out what was within. It was found that everyone had just taken flight at the news that the army was coming to sweep upon them.

This is how it was known. Two old women were still there, as well as an old man and a young boy. Monsieur de Tracy wished to spare their lives, but the two women preferred to throw themselves into the fire rather than see their village burn and all their goods destroyed. The child, who is very pretty, was brought here. The old man was found under a canoe, where he had hidden himself when he heard the drums, imagining that they were demons and believing that the French did not intend to destroy them but to use their demons—it was thus he called the drums—to terrify them and chase them away. He said the Iroquois of the other villages had retired to this last one, which was the best and the strongest, that they had armed themselves with weapons and food to resist the French and even made a great provision of water to put out the fire in case the village should be set ablaze. But when they saw the huge army, which seemed more than four thousand men, they were so afraid that the chief rose and said to the others, 'Brothers, let us flee. Everyone is against us.'

With these words he fled, and all the others followed him. They were not mistaken in their belief that the army was so numerous; it seemed so even to the French, and Monsieur [Jean-Baptiste Legardeur] de Repentigny, who led our French habitants, assured me that, when he climbed a mountain to discover whether there were any enemies, he cast his eyes upon our army, which appeared to be so numerous that he believed the good angels had joined with it, at which he was quite bewildered—those are his terms.

Be that as it may, God has done for our men what he did of old for his people, who cast such fear into the hearts of their enemies that they were victorious over them without doing battle. It is certain that there is something of the prodigious in all this affair for, if the Iroquois had held firm, they would have caused our army great difficulty and delayed it con-siderably—fortified and armed as they were, and bold and proud as they are. For in our experience, the Agneronons [Mohawks], the Iroquois nation we are speaking of, yield to no-one. None of their neighbours dare to contradict them; all must submit to their counsels, and they succeed in all their enterprises by trickery and cruelty. But this rout has reduced them to the ultimate humiliation to which a nation can be reduced.[139]

Maybe it's just me, but I have a hard time visualizing two old women throwing themselves into the fire because they were upset at their village being destroyed. I am more inclined to believe that the soldiers were kind enough to offer them assistance in that regard! Although she had only recently prayed for the success of the army, l'Incarnation expressed a glimmer of concern for the Mohawks:

What will become of them? Where will they go? Their villages have been burned; their country has been sacked. The season is too far advanced for them to rebuild their villages. The little grain that remains from the firing of their crops will not be enough to nourish them, they being to the number of three thousand. If they go to the other nations, they will not be received for fear of causing famine; and besides, the other nations would scorn to incur their indignation and put themselves in danger of a like misfortune. It is not yet known where the Agneronons have gone. If in their flight they encounter the Loup nation [Mahicans], their enemies, they are lost without resource.[140]

She goes on to reveal that the French had intended to advance to the Oneida villages and do the same to them, but due to the lateness of the season, they turned back. When they arrived at a lake they found "boats made of great hollowed trees" which the Mohawks had hidden in tall grass, and used them to transport their troops. Her account of the expedition, like the Sullivan-Clinton campaign more than a century later, reveals the bounty of Iroquois village life:

It is a marvellous thing to hear tell of the beauty and goodness of that country. There is a great cleared expanse, with very beautiful meadows, where the grass grows high as a man. The canes, or stalks, of the Indian corn are ten, twelve, or thirteen feet in height; the ears are of great cubit, and on each ear are more than four thousand kernels. Squash, which are equal to the rainette of apples of France (of which they have the taste), and beans grow there in abundance. The Iroquois were provided with all this, and, as I have said already, they had enough to nourish all Canada for two years. We have good soil here but there it is comparably better. This will be apparent if the King desires French colonies to be established there.

The cabins that were sacked and burnt were well built and magnificently ornamented; no-one would ever have believed it. They were filled with carpentry tools and others that they used to decorate their cabins and furniture. All these were carried off, as well as good four hundred pots and the remainder of their wealth.[141]

With the escape of the Mohawks, Monsieur de Tracy failed to satiate his desire for blood atonement for the loss of his soldiers at Fort Saint-Anne earlier in the year. Marie de l'Incarnation tells us that this price would be paid:

> There were several captives from the Iroquois nations here; upon the return of the army, Monsieur de Tracy had one of them hanged, giving the others to understand that this was because he had broken the peace and caused the misfortune of the Agneronons by the evil counsel he had given them. This greatly startled the barbarians, who trembled like children in their fear that as much would be done to them.
>
> The Flemish Bastard feared it more than the others because he was the most famous among the Iroquois. Monsieur de Tracy nevertheless spared his life and sent him in search of his fugitive people, with the mandate to tell them that if they stirred again he would go back to see them and this time they would not get off so lightly. He also sent three or four men of each nation to take them the news of what has happened to the Agneronons and tell them they must make their intentions known, failing which he will hang all of their people that are still here. They made fine promises as they departed. I do not know whether they will keep them.[142]

Finally, she tells us of an unusual occurrence that happened in New France while the troops in the midst of their attack:

> At the very moment that our Frenchmen were burning the Iroquois villages, it seemed that God wished to give us news of this himself by means of several fires that broke out in our forts and even in ours in Quebec.
>
> In one of the forts that had been built on the road of the Iroquois, the soldiers guarding it almost died of fear. They saw a large opening in the air and, in this opening, fires whence came doleful voices and dreadful screams. These were perhaps the demons, enraged that a country of which they had been the grand masters for so long had been depeopled and Masses said and God's praises sung in a place

where there had never been anything but impurities and abomination.

I recommend the conversion of those barbarians to your prayers. God has destroyed them without there being a single one of them lost. Perhaps he has humbled them only for their salvation.[143]

This would not be the last time the French would devastate the Mohawk villages. Count Frontenac would lead another army on snowshoes into the Mohawk Valley in January of 1693 and repeat Monsieur de Tracy's scorched earth tactics. Both of these genocidal acts are footnotes in history today. In fact, few Mohawks today are even aware that it happened the first time, let alone that it was repeated. I suspect that it was the trauma of seeing their world set ablaze that prompted so many Mohawks to relocate to New France, where they could prove to "Onontio" that they had been sufficiently cowed and were no longer a threat to the French—and where they could keep an eye on future troop movements of an adversary who had already demonstrated the resolve to wipe us from the face of the earth forever.

15

A LAYER OF ASH

Centuries after the destruction of the Mohawk villages in 1666, archaeologists found evidence of the conflagration of the first village at what is known as the Freeman site. Donald Rumrill describes it as being located almost four miles west of Fultonville and a mile from the Mohawk River. The site was largely destroyed by home construction. Fortunately, Dr. Kingston Larner was able to do a minimal sampling of the area before the owner began building:

> One of the most revealing results of this endeavor was the exposing of a layer of ash at the occupation level and almost all of the post molds encountered were found to have been charred signifying that the village had burned or been burned, probably the latter.
>
> ....
>
> One corner bastion was also revealed by the excavation.
>
> ....
>
> A new name appears in the New York colonial documents and elsewhere as the first castle of the Mohawks in 1659—that of Kaghnuwage where meetings were held between the Dutch and the Mohawks September 24, 1659. Seven years later the Marquis DeTracy uses the name Andaraque as the easternmost castle. The names have distinctive similarities in pronunciation using the combined patois of French and Mohawk tongues. The Freeman site also appears to have been abandoned rather abruptly since large chunks of burned wood and charcoal are in the hearths as well as one pile of fresh water clams that were never opened!
>
> DeTracy says in his account,

> > ...while the distance could be seen the barbarians, loudly hooting on the mountain(?) and discharging many wasted shots at our soldiers.

There is a high hill (mountain?) to the southeast of the site that fits the scenario very well.

Seventeen Hollanders delivered presents to the Mohawks on September 24, 1659 in the "first castle of the Mohawks called Kaghnuwage". In the speeches it was noted that the Mohawks "were very busy cutting wood to build your fort" for which the Dutch were requested to supply horses. They refused, saying it was not feasible because "the hills were too high and steep" and the Dutch themselves "could not carry the palisades". This suggests an interpretation that some, at least, of the houses in the new village at Kaghnuwage were already in place and being lived in and the Indians wanted assistance with the much larger, and, therefore, heavier trees used in palisading their castle. This, then, in effect, establishes the beginning year of the Freeman site village and puts it absolutely in the proper place and time framework to be DeTracy's Andaraque![144]

Rumrill substantiates these documentary references with other items found in Larner's excavation to confirm the village's date of occupation:

Whereas my choice for the predecessor of Kaghnuwage, Printup, was profuse with Jesuit rings and medals, etc., as does the successor, the Fox Farm site, there have not been any at all revealed so far from the Freeman site. From 1655 to 1659 the Jesuits had fairly free access to the Mohawk Valley if they so desired and had established missions from time to time

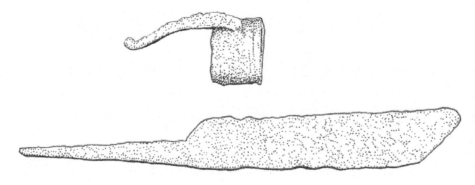

Metal scabbard part and knife blade from Fox Farm Archaeological Site. Kingston Larner collection, courtesy Dr. Paul Huey. Sketch by the author.

through 1657-58. From 1659 until 1667 no one from any of the blackrobes orders were in the valley for any reason. Therefore, no religious rings, medals, crucifixes, etc. would be expected to be found at this particular Kaghnuwage.

A 1632 double tournois coin was recovered here, a significant item for the 1663-1682 period...

A trade artifact similarity to Printup, Mitchell, Smith, and Janie sites shows up on Freeman in the form of the brass jew's-harp with the capital R and five notches on the tangs. The brass arrow points range from imperforate to single and double perforations to bifurcated, stemmed, and stylized examples. These indicate that even in the 1660's the Mohawks were not yet completely modernized with firearms for hunting and warfare. Seven Madison flint points were also found.

There were ten pieces of Indian pottery recovered at Freeman, all but one a rimsherd and all local Late Woodland motifs. Even though none were found at Printup, these pieces do not denote a double occupation of this site but rather that the art had not been lost as yet. Indeed, native pottery was

Metal utensils and miniature cup from the Freeman Archaeological Site. Artifacts from the Rumrill Collection courtesy of the New York State Museum, Albany, NY. Sketch by the author.

also found at the Veeder site which in all probability was in existence as late as 1693.

....

Also lacking were amounts of gun parts but, then, only a small percentage of the site was examined. One of the items recovered, however, was a beautiful flintlock hammer, an exact twin of type I, which Mayer places in the 1660-1680 time period. Several gunspalls were unearthed, mostly of the honey colored French variety; however, two were of what appears to be English flint. Two iron remnants of a sword scabbard were found during the excavation and several knives, all of which fit into Hagerty's representation of 1660-1677 on Oneida sites.[145]

Although Dean Snow's account of Freeman is essentially the same as what Rumrill presents, he includes a photograph of a broken effigy pipe found at Freeman which seems to have a hooded face looking back at the smoker. I can't for the life of me figure out what that could mean.

Rumrill mentions the Fox Farm site as being the successor of the Freeman site. This is located roughly two miles southwest of the Caughnawaga site at the Káteri shrine in Fonda.

After the DeTracy raids on the Mohawks in 1666, most, if not all, of the villages were reestablished but, this time, on the north side of the river. The farthest easterly of these at first was at the Fox Farm site which is a little over 400 meters from the water's edge. I make a point of this measurement since it also is most likely the first "town" that Wentworth Greenhalgh visited on his journey through the Mohawk Valley from May 28, 1677 to July 14, 1677, which he named Cahaniaga.

Hooded effigy pipe from Freeman Archaeological Site. Artifact from the Fort Plain Museum collection. Sketch by the author.

Four hundred meters is a long bow shot on the level but the Fox Farm site location is over 30 meters higher than the river and that's how Greenhalgh describes Cahaniaga—"situate upon the edge of a hill, about a bow shot from the river". Perfect description, and the only site on the north side of the river to fit this representation except for one I've given the name of Turtle Pond from approximately the same time period.... Greenhalgh continues in his portrayal of Cahaniaga as being "double stockadoed round, has four ports about four feet wide apiece, and contains about twenty four houses".

The Fox Farm was a fairly large site. The huge gravel pit that has taken its place is just about the outline of the village proper according to the people that mined the gravel from it. They described to me the "Indian dirt" house outlines as well as the many deep pits that were revealed in their excavation. No one will ever know whether there were twenty four houses and a double stockade to ascertain the basic facts to support the suggestion that this was, indeed, Cahaniaga.[146]

Glass trade beads from the Fox Farm Archaeological Site. Artifacts from the Rumrill Collection courtesy of the New York State Museum, Albany, NY. Sketch by the author.

Snow provides an overview of recovered artifacts:

Key artifacts include iron mouth harps, brass mouth harps, iron keys, iron gun parts, brass points, iron hooks, kaolin pipes, cross and orb kaolin pipes, EB kaolin pipes, stamped Jesuit rings, a Louis XIII coin, rum bottles, conch shell fragments, hawk bells, pewter spoons and buttons, brass kettles, brass scrap, lead shot, iron awls, thimbles, shell wampum, and iron nails.

....

The bead assemblage is dominated by round red beads. Only a few round black beads have been recovered.

....

Glass beads are useful for dating sites belonging to this period, but only if sufficiently large samples are available. Round red beads had been available since 1580, but they dominate assemblages after 1666. Round black beads, also available since 1580, are found in small numbers, but come to replace red beads as the dominant type after 1679.

There is much artifact fallout from earlier periods, including some anachronistic gun parts. Rumrill has found a snaphaunce hammer, a snaphaunce pan cover, and the top flint vise jaw of a Spanish *miquilet*. However, the redwood beads, cross and orb kaolin pipes, and stamped Jesuit rings would seem to put this site clearly in the series established after 1666 on the north bank of the Mohawk River. The lack of HG kaolin pipes, large number of black beads, or wire-wound beads leads to the conclusion that the site was abandoned by 1679. Rumrill gives it the range of A.D. 1666-1683. John McCashion, who argued on the basis of trade pipe data, put the terminal date of occupation for both White Orchard and Fox Farm at 1682. The site fit the period A.D. 1666-1679, at the end of which the Jesuits, many Catholic Mohawks, and probably most of the Huron immigrants left the valley.

....

The site has been heavily damaged and almost completely destroyed by gravel mining. Topsoil from the site was pushed to the side before gravel operations began, and this displaced soil still produces artifacts. A sidehill midden still survives, and although it has been damaged, it deserves preservation.[147]

The gravel mining operation that destroyed much of the remains of Káteri Tekahkwí:tha's third village has long since been abandoned. There are only trees and bushes there today. Of the Fox farm, only the aging barns and a cornfield remain. A few beads may be churned up by the plows from time to time, but there is otherwise no evidence of the thriving Mohawk village that sprang up on the site in 1667.

16

RETURN OF THE
BLACK ROBES

In July of 1667, New France sent Fathers Jacques Frémin, Jean Pierron and Jacques Bruyas to the new Mohawk villages, now located north of the Mohawk River. Bruyas would then travel on to the Oneidas. It was to be a new era for relations between the Iroquois Confederacy and New France, but the *Jesuit Relations* tell us that the Mohawks were still cautious about what was approaching them from Lake Champlain:

> The whole country of the Iroquois was at that time so overcome with fear of a new French army, that for several days fourteen warriors had been constantly on the watch at the entrance to this Lake, in order to discover the army's line of march, and bear news of it with all haste to the whole Nation. Their purpose was to lay ambuscades for it in the woods, by means of which they intended to attack it at an advantage, and harass it in the defiles; accordingly, there was also a third band posted there, for the purpose of making this reconnoissance. But, by great good fortune for them and for us, instead of being enemies to them, we were Angels of peace; while on their part, from being Lions as they had been, they became our menials, and served us very opportunely as porters,—being furnished us by Providence to take charge of our baggage, which we would have had much difficulty in transporting to their country by land.
>
> We proceeded accordingly in company, by short marches, and came to within three-quarters of a league of their chief Village, called Gandaouagué, the one which the late Father Jogues watered with his blood, and where he was so maltreated during eighteen months of captivity. We were received there with the customary ceremonies, and with all imaginable honor. We were conducted to the cabin of the foremost Captain, where all the people crowded in, to contemplate us

at their ease,—quite delighted to see among them Frenchmen, so peaceably inclined, who not long before had made their appearance there as if infuriated, setting fire to everything. The first care of Father Fremin was to go through the cabins, and find the Huron and Algonquin captives, who alone compose two-thirds of the Village. He baptized at once ten of their children, offering to God these blessed first-fruits of the new Mission.[148]

The *Relation* mentions the baptism of a Mohawk woman dying from injuries she received from the Mahicans. We then hear about a Mohawk woman who followed the priests from one village to the next hoping for baptism—and then suffered the abuse of her relatives and neighbors who saw the illness of her son, the death of her husband (at the hands of the Mahicans), and, later, her own illness as being directly connected to her baptism.[149]

Resuming the narrative of their arrival, the priests describe their visit to two other newly-rebuilt villages. The Mohawks had apparently survived the winter, contrary to Marie de l'Incarnation's dismal forecast:

> From Gandaouagué we went on to another Village, two leagues distant, where we were received even more kindly than at the first one; this place we consecrated by the Baptism of three children, one of whom, Orphaned of both parents, was at the point of death. Was not this a rich recompense in advance for our past labors, and a powerful incentive to embrace with courage those which should present themselves in the future?
>
> However, we had to leave this second Village, in order to journey on to the Capital of this whole country, called Tionnontoguen,—which the Iroquois have rebuilt, at a quarter of a league from that which the French burned down last year. We were escorted thither by two hundred men, who marched in good order; we went last, immediately in front of the hoary Heads and the most considerable men of the country. This march was executed with an admirable gravity until, when we had arrived quite near the Village, every one halted, and we were complimented by the most eloquent man

of the Nation, who was awaiting us with the other Deputies. After this, he conducted us into the Village, where we were received with the discharge of all the artillery,—each one firing from his Cabin, and two swivel-guns being discharged at the two ends of the Village.

The entire harangue which this man made us consisted of these few words: that they were glad that the Frenchman was coming to clear the air from the mists with which the nation of the Wolves was clouding it, and to restore calm to their minds by the assurance of peace that our arrival gave them. After this followed the feast, which consisted of a dish of porridge made with Indian corn, cooked in water, with a little smoked fish, and, for dessert, a basket of squashes.

Perhaps some will be astonished that Missionaries accept honors which are paid them with so much ceremony, and are present at feasts with which these peoples are accustomed to regale their Ambassadors. But both these honors and these feasts are after the manner of the Savages,—that is to say, of such a nature that they conflict neither with humility nor with Christian temperance; on the contrary, they furnish opportunities to practice advantageously both these virtues. We must then hold St. Paul's opinion: *Scio et humiliari, scio et abundare, et satiari et esurire*.

The day of the Exaltation of the Holy Cross having been fixed upon for making our presents,—that is to say, for speaking in public on the subject of our coming,—all the six Villages of Agnié assembled here, men, women, children, and old men. After having begun the ceremony by the *Veni Creator*, the chanting of which was accompanied by the notes of a small musical instrument, which these peoples listen to with pleasure and wonder, Father Fremin made a harangue before all this great assembly, adapting himself in discourse and gestures to the usage of their most celebrated Orators, who speak not less by gesticulation than by language. He made them see the great blessings produced by peace, and the evils that accompany war—of which they had felt the effects, a year before, in the destruction of their Village by fire. He reproached them for the acts of perfidy and cruelty that they had committed, with such barbarity, upon our Frenchmen, without having received any ill treatment from these. Then he declared to them that he came for the very purpose of changing this barbarous disposition, by teaching them to live like men, and then to be Christians; and that our great Onnontio would then receive them as his subjects, and would take them thenceforth under his Royal protection, as he had all the other tribes of those regions; and that, moreover, they must take good heed in the future not to commit any act of hostility, either upon us or upon our allies.[150]

Father Frémin went on to use a wampum belt to convey his message of "peace" to the Mohawks who had gathered to hear him speak:

But, in order to inspire them with greater terror, and make more impression on their minds, as these peoples are greatly influenced by external phenomena, the Father caused to be erected, in the middle of the place where the Council was being held, a pole forty or fifty feet in length, from the top of which hung a Porcelain necklace. He declared that, in like manner, should be hanged the first of the Iroquois who should come to kill a Frenchman or any one of our Allies; and that they had already had an example shown them in the public execution, which took place at Quebec in the preceding year, of a man of their country who had violated some of the terms of peace.

It is incredible how much this present, so unusual, astounded them all. They remained for a long time with their heads down, without daring either to look at this spectacle or to talk about it, until the most prominent and most eloquent of their Orators—having recovered his spirits—arose and performed all the apish tricks imaginable about this pole, to show his astonishment. It is impossible to describe all the gesticulations made by this man, who was more than sixty years old. What looks of surprise at the sight of this spectacle, as if he had not known its meaning! What exclamations, upon finding out its secret and interpretation! How often he seized himself by the throat with both his hands, in a horrible manner,— squeezing it tightly to represent, and at the same time to inspire a horror of, this kind of death, in the multitude of people who surrounded us! In a word, he employed all the artifices of the most excellent Orators, with surprising eloquence; and, after discoursing on this theme a very long time, continually manifesting mental traits which were out of the ordinary, he ended by delivering to us the captives for whom we asked, and giving us the choice of a site for the erection of our Chapel, in the construction of which they offered to work with all diligence. They delivered to us also a Frenchman whom they had held a prisoner for some time, and promised us the liberty of twelve Algonquins,—part from the Nation of the Nez Percez, part from that of the Outaouacs,—whom they will put into our hands, to send back each to his own country.[151]

Where they had once been subjected to torture and death, the Jesuits were now making threats of execution—and getting away with it. Fear of another French army burning their villages to the ground had sufficiently cowed the Mohawks, but the fight was not out of them completely. According to the *Relation* of Father Jean Pierron,

One of the most important things I have to Write is the attack on Gandaouagué, which is one of our best Villages, and situated nearest to the enemy's country. On the eighteenth of August, 1669, three hundred of the Nation of the Loups—who live along the Sea, toward Baston, in new England—presented themselves at daybreak before the Palisade, and began to make so furious a discharge of musketry that the balls, piercing both the stockade and the cabins, soon awakened men, women, and children, almost all of whom were, at the time, sound asleep. The men at once took gun and hatchet in hand; and, while they defended the palisade, the women began, some to make bullets, and others to arm themselves with knives and defensive weapons, in view of an irruption.[152]

The Mohawks went on to repel this attack, but were irritated by Pierron's attempt to administer to the enemy warriors they brought back to their village:

While I was earnestly talking to them about their salvation, I heard some of the Iroquois saying to one another, 'Seest thou how he loves our enemies?' and others adding that I ought to let people who had done them so many injuries burn in hell also. But there were some among them who acknowledged that I was doing well to instruct them; and that man in his vengeance ought not to carry his resentment beyond the limits of his enemy's life.[153]

The *Jesuit Relations* contain many more accounts of the interaction between the priests and their Mohawk hosts—far too many to recount here. These are now available on the internet for those who don't have access to them in book form. Many of them have been included in the excellent compilation, *In Mohawk Country: Early Narratives of a Native People* (1996). The reader will not lack for further examples of how far Jesuits were willing to go to dissuade their Indian hosts from their traditional beliefs and practices, as we see in the writing of Father Pierron:

Our elders having invited me to their ceremony for the dead, which was to take place at Gandaouagué, I repaired thither on purpose to gratify them. The assembly was composed of the Onnontagué, of some Ouneiouts, and of all the more important men of Agnié. Each tribe was separated from the others, according to their custom. While waiting for the Onnontagué to speak, our Agniés were telling one another their fables and superstitions. I joined them and mingling adroitly some words of truth among their lies, I made them see clearly how ridiculous their superstitions were. A Captain who was a friend of mine, finding it hard to brook this sort of insult, wished to impose silence on me; but I believed that in a matter of Religion and in a crisis of such importance, I ought not to suffer any one to close my mouth. As, furthermore, I was not ignorant of the authority I had among these people, I said to this Captain, with considerable firmness: 'Art thou well aware that thou offerest me the keenest affront that I can ever receive? But who art thou, to bid me be silent, and did I come here to obey thee? If I had treated thee in this way at Quebec, wouldst thou not have reason to complain of it? But wherein have I spoken amiss, to close my mouth in this manner? And if I told the truth, wherefore art thou unwilling that it should be heard?"[154]

The Jesuits came to the Mohawks to pry them away not only from their "fables and superstitions," but from the valley they called home. The same year the missionaries arrived in the Mohawk villages, the French established an Indian mission on the banks of the St. Lawrence River opposite Montréal at Laprairie. Historical sources identify this community as *Kentake*, but it would be properly rendered today as *Kahentà:ke*.

Father Chauchetière, writing in *Annual Narrative of The Mission of the Sault, from Its foundation until the year 1686*, described the origins of this new community:

> The time of the wars between the french and the Iroquois being past, we saw the prophecy of Isaias literally fulfilled: "The bears and the lions shall dwell with the lambs." We saw the iroquois come to seek the friendship of the french; we saw the french go on missions to the country of the iroquois. That was the time when every one thought of making himself a home on the lands of new france. Montreal, which was the great theater of the war, became a fertile field. People even crossed the St. Lawrence river, and established opposite montreal the seigniory of la prairie—a place chosen by God for forming there one of the fairest missions that has been seen in Canada. The french prepared the place, repairing thither to build a village, which began in the year 1667.[155]

Jesuit Father Jean de Lamberville, the superior of the Iroquois missions, explained the strategy behind this new community in the *Relations* of 1672-1673:

> I am convinced that to make them good christians in their own country is a difficult thing, and one that will take a long time to accomplish; but if we could gradually detach Them from Their dwelling-place, and attract Them to Our huron Colonies, it would be very easy to make worthy Christians of them in a short time.[156]

17

BAPTISM BY FIRE

Unlike the *Jesuit Relations*, which were typically written on an annual basis, Fathers Chauchetière and Cholenec wrote their biographies of Káteri Tekahkwí:tha several years after the fact, drawing from memory as well as interviews with others who knew her personally. They wrote in a way that emphasized her holiness and sainthood, by contrasting her innate goodness with the sinfulness of her Mohawk kin. This has had the effect of turning our own people off from these Jesuit biographies, and thereby closing a window into a very crucial period of our collective history.

In addition to valuable information about Mohawk life in the mid- to late-17th century, we find in their writings an indication of how much turmoil the presence of New France's missionaries had brought to our communities, something that would eventually result in a major fissure in the "Land of Flint."

Tekahkwí:tha first came to know the Jesuits who came to Mohawk Country in 1667. According to Chauchetière, it was an uneventful encounter that nonetheless foreshadowed what was to come:

> Peace was made between the savages and the French, and several Jesuit Fathers [Fathers Bruyas, Frémin, Pierron] were sent among the savages to preach the faith. The priests arrived in the village of the Iroquois at a time of a drinking debauch, and since the savages were in no condition to receive the Fathers in the main village, as should have been done, they lodged them at the small village of Gandaouague, where Katharine lived. Katharine's uncle, as one of the principal elders of the village, received the Jesuits. Katharine, who was in the lodge, was required to render small services to the priests. Providence, which manages all these things, seemed to be working in Katharine's behalf, allowing her to see the Fathers, who one day were to baptize her.[157]

Later on in the same text, Father Chauchetière reveals that the young maiden's uncle kept her from doing more than just waiting on the priests:

The Reverend Fathers Frémin, Bruyas, and Pierron and certain other Jesuits passed some years among the Mohawks without becoming acquainted with Katharine. This was partly due to the malice of her uncle, who did his utmost to prevent his people from coming to pray to God at Montreal—although he allowed them to pray in their village. Perhaps it was also due to Katharine's shyness, for she did not dare to go to the Fathers for instruction.[158]

Just as the New Testament gospels tend to disagree with one another on minor details, so too do the biographies of Chauchetière and Cholenec. For instance, Cholenec reads much more into this initial encounter between Tekahkwí:tha and the priests:

> This unseasonable period, however, procured for the young Tegahkouita the advantage of making early acquaintance with those of whom God wished to make use to conduct her to the highest degree of perfection. She was charged with the task of lodging the missionaries and attending to their wants. The modesty and sweetness with which she acquitted herself of this duty touched her new guests, while on her part she was struck with their affable manners, their regularity in prayer, and the other exercises into which they divided the day. God even then disposed her to the grace of Baptism, for which she would have asked, if the missionaries had remained longer in her village.[159]

She would not be baptized until a new priest arrived in her village, as told by Chauchetière:

> When Father James de Lamberville was among the Mohawks, God cast His merciful eyes on Katharine's lodge and on her person, because this lodge had received the Fathers when a few years before they first brought the faith to the land of the Iroquois. Katharine had been a pagan for eighteen years, there-fore, when God sent her an illness which was to protect her from sin and which inspired Father de Lamberville to go to instruct the girl for Baptism.

As it was spring, all who were in the lodge went according to custom to cultivate their fields. Katharine had gone many times, for she was not in the habit of staying in the lodge and doing nothing while the others worked, but a sore foot and her ailment forced her to rest a few days, for she was not able to walk. The missionary Father, who knew that no one of that lodge was idle, never entered it, and above all because Katharine's uncle did not like the French at Montreal.

In passing through the village, the Father had come to Katharine's lodge and felt impelled to enter it. He found Katharine within. There never was a more fortunate meeting: fortunate for the girl, who wished to speak to the priest and did not dare to go to him; fortunate for the priest, who found a treasure where he did not expect to find one. The first words Katharine spoke to the Father revealed the feelings of her heart; but she explained to the Father what her uncle might do to keep her from being baptized, since he feared she would do as all the others and leave the country. The Father encouraged her, but was content for the time to invite her to come to the chapel to pray; This first exhortation had a great effect, because God so blessed it, that when Katharine was well again she did not fail to come there and pray to God. There were only two places in the world to which she went, her lodge and the church. Until her death she persevered in frequenting these two places only, so that those who sought her, went nowhere else to find her. At first no one caused her any trouble. They let her go and come and pray as others did, and some believed that if her lodge was not opposed to the prayer, it was because Katharine's mother, that good Algonquin of whom we have already spoken, had practised that habit there until her death, so that the savages had probably become accustomed to see her pray.[160]

Father James de Lamberville, who was mentioned in this quote, gives us his own account of this encounter:

For several years I did not know her, but one day, having found her in her cabin where she was confined through some foot-trouble, I spoke to her of Christianity and I found her so docile that I urged her to be instructed and to attend chapel, which she did with wonderful assiduity after she had been cured. When I found her so faithful I inquired as to her conduct in the cabin; all spoke well of her. In fact, I noticed that she had none of the vices of the girls of her age; this encouraged me to instruct her regularly. Finally after having taught her her prayers, and seeing that she was resolved to live in a Christian manner, I gave her Baptism on Easter Day itself in the year 1676. Since that time I can say I have found nothing in her in which she would seem to have relaxed in the slightest degree from her first fervor.[161]

Chauchetière resumes his narrative:

The priest chose Easter Sunday as the time and the chapel as the place for such a solemn Baptism. Together with two others Katharine was baptized with all the ceremonies of the Church. She was given the name of Katharine. Many savages before and after her have been called by that name, but not one has lived up to it in the manner of the Good Katharine Tekakwitha.

> ....

Not only did Katharine practise her faith in such a manner that her confessor declares she never once relaxed from her original fervor, but her extraordinary virtue was remarked by everyone, as much by the heathens as the faithful. The Christians observed her exactitude in obeying the rules of life which the priest had prescribed: that is to say, to go every day to prayer morning and evening and every Sunday to assist at Mass, and (naming what she must avoid), not to assist at the "dream feasts," nor at dances nor at other gatherings among the savages which were contrary to purity; nor yet at the liquor debauches of the heathens.[162]

The conversion of Mohawks—and their eventual removal to the new settlement at Laprairie—was causing turmoil in the villages. The most notable of these was a warrior known by several names: *Atahsà:ta*, or "a

Shadow," Kryn, Joseph *Togouiroui,* and the "Great Mohawk." It was he who led the successful defense against the Mahican attack of 1669. He and 42 others had left the Mohawk Valley for Canada in 1673.[163] In his history of the Mission of St. François Xavier, Chauchetière describes departure of Atahsà:ta as well as the impact it had on the Mohawk population:

> Having gained many persons, he sets the day for the general departure. When evening comes, he divulges the matter, and in a loud voice bids farewell in the midst of the village, and orders his people to pack their bundles. A father even joins them to lead them away. The rank, the zeal, and the spirit of God which this man possessed shut the mouths of all the elders, who were in their hearts enraged at seeing such bold-ness and not knowing whom to blame. They would at once have broken the head of another man, who had less authority. This farewell being finished, about forty persons are seen to depart,—men, women, and children, leaving their fatherland to come to make themselves Christians at montreal. This first shock given to infidelity has depopulated the country of anié; for it succeeded so well that, from that time, people have come down from the iroquois in great bands, in order to live at la prairie; and in less than Seven years the warriors of Anié have become more numerous at montreal than they are in their own country. That enrages both the elders of the villages and the flemings of manate and orange. In a short time, less than a year or two, 200 persons were thus added to the number of the Christians of la prairie.[164]

Father Cholenec informs us that, "Katharine had an older sister by adoption who had for some years been living at this mission with her husband."[165] It must have been particularly galling to have a second daughter of their most outspoken chief fall under the sway of the "Black Robes." As Chauchetière relates, Káteri's family went to great lengths to discourage her from following in her sister's footsteps:

> Her lodge began to persecute her, saying that since she was a Christian she had become lazy, for she did not work in the

fields on Sunday. They rebuked her for this pretended negligence and later ill-treated her in various ways. One way, common in this country, was to make her give up the rosary. Katharine said that she would rather die than give it up.

There were some who dared not declare themselves when they were the only Christians in their lodges, but Katharine showed an extraordinary strength of spirit against human respect when the children, pointing their fingers at her, no longer called her by her Indian name. They called her by the name of Christian, in derision, as one would speak to a dog; and this lasted such a long time that they forgot her name, giving her none other than "The Christian," because she was the only one baptized in her lodge. Far from lamenting the contempt they showed her, Katharine considered herself fortunate to have lost her name.

She had much to suffer from the jeers of the sorcerers, of the drunkards and from all enemies of *The Prayer*, and of her uncle. One day they contrived a plan to make her surrender her good resolutions. A young man was bribed and was sent into the lodge by the uncle with a tomahawk to pretend to kill this Christian, perhaps with the intention of terrifying her and preventing her from following the others whom the Great Mohawk carried off to dwell in Laprairie.[166]

Cholenec, writing in 1715, elaborates on these abuses:

Whenever she went to the chapel they caused her to be followed with showers of stones cast by drunken people, or those who feigned to be so, so that, to avoid their insults she was often obliged to take the most circuitous paths. This extended even to the children, who pointed their fingers at her, hooted after her, and in derision called her "The Christian." One day, when she had retired to her cabin, a young man entered abruptly, his eyes darting with rage, and a hatchet in his hand, which he raised as if to strike her. Perhaps he had no other design than to frighten her. But whatever might have been the Indian's intention, Katharine contented herself with modestly bowing her head, without showing the least emotion. This intrepidity, so little expected, astonished the Indian to such a degree that he immediately took to flight, as if he had been himself terrified by some invisible power.[167]

Although the Jesuit biographies are remarkably consistent with one another, one might conclude by comparing these two accounts that this incident had taken on much more dramatic proportions over time![168]

We resume the narrative of Father Chauchetière, who tells us that the young maiden's virtue was impugned by accusations of adultery during this time:

> Finally, the last persecution she suffered was simply a calumny which was invented to effect complete ruin of her reputation with the priest who directed her, and to throw her into despair of her salvation.
>
> It was in spring, when, during the hunting season, she went near the Dutch settlement with her relatives and her uncle. The wife of one hunter disliked Katharine, perhaps because her virtuous life was a reproach to the different life which this heathen led. This woman observed all Katharine's actions and words in order to find some fault with them. It is a common custom among the savages to treat an uncle as a father and to call him by the same name—father. It happened one day that Katharine, speaking of this old man in company with others, named him without using the name of "father" or "my father." The woman noticed this and rashly judged Katharine, saying that Katharine had sinned with her husband. She did not fail to go to Father de Lamberville and tell him that she whom he esteemed so highly had sinned. The Father wished to examine the reasons the woman had for treating a good Christian in such a manner. Having found that the strongest reason was that which I have just mentioned, he reproached her severely for her slanderous tongue; but he spoke to Katharine and instructed her on sin and the pains of hell which God has prepared to punish it, and finally he questioned her. Katharine replied firmly and modestly that never had she fallen into this sin, neither on this occasion nor on any other; and that she was not afraid of being damned, but much more of not having

enough courage to let herself be slain rather than to work in the fields on Sundays. She believed she had not done enough by going entire days without eating, for they hid all there was to eat in the lodge and left her nothing that was prepared for the day, in order that hunger might oblige her to go to the fields where they would have forced her to work.[169]

Father James de Lamberville tells us that there was really only one solution to Káteri's plight—to join those who had already made the journey to Canada:

I regretted only that so pure a soul and one so disposed to receive the impress of the Holy Spirit should remain in a land subject to all sorts of vice, and where the mere effort to resist the attacks of the enemies of Christianity is no mean achievement. I spoke of this to her sometimes, especially when she came to explain to me of the displeasure shown her by those of her cabin, for after trying to console her I told her of the peace enjoyed by the Christians of Sault Saint Francis Xavier— peace in which, were she there, she would find more sweetness in a day than she could enjoy in a year by remaining here.[170]

Chauchetière relates that this was not the first time the thought crossed the young maiden's mind:

She often desired to leave the country, but did not dare mention it. The Christians who came from Laprairie to the Iroquois brought her consolation, as when the Great Mohawk visited them; but when they returned without her, her grief was extreme.[171]

Káteri's misery was not to last. A guardian angel was already putting into motion a plan for her deliverance.

18

A Lily Among Thorns

A Mohawk elder—who only grudgingly allows me to call her that—told me that when she was young, she would often ask where the term "Lily of the Mohawks" came from, and was told by her elders that after the death of Káteri Tekahkwí:tha, lilies sprouted from her grave. Although the Jesuit biographers make no mention of this, it might very well be so.

The Jesuit writings suggest a more mundane and political origin for this moniker. The *fleur-de-lys*, or "lily flower," is commonly regarded as a heraldic symbol of the French monarchy. Four of them are depicted in the flag of Quebec. It has been suggested that the stylized lily is representative of the Holy Trinity as well as the Virgin Mary.[172]

As noted in a previous chapter, a Jesuit priest invoked the term when he wrote that a new governor had arrived from France "to plant Lilies on the ashes of the Iroquois."[173] It is therefore not surprising to see Father Chauchetière apply this term to Káteri:

> I have up to the present written of Katharine as a lily among thorns, but now I shall relate how God transplanted this beautiful lily and placed it in a garden full of flowers, that is to say, in the Mission of the Sault, where there have been, are, and always will be holy people renowned for virtue.[174]

Chauchetière was borrowing from scripture for this epithet. Specifically, he was citing the Song of Solomon 2:2 from the Old Testament: "As the lily among thorns, so is my love among the daughters." The priest's use of scripture to describe Káteri is undoubtedly the origin of the expression by which she is universally known, "Lily of the Mohawks." If it isn't already obvious, her fellow Mohawks—and her family in particular—would be the thorns.

How the lily escaped these thorns is explained by Father Cholenec:

> Divine Providence soon showed the way. Katharine had an older sister by adoption who had for some years been living at this mission with her husband. Her desire to have Katharine

share their happiness led her to make her husband depart with several others who went to see their relatives, so that Katharine might be brought there. This man explained his purpose to her when he arrived and Katharine felt a joy it would be difficult to express. Her aunts seemed willing that she should go, but everything was to be feared from her uncle, who was very powerful in the village and who strongly opposed these transmigrations which unpeopled his country to populate ours.[175]

Father de Lamberville, who was a participant in her escape, provides us with the details:

Among some of the Christians of the Mission of Sault Saint Francis Xavier who came to the Iroquois to see their relatives, was one of the most important of the Oneidas called Ogenheratarihiens. He entered my cabin, where forthwith a crowd of people, as is the custom of the country, came to greet this newcomer, and among them Katharine. This man, seeing them assembled, began to talk to them of Christianity and of the happiness of those who had come to live at Sault Saint Francis Xavier. Katharine alone, as if God had addressed to her the words of this preacher, was touched by them. She sought me out and told me she was determined to carry out what I had so often advised her. She begged me earnestly to take proper measures to restrain her relatives who wished to stop her. I put her under the care of Ogenheratarihiens who strongly confirmed her in her resolution. This fervent Christian and another Mohawk Indian who was related to Katharine, conducted her escape very skillfully. Some one had gone to warn one of her uncles, the most important man in the village, who was utterly opposed to any of his compatriots going to the Mission of the Sault. He was then with the Dutch, neighbors of the Iroquois, where she should embark; nevertheless he could not find her in spite of his diligent search.[176]

Thus ends Father de Lamberville's contribution to the contemporary biographies. Chauchetière and Cholenec pick up the story where he leaves off.

P. KARWIRAKERON
MONTOUR 00

Chauchetière provides a lengthy biography of *Ogenheratarihiens*, whose Indian name was translated by the Jesuits as "Hot Ashes" or "Hot Powder." Today we would render it in Mohawk as *O'kenhratarîhen*. He was also known as Louis *Garonhiague*, which we easily recognize as Karonhià:ke, the Mohawk word for Sky World and Heaven. Hot Ashes was a notable Oneida war captain who followed his Christian wife to the Mission of the Sault and eventually became a Christian himself. He became as fervent a Christian as he was a warrior, according to Chauchetière:

> Such was the man whom God had chosen to take Katharine from the Iroquois. She hoped to leave this land of Sodom and to serve God in peace at the Mission of the Sault. Hot Ashes went first to the Mohawks to join Katharine's cousin and another savage from the Huron Mission of Lorette. They set out with Hot Ashes to rescue one of God's chosen ones.
>
> On their arrival they went to the church to begin their visit by prayer. Father James de Lamberville, who loved such visits and who considered, as he said, these Christians from the Sault similar to Angels from God, received the three himself. The spirit of Christianity and the mortification of their passions were depicted on the countenances of these new apostles. But the savages were drawn more by curiosity than by the appearance of their visitors. The elders were the first to visit the newcomers from Montreal. By a stroke of Providence, Katharine's uncle was then with the Dutch, a circumstance which facilitated her departure. When the audience was sufficiently large, Hot Ashes spoke to them. He reminded them that he had formerly been a Oneida chief, a warrior and one of themselves; but (he told them), in those days he had been nothing but a dog, and had only begun to be a man in the last few months. He also said many other touching things by which Katharine profited more than anyone. The elders left one after another until the preacher was almost alone.
>
> Katharine could not tear herself away from these newcomers. She told the priest that she must go away even though it cost her her life. Father de Lamberville spoke to Hot Ashes and his companions and the chief replied that there would be

room in the canoe for her, since he intended to go to the Oneidas and preach the faith among the Iroquois nations. This plan was no sooner decided upon than it was put into action. Katharine embarked secretly with the two companions of Hot Ashes and started on the way toward the Dutch.[177]

As Káteri's Jesuit biographers rarely provide the context of the events they describe, we must turn to *The Livingston Indian Records* (1956) to learn that the Five Nations were holding councils with the colonies of Maryland and Virginia that summer in Albany. They discussed the return of prisoners and strengthening the Covenant Chain of Peace and Friendship. One such meeting was held on August 6, 1677, with 8 Mohawk chiefs, whose names are given as *Canneachko, Aihagari, Roote, Cassenossacha, Cannondacgoo, Odiana, Tagansariggo,* and *Semachegi.* A portion of their speech is as follows:

They say with a present, "We are glad that the King's Governors of Maryland and Virginia have sent you hither to speak with the Maquess [Mohawks], as also that the Governor General has been pleased to [designate] and appoint this place to speak with all nations in peace. Finding this fit place for the same, for which we do return his honor hearty thanks, especially that his honor has been pleased to grant you the privilege for to speak with us here. Seeing that the Governor General & we are one, and one heart and one head, for the covenant that is betwixt the Governor General and us is inviolable, yea, so strong that if the very thunder should break upon the Covenant Chain it would not break it [asunder.] We are likewise glad that we have heard you speak and now we shall answer. That in case any of our Indians should injure any Christians or Indians in your parts or your Christians or Indians do any damage to our Indians, we desire that on both sides the matter may be composed, and that which is past to buried in oblivion. They say further that the Seneks [Senecas] were upon the journey to come hither with six hundred men, but for fear turned back again. But we were not afraid to come here." Do give thereupon one dressed elk skin and one beaver.[178]

The "saint among savages" theme is truly international.

The priests were undoubtedly aware of these councils. Is it possible that they saw these peace overtures with the English colonies as a threat to French interests? Did they step up their efforts to draw the Mohawks and other Iroquois to Canada? And if so, how much faith can we put in their dramatic description of Káteri's escape?

One of the curious things about the narratives of Káteri Tekahkwí:tha's life is the fact that they do not mention the names of any of her parents, natural or adoptive. Certainly, this information could have been ascertained by the Jesuits, who had access to many people who would have known. Her uncle, a leading chief of the Mohawk village, may well have been one of the chiefs mentioned by name in councils with the French, Dutch, or English, but unless some rare document turns up somewhere, we will probably never know. He remains a faceless, nameless villain.

> The Divine Providence which guides the saints along roads unknown to men, conducted Katharine to the Sault in an extraordinary manner without being discovered. When it became known that the three visitors from Montreal were returning and that Katharine was no longer in the lodge, suspicion was aroused. Messengers hastened to the Dutch to carry this news to Katharine's uncle. Being a wicked man and an enemy of all who came from Montreal, the uncle set out to find the travelers, and if possible, as he said, to kill them. He loaded his gun with three bullets for the purpose, but although he searched thoroughly for his niece, the party eluded him by disembarking and hiding in the woods.[179]

A Mohawk chief would certainly be justified in wanting to stem the flow of migration to Canada, considering the losses his population had already suffered from war and disease. It is also understandable that a parent would be alarmed by his young daughter sneaking off with strange men, and might be inclined to pursue them. Chauchetière tells us that eventually he did manage to overtake the party:

As they were near the Dutch, Katharine's cousin decided to go to them for bread. He left his sister-in-law, Katharine, with the savage from the Mission of Lorette, who had lived many years in continency with his wife in a cabin by themselves. Katharine's uncle was approaching as the other left.

Her brother-in-law saw the old man, but he was too near to avoid him without making himself known. Accordingly he continued on his way, but since Katharine's uncle did not know those for whom he was looking, they passed each other. When Katharine's brother-in-law returned from the Dutch, he told her of his adventure and Katharine interpreted it as a special sign of the Providence of God for her; and so she was encouraged to give herself entirely to God and to make use of the opportunities which He sent her to compass her salvation. Her journey was a continual prayer and the joy which she felt in approaching Montreal cannot be put into words.[180]

Cholenec's account differs slightly in detail. One thing it has in common is that it undermines the notion that the uncle of Káteri was filled with homicidal rage:

They saw him coming from afar, and as they were doubtful as to his plans, they hid Katharine in the woods, while the others sat down by the road as if to eat. Coming upon them, he asked them very abruptly where his niece was. They answered that they had seen her in the village and that they could not tell him anything else about her, whereupon the old man, God doubtlessly wishing it to be so, turned back without making any further effort to find her.[181]

If this were a trial, the uncle's defense team would certainly point out that there would be no point in loading a 17th century musket with three bullets as if it were a revolver. They would then challenge the Jesuit testimony as hearsay and ask that all charges be dropped for lack of evidence!

19

JOURNEY TO THE VILLAGE OF PRAYER

We will now focus on another aspect of the story that rarely gets attention: the specific route our heroes took to reach Canada.

While he is certainly the most colorful writer of the three Jesuit authors, Chauchetière's description of Káteri's escape falls short of telling us anything about the geographical setting of the story. All we know is that the "confrontation" with her uncle took place somewhere in the vicinity of a Dutch settlement, most likely Schenectady.

There is no question that they traveled to Canada via Lake George, Lake Champlain, and the Richelieu River. But how did they get to that corridor? The Mohawk River would have led them to the Hudson River, which would have taken them northward to an area where a portage might have been possible. Our sources suggest a more direct route over land was favored by most travelers. This was, after all, how the French army and the Jesuits had come to the Mohawk Valley.

Ellen H. Walworth, author of *The Life and Times of Kateri Tekakwitha, The Lily of the Mohawks* (1891), offers this suggestion:

> Their probable route to Lake George was through what is now the township of Galway in Saratoga County, and thence up the valley of the Kayaderosseras Creek, skirting the eastern side of the long mountain-ridge that carries Lake Desolation high on its back. Through this region one can travel almost in a straight line of open country from Amsterdam on the Mohawk to Jessup's landing on the Hudson. There the river is fordable, just above Palmer's Falls and below the old scow-ferry. A well-worn trail followed the eastern bank of the river from there to Luzerne, and then turned northeast, through a beautiful valley, to the mountainous shores of Lake George.[182]

Recently, Diego Paoletti of Montréal posted an alternative route on his website, *The Life of Catherine Tekakwitha:*

The most probable route was the Mohawk River from Gandaouage, or Fonda. When reaching the vicinity of Fort Orange, or Albany from the Mohawk River (a distance of about 5 km, or 3.1 miles), that Catherine Tekakwitha and the Native from the Mission of Lorette waited on the riverside of Mohawk River for her brother-in-law, who went to get bread in Fort Orange. The final would-be calculation of the distance and time travelled by her brother-in-law to Fort Orange and back to the riverside of the Mohawk River are not included. Then, they resumed their voyage on the Mohawk River and on the Hudson River.

Then, before reaching the falls on the Hudson River that they crossed the forest (a distance of about 16 km, or 10 miles), and her brother-in-law and the Native from the Mission of Lorette had carried their canoe through the forest until they reached Lake George or Lake du Saint Sacrament.[183]

One source gives the Iroquois name for today's Lake George as *Andiatarocte*, which translates as "Lake Shut In." The modern form would be *Kaniá:taro'kte* or *Aniá:taro'kte*, or "End of the Lake." It was Father Isaac Jogues who named it Lac du Saint-Sacrement, or Lake of the Holy Sacrament.[184]

When Káteri and her companions reached the lake, they must have found the canoe the rescuers had left there on their way to Mohawk Country. This was probably an elm-bark canoe like the Iroquois typically used, a somewhat crude vessel with crimps in the sides and a straight edge at both ends, made of a single piece of bark. They may well have bartered with friendly Algonquin Indians and procured a sleeker birch bark canoe, which would have been very cosmopolitan of them. Whatever the case, our trio of travelers began their journey northward, passing by the site of many future battles. Is it possible to see the ghosts of the not-yet dead? If so, they would have seen plenty of them at the site of the future Fort William Henry, where notable clashes in the French and Indian War took place some eight decades later.

Reaching the end of the 32-mile lake, our intrepid travelers would have descended the La Chute River that joins Lake George to Lake Champlain, portaging around the waterfalls found there. This is where Samuel Champlain and his annoying Indian allies chased down and killed our alleged Mohawk ancestors some 68 years earlier. They would have also passed a location mentioned by Jesuit Fathers Frémin, Pierron, and Bruyas on their journey to Mohawk Country in 1667:

> Arriving within three-quarters of a league of the Falls by which Lake St. Sacrement empties, we all halted at this spot, without knowing why, until we saw our Savages at the water-side gathering up flints, which were almost all cut into shape. We did not at that time reflect upon this, but have since then learned the meaning of the mystery; for our Iroquois told us that they never fail to halt at this place, to pay homage to a race of invisible men who dwell there at the bottom of the lake. These beings occupy themselves in preparing flints, nearly all cut, for the passers-by, provided the latter pay their respects to them by giving them tobacco. If they give these beings much of it, the latter give them a liberal supply of these stones. These water-men travel in canoes, as do the Iroquois; and, when their great Captain proceeds to throw himself into the water to enter his Palace, he makes so loud a noise that he fills with fear the minds of those who have no knowledge of this great Spirit and of these little men. At the recital of this fable, which our Iroquois told us in all seriousness, we asked them if they did not also give some tobacco to the great spirit of Heaven, and to those who dwell with him. The answer was that they do not need any, as do people on the earth. The occasion of this ridiculous story is the fact that the Lake is, in reality, often agitated by very frightful tempests, which cause fearful waves … and when the wind comes from the direction of the Lake, it drives on this beach a quantity of stones which are hard, and capable of striking fire.[185]

Our three heroes, of course, would have paid no mind to these old superstitions, having a great many new superstitions to care about instead. Nor would they have given a second thought to a small rock jutting out of the water between Shelburne Point and Juniper Island, not far from Burlington, Vermont. This is known as Rock Dunder, a favorite resting spot for seagulls. There is an interesting story that goes with this rock, which is worth relating here.

You will recall from an earlier chapter that when the French first attempted an invasion of Mohawk Country in the winter of 1666, they got lost near the Dutch town of Schenectady and were saved by the quick thinking of Arendt van Curler, known to the Mohawk as Corlaer and to the French as Corlat. He convinced the Mohawks not to attack them, and then provided them with enough provisions to make it back to Canada. Cadwallader Colden tells us that once peace was made between the Mohawks and the French in 1667,

> The French Governor, in order to Reward so signal a Service, invited Corlaer to Canada, and, no doubt, with design to make use of his Interest in some Project, in favour of the French Colony; but as he went through the Lake (by the French call'd Champlain) his Canoe was Overset, and he drowned. From this Accident that Lake has ever since been call'd Corlaers Lake by the People of New-York.
>
> There is a Rock in this Lake, on which the Waves dash and fly up to a very great height, when the Wind blows strong; the Indians fancy, that an Old Indian lives under this Rock, who has the Power of the Winds, and therefore as they pass this Rock in their Voyages through this Lake, they always throw a Pipe or some Tobacco, or something else to this Old Indian, and pray a favourable Wind. The English that often pass with them, sometimes laugh at them; but they are sure to be told of Corlaers Death with a grave air. *Your great Countryman Corlaer (say they) as he passed by this Rock, jested at our Fathers making Presents to this Old Indian, and in derision turn'd up his Back-side towards the Rock, but this Affront cost him his Life.*[186]

This rock was known to the Mohawks and later colonists as *Rogeo,* or *Rotsio,* and it eventually became a boundary marker between the Iroquois and the "Canada Indians."[187] Today this name would be rendered as *Rotsíhne.* It is also significant to Abenaki Indians, who call it *Odziozo,* the spirit being who created Lake Champlain.[188]

Eventually our travelers would have completed the journey up Lake Champlain and reached the Richelieu River, where they would have descended past the three French forts along the way: Fort St. Jean, Fort St. Therese, and Fort St. Louis. Beyond the third fort they would have

taken their canoe out of the water and followed a shortcut to the banks
of the St. Lawrence River opposite Montréal Island, otherwise they
would have to travel all the way to where the Richelieu met the
St. Lawrence, and then paddle many miles upstream. The trail is found
on a well-known map of the region made in 1666 by Monsieur de Tracy.

Our Jesuit biographers do not disclose which route they actually took,
but Diego Paoletti has an alternative for this last leg of the journey on
his website:

> When in the area of (Saint-Paul-de-) l'Île-aux-Noix they went
> through the forest of the Montérégie region (a distance of
> about 11 km, or 6.9 miles). They went by land from there,
> because further there were the Saint-Jean Rapids on the
> Richelieu River. Île-aux-Noix was known before the arrival of
> the Europeans and settled by Native people on a regular,
> seasonal basis. The location of the island and the area sur-
> rounding the island were a known hunting and fishing grounds.
>
> Again, her brother-in-law and the Native from the Mission
> of Lorette had carried their canoe. They crossed through the
> rivers of the Montérégie region forest with their canoe until
> they reached the river de la Tortue, or the river Saint-Régis.
> They sailed the river de la Tortue and into the Saint-Laurent
> River, or The Great River. They sailed south along the shore
> of the Saint-Laurent River to the Mission of the Sault (a
> distance of about 2 km, or 1.25 miles). They sailed in the
> canoe most of their voyage, because the forests were dense.
>
> In the portrait by Father Chauchetière of Catherine
> Tekakwitha, that he painted them in a canoe in front of a
> church that depicted the chapel of the Mission of Saint
> Francis Xavier at the Sault.
>
> Thus, they travelled about at least a distance of at 220 km,
> or 137 miles and also 2 km, or 1.25 miles on the Saint-Laurent
> River. If they travelled by day, which it had perhaps taken
> them about thirteen days (if they travelled about eight hours
> each day) to reach the Mission of the Sault.[189]

Our expedition has returned us to the place where we began, the
valley of the St. Lawrence River, where Jacques Cartier visited the

village of Hochelaga in the early 16th century. Incredible changes have taken place since then. In a village that lies somewhere on the banks of Kania'tarowá:nen, former enemies have become friends—just like the Huron and Mohawk who have led Káteri Tekahkwí:tha to this land. Instead of descending upon the valley to take captives, seize furs, and wage war, Mohawks have come to the St. Lawrence River to embrace a new faith, form new alliances, and begin a new era of our history.

20

THE NEW KAHNAWÀ:KE

Instead of taking Káteri to Laprairie, her rescuers brought her to a new village, this one located about six kilometers west in what is now Ville Sainte-Catherine. It was established in 1676 and named Kahnawà:ke, probably because so many of its residents had come from the village of the same name in the Mohawk Valley, and because it overlooked the rapids of the St. Lawrence River. A Jesuit, writing in 1677, noted the reason for the move from Laprairie:

> The Iroquois savages who had taken up their Residence at la prairie de la Magdeleine for the purpose of being Instructed, and of living there in a Christianlike manner, as they have done for many years, have always complained that those meadows were too damp for their Indian corn, and they have Urgently requested us to give them other lands, which they might more successfully Till.
>
> This was granted to them last year, and they were given the lands that are above la prairie de la Magdeleine, and bordering

Ville Sainte-Catherine shrine location circa 1920. Source: Historic Caughnawaga by E. J. Devine.

Aerial photo of Ville Sainte-Catherine circa 1949, before the St. Lawrence Seaway radically altered the landscape.

on sault st. Louis—whence this mission has derived the name of st. François Xavier du sault. They have settled there to continue the wholly Christian life that they previously led; and they have even progressed in the practice of all the virtues ...[190]

Father Chauchetière described the humble beginnings of the new mission in his *Annual Narrative of the Mission of the Sault:*

Poverty is not a scourge of the mission, but an adjunct which chastens it from time to time. It was so great last year, and has continued in such a way this year, that it obliged the mission to leave the land of la prairie for the purpose of seeking one a league and a quarter higher up, named the sault St. Louis, or

Satellite photo of modern Ville Sainte-Catherine. Shrine is located on mainland left of bridge at the center of the image.

that of St. Xavier, from the appellation of the mission. Our Lord assuredly wishes to honor his poverty in that of the Savages; for it is a companion which follows them everywhere. Neither do they ask to be delivered from it, as from the other temptations of life, because it increases their merit. Be this as it may, it is the reason which obliged the mission to change its abode,—which occurred nine years ago, in the month of July. This was not accomplished without a great deal of trouble. The missionaries had no other accommodation than a sorry lodge, and for chapel a cabin of bark, in which the superior of the mission dwelt in a corner arranged for the purpose.[191]

He described the mission's geography in 1682:

We are in a very high and beautiful location, with a fine view, 60 leagues Distant from Quebec,—which is called "the Iroquois mission." It is the finest mission in Canada, and, as regards piety and devotion, resembles one of the best Churches in france.

The river St. Lawrence here forms a Lake two leagues wide;
and The place where we are is so high that the waters of this
great river fall here with a loud roar, and roll over many
Cascades, which, frighten one to look at. The water foams As
you see it do under a mill-Wheel. We nevertheless readily pass
over it every Day in our Bark Canoes; and I cannot help saying
that one must be crazy to run the rapids as we do, without any
Fear of being drowned.[192]

Today the site is identified by a cenotaph marking Káteri's first burial
site. This is located across the street from a modern church, La Paroisse
Sainte-Catherine d'Alexandrie. The white marble cenotaph is still
maintained, even though Káteri's remains are now located in the St.
François Xavier Church on the modern-day Kahnawà:ke reserve several
miles west. East of this small memorial is a bridge to the locks of the St.
Lawrence Seaway, a massive structure that completely blocks the view of
the Montréal skyline on the opposite shore of the St. Lawrence River.

It is hard to imagine what it must have looked like in the late 17th
century, although there are aerial photographs taken before the Seaway
construction that allow us to visually reconstruct the area to a certain
degree.[193] There are also photographs that appear in Father E. J. Devine's
Historic Caughnawaga (1922).[194] I have been unable to determine if there
have been any archaeological surveys of this particular village site,
although a later site, *Kanatakwén:ke* (1696-1716), was hastily surveyed
during the construction of the Seaway.[195] Father Chauchetière made
several drawings of the mission that have been reproduced in various
books.[196] Finally, there is Father Cholenec's description, published in the
Jesuit Relations, which helps paint our picture: "The mission of st.
François Xavier du sault consists of 22 Huron and Iroquois Cabins, in
addition to the Chapel and to our house."[197]

We can only imagine what it must have been like for Káteri
Tekahkwí:tha to finally arrive at her new home on the St. Lawrence
River after so long and harsh a journey, and so trying an experience in
her former village. Father Chauchetière can hardly contain himself in
relating her arrival:

Behold then this young Indian maiden, twenty-one years old,
who has remained saintly and pure, triumphing over the vice

The "hortatory" wampum belt given by Christian Huron to the Iroquois of Kahnawà:ke in 1677. Reproduction and photo by the author.

and licentiousness which corrupted all the Iroquois. Behold the Genevieve of Canada, the treasure of the Sault, who has sanctified the roads between the Mohawks and Montreal, along which many chosen souls have passed after her. When she found herself far from her own country and realized that she need no longer fear her uncle, she gave herself entirely to God, leaving the future in His hands. She arrived in the autumn of 1677, having made an uninterrupted journey because of her great longing to reach her destination.

When she arrived she gave the priests [Fathers Frémin and Cholenec] the letters which Father James de Lamberville had written. After reading them, they were delighted to receive her, for these were the words of the letter: "I send you a treasure, guard it well." Her face, however, told more than the letters. It is impossible to portray the joy she experienced in being in the land of sunshine, freed from the anxiety she had felt at not being able to serve God as she wished, in being released from the persecutions she had endured in the lodge in her own country, in having holy companions and in being able to hear several Masses a day, and above all in being able to receive Holy Communion frequently.

Although the chapel at the Sault was made only of bark, she satisfied her desire for prayer by spending her leisure time there, for even then she had more devotion than the older Christians. We are now to see how she took the place of another Katharine, who is buried at Laprairie and who had died such a short time before the arrival of this Katharine, that when anyone wished to say that a person was a good Christian, he said that such a person resembled Katharine Ganneaktewa.[198]

Father Cholenec's account differs in the wording of the letter sent with Káteri by Father de Lamberville:

> Reverend Father Frémin, one of the great missionaries of Canada, was then in charge of the mission; Father Chauchetière and I were there with him. Katharine was directed to me by Father James de Lamberville; the letter she brought from him contained this passage: "Katharine Tegakoüita is going to live at the Sault. Will you kindly undertake to direct her? You will soon know what a treasure we have sent you. Guard it well! May it profit in your hands, for the glory of God and the salvation of a soul that is certainly very dear to Him."[199]

Father Chauchetière was himself a new arrival to the village, having arrived only a few months before Káteri. He was 32 years old at the time of her arrival. Father Cholenec was 36, and Father Frémin, who was in charge of the mission, was 49. Cholenec was Káteri's "ordinary confessor" and had a great deal of personal interaction with her during her time at the new Kahnawà:ke. He wrote a full biography of Káteri about ten years after Chauchetière wrote his in 1686. In the chapters that follow, we will quote from these manuscripts as well as several other letters in which they documented her life.

We will resume Cholenec's description of the mission that appears in the *Jesuit Relations*. Here he marvels at the piety of the inhabitants:

> It is a fine Thing, and one that doubtless causes much Joy to the whole of paradise, to see the peace, the gentleness, the union, the piety, the devotion, and the fervor of our savages in this new settlement. As their devotions are no longer hindered by contact with the french, we can say that the liberty that they now enjoy of doing Things in season and in their own fashion has served to increase and to strengthen devotion, inasmuch as it produces order and Regularity. This may be Observed at a glance, throughout the week, but above all on Sunday, which they devote entirely to God and to the salvation of their Souls.
>
> ....
>
> On Sunday Morning the Father says Mass at 8 o'clock. The savages Sing through nearly the whole of it, the men on one

side and the women on the other, alternately and in 2 choirs. This they always do, at present, when they Sing in the Chapel,—in which also, for that purpose, the men are always placed on The Gospel side, and all the women on The other.

....

O My Father! What glory for God; what Joy for all paradise; what Edification for all the french who see this beautiful order, and who Hear those holy and Celestial harmonies! They are all Charmed to see it, and afterward publish it everywhere; and assuredly they have Reason to do so. Indeed, for my part, I admit that, of all that I have Hitherto seen among them, Nothing has so Delighted me as thus to hear these savages Sing God's praises at their vespers. For they do it, both men and women, with such devotion and Modesty that I may say, without exaggeration and in pure truth, that our church then resembles a Choir of Religious rather than a Chapel of savages.[200]

We can only wonder how moved Káteri was to be shown her new place of worship, which was at that time a crude structure of bark and logs, not much different from the longhouses of the Indians. In his narrative of the mission for the year 1677, Father Chauchetière describes a curious ornamentation, a gift of Christian Hurons, which she undoubtedly saw there:

This year will be remarkable for a celebrated present which was sent from lorette to the Sault. It was a hortatory collar which conveyed the voice of the Lorette people to those of the Sault, encouraging them to accept the faith in good earnest, and to build a chapel as soon as possible; and it also exhorted them to combat the various demons who conspired for the ruin of both missions. This collar was at once attached to one of the beams of the chapel, which is above the top of the altar, so that the people might always behold it and hear that voice.[201]

This "hortatory collar" was undoubtedly the wampum belt that was displayed at the church in Kahnawà:ke until it disappeared in the early 1970's. It was a purple belt with white emblems depicting a cross in the center and a chain of three rectangles on each side. A wampum belt weaver herself, Káteri could not have missed the implication of the symbols arrayed on the belt: instead of being united by a pine tree or heart at the center, as they were in the *Aionwà:tha Belt* of the Five Nations, the icons on this belt were united by the cross of Jesus Christ. There was just one difference: there was no "path of peace" directly linking the outside nations to the cross at the center. It stood alone, unattached—as if to tell everyone that the true connection was yet to be made.

21

Divine Fire

Her biographers hold nothing back when they describe how elated Káteri Tekahkwí:tha was to arrive at the new Kahnawà:ke, a place where she was surrounded by people who were just as devout. Many of them were people from her own village in the Mohawk Valley.

"She compared what they were here with what they had been there, and then reflecting gravely on their happiness and on her own, she felt an unbelievable joy to find herself, after a fortunate exile from another Egypt, happily transplanted to this promised land, where she finally found what she had sought for such a long time, without even knowing what it was," wrote Father Cholenec. "She could not speak of it to us without ecstasies."[202]

She took up residence with her older sister and her family. The mistress of this lodge was Anastasia Degonhatsihongo—*Kanáhstatsi Tekonwatsenhón:ko*, or "She Hit its Fire"—who knew Káteri and her mother in the Mohawk Valley. Kanáhstatsi was one of the first Mohawk converts. "She was one of the pillars of the mission, a most fervent member of the confraternity of the Holy Family, and of the entire village, the one who knew best how to instruct," wrote Cholenec.[203]

Father Chauchetière described Káteri's tutelage:

> She learned first the ordinary exercises of the mission, for the feast days and for the work days. She learned more in one week than the others had in several years. She was never idle for a moment, whether she was in the lodge, in the fields, or in the forest. One saw her, rosary in hand, with her dear instructress, going and coming, carrying her share of the wood. The most menial occupations were raised by the fervor and spirit with which Katharine did them. She never separated from Anastasia because she learned more when the two went together for wood than at any other time. Her manner of action made Anastasia say that Katharine never lost sight of God.[204]

Kanáhstatsi Tekonwatsenhón:ko, Káteri's new "mother."

It wasn't long before the newcomer attracted notice. Chauchetière describes one early encounter:

> A young man visiting one day in the lodge, saw Katharine sitting near her instructress, Anastasia Tegonhatsihongo, whom she also called mother. He remarked jokingly, "It is said this one has sore eyes," and at the same time took the end of her blankets and uncovered her face. This act of uncovering her head made Katharine blush, but without becoming angry she gathered up her blanket and listened patiently to her mother, who was instructing her. Her enduring patience made her incapable of being uncharitable, or of complaining about anyone.[205]

Father Cholenec noted how rapidly she progressed:

> As she was noble and generous of heart and quick of spirit, and since, as far as we were able to discover, she possessed an insatiable desire to learn what was good, and an equal ardor to put into practice what she had once learned, her well-disposed soul caught fire, and, placing her own strength to the work, she began to practice the things she saw the others doing. She did them so well and with such noticeable progress that within less than a few weeks she distinguished herself among all the girls and women of the mission. She soon gained the esteem and admiration of everybody, so that Katharine Tegakoüita, after having been preserved for more than twenty years among the wicked and the sinful, now soon became a saint here among the just and the faithful.
>
> It is, doubtless, surprising to see how far this young girl advanced in piety during the two years and a half (approximately) that she lived at the Sault, but it is more astonishing still that she possessed such virtue almost from the very beginning. It may in truth be said of her that she never was a novice in the exercise of virtue, but that she had been accomplished in it from the beginning and that she attained perfection with such rapidity that she had the Holy Ghost for her teacher.[206]

Most Iroquois converts had to wait several years before they could be granted the grace of First Communion. Not so with Káteri, who received this sacrament on her first Christmas at the Sault:[207]

> This rule did not hold for Katharine; she was too well disposed and desired with too great an eagerness to receive Our Lord, to be deprived of this great grace, so she was promised some time before the feast that she might receive Him on Christmas, after she had been instructed in the mystery.
>
> She received the good news with all imaginable joy, and prepared herself for the great event with an increase of devotion suitable to the exalted idea she had of it. It must be admitted, however, that it was at this First Communion that all her fervor was renewed. The ground was so well prepared that only the approach of this divine fire was necessary, to receive all its warmth. She approached or rather surrendered herself to this furnace of sacred love that burns on our altars, and she came out of it so glowing with its divine fire that only Our Lord knew what passed between Himself and His dear spouse during her First Communion. All that we can say is that from that day forward she appeared different to us, because she remained so full of God and of love of Him.[208]

Later in his manuscript, Cholenec elaborated on the effect this "divine fire" had on her countenance:

> It has been told of several Saints, that at times their hearts were so inflamed with divine love, that in spite of the efforts they took to hide this sacred fire, which consumed them from within, they were unable to prevent the escape of some of its sparks. Such was Katharine's love. This young girl, although only an untutored Indian, was so filled with the spirit of God, and tasted such sweetness in its possession, that her entire exterior gave testimony of it; her eyes, her gestures, her words, were filled with divine love at such moments. If one were with her, it did not take long to be touched by it, and to become warmed with this heavenly fire.[209]

Cholenec goes on to say that the women of the village were drawn to Káteri's radiance:

> This fact, moreover, was so well known in the village that at the time of general Communion the most devout women hastened to place themselves near her in church, claiming that the mere sight of her exterior was so devotional and ardent at those times that her example inspired them and served as an excellent preparation for approaching the Holy Table in a proper manner.[210]

Cholenec notes that her fervor doubled once she had taken Communion:

> Every morning, winter and summer, she was in our church at four o'clock and often she arrived even before the bell which rings every day at that hour. She remained there several hours in succession in prayer, though her tongue played small part in it. Ordinarily she prayed only with eyes and heart—her eyes suffused with tears, and her heart incessantly giving forth ardent sighs. She was always as if lifted out of herself when she prayed and conversed with Our Lord. Her fervor was no less evident in the confessions which she made every eight days or sometimes oftener. She passed an entire hour in the church weeping and sighing while she prepared herself, and when she began her confession it was always with such loud sobs that she would have given her confessor much difficulty in understanding her, had he not otherwise known her angelical innocence. She thought herself the greatest sinner in the world. It was with such sentiments of humility that she made all her confessions.[211]

Káteri was "filled with God and his Holy love."

> One had not to be long in her company to feel it and to be surrounded by it as she was. All her joy was to think upon Our Lord and to converse familiarly with Him. She passed almost the entire day, on Sundays and feast days, praying at the foot of the altar, and on working days she often came there to offer

up her work. If sometimes asked, "Katharine, do you love Our Lord?"—it was enough to see her immediately quite overcome. "Ah, my Father! Ah, my Father!" she would say, and she could say no more.[212]

Chauchetière noted that she had a favorite saying that summed up her virtues completely: "Who will teach me what is most agreeable to God, so that I may do it?"[213]

He also informs us the people of the village had a favorite saying about her as well: "It became a common thing in the village to say that Katharine was never any place but in her cabin or in the church, and that she knew but two roads: to her field and to her cabin."[214]

Alas, this idyllic moment in time was soon to pass, for a new trial was about to begin. The majority of the Indians went out on extended hunts each winter, and Káteri would be no different.

After the festival of Christmas it was the proper season for the hunt. She was unable to excuse herself from following her sister and brother-in-law into the forest. She then made it apparent that one is able to serve God in all places where His Providence calls. She did not relax any of her ordinary exercises, while her piety even suggested holy practices to substitute in place of those which were incompatible with living in the forests. There was a time set apart for everything. In the morning she applied herself to her prayers, and concluded with those which the Indians make in common according to their custom. In the evening she renewed them, continuing until the night was far advanced. While the Indians were eating breakfast to strengthen themselves to endure the chase through the whole day, she retired to some secret place to offer up her devotions, for this was a little before the time when they were accustomed to hear Mass at the mission. She had fixed a cross in the trunk of a tree which she found by the side of a stream, and this solitary spot was her oratory. There she placed herself in spirit at the foot of the altar. She united her soul with that of the priest, prayed her guardian angel to be present for her at that Holy Sacrifice and to apply to her its benefits. The rest of the day she spent in laboring with the others of her sex, but to banish all frivolous discourse and preserve her union with God, she always introduced some religious conversation, or perhaps invited them to sing hymns or anthems in praise of their Lord. Her meals were very simple, and often she did not eat till the end of the day. At other times she secretly mixed ashes with the food provided for her, so as to deprive it of everything that might afford pleasure to the taste. This is a self-mortification which she always practised whenever she could do so without being seen.

This sojourn in the forests was not very agreeable to Katharine, although generally pleasant to the Indian women, because, freed from domestic cares, they pass their time in amusements and feasting. She longed without ceasing for the time when they are accustomed to return to the village. The church, the presence of Jesus Christ in the august Sacrament of the Altar, the Holy Sacrifice of the Mass, the frequent exhortations, and the other exercises of the mission, of which she was deprived while engaged in the chase—these were the only objects which interested her. She had no taste for anything else. She therefore formed the determination, that if she lived to return once more to the mission, she would never again leave it.[215]

Chauchetière tells us that a "great calumny" greeted her return:

The trial was never more severe than that which she had at the Sault at the return of the winter hunt. And for two reasons: first, because she believed herself safe from calumny in leaving the Iroquois; and secondly, because she was accused of a thing of which she was innocent, one which deeply grieved her. A married woman, a good Christian, but somewhat given to backbiting, formed a very unfavorable judgment of Katharine, based entirely on appearance. The facts were that her husband, returning one evening very tired from the hunt, in which he had chased an elk all day, entered the lodge at a late hour. Everyone being in bed, he threw himself on the first place that he found and fell asleep through exhaustion. The next morning the wife seeing him asleep on a mat at one side, and not knowing the facts, looked further to see who was near him. Perceiving Katharine, she judged ill of her and the husband. Her suspicions were confirmed by some words of her husband, namely, that he had a canoe at the river which needed mending by some of the women, and as the time to depart was approaching, he asked Katharine to mend it. Although these thoughts remained with her, she had enough wisdom not to speak of them before arriving at the village. She went to find the Father, to tell him of her suspicions and of the reason for her judgment. The priest, who was wary in so delicate a matter, one in which there was a semblance of probability, spoke to Katharine as much to question as to exhort her. Whatever Katharine might say then, she was not entirely believed. Her instructress spoke to her again to remedy the evil, if there was one, or to prevent it. Katharine had never suffered so much as on this occasion, and what hurt her most was that the Father seemed not to believe her, but accused her as if she had been guilty.[216]

Chauchetière's account suggests that Father Cholenec believed the accusation, a point which he (writing about himself in the third person) disputes in his own version:

It is God's way with His elect to put their virtue to the test by similar happenings, and to render it perfect in the fire of tribulation, allowing it to be blackened by slander and even by hideous calumnies. *As gold in the furnace* (Wis. 3:6). In this case He even permitted that the missionary should not take Katharine's part in the beginning. If on one hand this chaste girl's horror of impurity, and if her innocence of life, which he did not ignore, made him judge that perhaps she was not guilty, on the other hand, the report of a woman whom he knew to be one of the best and most virtuous of the mission, persuaded him that the one of whom she spoke might not be quite innocent. In order to enlighten himself in this delicate matter, he decided to have Katharine herself come to him. He had such a good opinion of her, and was so sure of her sincerity, that he decided not to make the matter known, but to listen to what she had to say, and to take her word for it. He spoke to her, therefore, disclosing what was said of her and asked her what was the truth of the matter. Katharine contented herself by merely denying the fact, without showing any emotion about it, because she knew herself to be absolutely innocent. This great tranquility of soul in a matter which would naturally be so sensitive to her, justified her perfectly in the mind of the missionary, who had already decided in her favor. This was not the case, however, with the Indian woman, her accuser, and with a few others who somehow knew of the affair. God allowed it to be thus in order to augment the crown and the merit of His faithful Servant, because after she had left her relatives, her country, and all the advantages she might have found in a good marriage, after having sacrificed all this to Our Lord, it only remained for her to sacrifice her honor and reputation, which she generously gave up for Him on this occasion. She was glad to see herself held in contempt, and to pass as a great sinner, and for this reason, far from hastening to discover who had spoken ill of her, she allowed the matter to die away as though it had concerned someone else, and all the vengeance she took was to pray to God for them.[217]

Káteri had already been through this before in the Mohawk Valley. As noted in an earlier chapter, her aunt had accused her of having an incestuous relationship with her uncle, an accusation that was not given much credence by the priest, Father James de Lamberville. This latest incident served only to confirm in Káteri the conviction that she should never return to the winter hunt, no matter how much she should suffer by remaining in the village. It also emboldened her resistance to marriage, something that was practically unheard of even in the village of Kahnawà:ke. Fortunately for Káteri, she would soon meet someone who would help her stand firm in her convictions: a woman of the *Standing Stone*.

Wari Teres Tekaienkwé nhtha, Káteri's new friend.

22

Wari Teres
Tekaien'kwénhtha

The "Praying Indians" typically returned from the hunt in time for Holy Week. Father Cholenec tells us, "It was the first time Katharine celebrated it with us for the great good of her soul."

> She assisted at all the services of Holy Week, and admired all these solemn ceremonies, receiving from them a new esteem for religion. She was so touched by sweetness and consolation that she shed many tears, especially on Good Friday during the sermon on the Passion of Our Lord. Her heart melted at the thought of the suffering of the Divine Savior; she thanked Him a thousand times for it, she adored and kissed His cross with feelings of the most tender gratefulness and the most ardent love. She attached herself to the cross that day with Him, taking the resolution to repeat on her virginal body the mortifications of Jesus Christ for the rest of her days, as if she had done nothing until then. On Easter Sunday she received Holy Communion for the second time, and did so with the same disposition and ardor and spiritual fruits she had on the feast of Christmas. To complete these benefits and spiritual graces, she received a second grace from the missionary on that day, which he accorded very rarely, and which proved the esteem he had for her virtue.[218]

That second grace was admission to the Holy Family, a devotion that was meant to maintain and increase the fervor of the Church. Monseigneur de Laval, the first Bishop of Quebec, had established the Holy Family for the French, but it soon made its way to Laprairie de la Madeleine and then to the Sault.

> It was decided, however, only to admit a few of the more fervent people of both sexes, so as to give a higher idea of it

and to oblige the members who were honored by such a great grace to respond by the holiness of their lives. In this they did not fail, because the Indians, once they have given themselves to God, are capable of the greatest and the most whole-hearted devotion. The small number of chosen souls upheld its new character by an exemplary piety, some were even so austere that the rest of the village looked upon them with a sort of veneration, and to call a person a saint or a member of the Holy Family was to say one and the same thing, so that they kept this name afterwards as a special sign in the mission. Katharine, who was still very young, and had only been at the Sault for approximately seven or eight months, was admitted to this small number, to which others were received only at an advanced age and after several years of probation.

But, as we have already pointed out, her virtue placed her above the rule for the ordinary people of the village, and they, moreover, far from being jealous, generally approved of her election. The members of the Holy Family especially showed their joy, looking upon Katharine as capable of sustaining of herself alone this saintly society by her good example. She was the only one who considered that she herself was unworthy, such humble ideas did she have of herself; but the more she thought of her unworthiness, the more she thought it a duty to work for her perfection, so as not to lower the fervor of the Confraternity, to which she gave a new renown by her own.[219]

Cholenec tells us that Káteri began to look upon her previous short-comings as "so many crimes and outrages against the Divine Majesty; and on account of them she chastised her body which was so innocent, looking upon it as guilty."

These shortcomings were one of the principal reasons for the austere life she led at the Sault and of that great thirst she had for mortification and suffering. Her instructress, on her part, contributed to this by speaking to her often of the pains of hell, of the terrible penances the saints imposed on themselves so as to avoid them, and which the Iroquois Christians had all the more reason to perform, because they had so often offended Our Lord amid the disorders of their country. She was still more spurred on to this by an accident that befell her at this time and which almost took her from our midst when we were just beginning to know her. One day, as she was cutting down a tree in the forest, it fell sooner than she expected. Her quickness saved her from being struck by the trunk, but one of the branches caught her as she fled, and hit her head with such force that it knocked her senseless. All thought at first she was dead, but she revived a little later, softly whispering: "O Jesus, I thank Thee for having rescued me from danger." The only conclusion she drew from it was that God had preserved her so that she might do penance for her sins.[220]

Káteri, always eager to imitate the teachings of the Jesuits, was about to embark on a life of penance and mortification, but this was something Kanáhstatsi could only encourage in her—she was far too old to do much more than that. As Cholenec says, "She needed a companion more of her own age, one who had the same resolution of giving herself entirely to God, and who was capable of leading the same kind of austere life that she herself had embraced."

Káteri did have a younger friend, as Cholenec stated in his original manuscript: "The first companion of Kateri was Jeanne Gouastraha, an Oneida. Jeanne Gouastraha had recently settled at the Sault with her husband, who was a Mohawk and her two children, who were a boy and a girl."[221]

For whatever reason, the editor of the *Positio* chose to leave this detail out of Cholenec's account, but Father Henri Béchard, S. J., documented the troubled life of Jeanne in his book, *The Original Caughnawaga Indians* (1976). Circumstances prevented this woman from staying at Kahnawà:ke for very long: Jeanne's husband had a weakness for alcohol and eventually left the mission of the Sault, never to return. Jeanne and her two small children moved to Lorette to live with her husband's family. They did not return to the Sault until four years after the death of Káteri.[222]

A new companion was soon to enter the life of Káteri, a widow who was perfectly suited for the rigors of mortification. She was an Oneida woman about thirty years old. Her name is given by the Jesuits as Mary Teresa *Tegaiaguenta*, but we would probably spell it today as *Wari Teres*

Tekaien'kwénhtha—"She Makes the Tobacco Fall." Wari Teres was a woman with a past, and what a past it was. She was baptized by Father Bruyas but had "degenerated" since then, and "the only thing Christian about her was her name," according to Cholenec. While living at Lapairie with her husband, who was not yet a Christian, she accompanied him on an ill-fated winter hunt:

> She [Mary Teresa] had departed at the beginning of the autumn with her husband and a young child, a son of her sister, to go hunting along the Ottawa River. On the road they were met by some other Iroquois with whom they joined, making in all eleven people, four men, four women, and three children. Ill luck ordained that snow fell very late that year, so that they were unable to hunt, and after they had eaten their provisions and the meat from an elk, which her husband had killed, they were soon reduced to hunger. First they ate some small skins which they had brought with them to make shoes, and later ate even their own shoes, and were finally reduced to herbs and the bark of trees, even as animals.
>
> In the meanwhile, her [Mary Teresa's] husband took sick and then two men of the group, a Mohawk and a Seneca, Tsonnontouan, went hunting, intending to return, at the very latest, in ten days. The Mohawk, indeed, returned within the appointed time, but alone, assuring them that his comrade had died of hunger; but it was not without reason that they suspected him of having killed his friend and subsisted on the flesh while he was away. They doubted him even more because he was in such good health, and because he admitted that he had killed no game. Because they had no longer hope of securing anything from these hunters, and since the man was no longer of any use, they wished to persuade the Christian woman to let her husband die, in order to save herself, her nephew and all the others. She would not consent to it and generously and steadily resisted it.
>
> They, therefore, abandoned her, together with her husband and nephew. Two days later the sick man died, regretting that he had not yet been baptized. After she had buried him, she sought the road again, carrying her nephew on her shoulders,

and in a few days rejoined the band who were seeking the road down the river to the French village. But they were so weak and exhausted after their twenty days of wandering, that at last they took the following resolution. In their last extremity, seeing their end before them, they decided to kill one of the number that the rest might live. They cast their eyes on the widow of the Seneca and his two children, and asked our Christian woman whether it were permissible to kill them, and what the Christian law was on this point, because she was the only one of the band who had been baptized. Not being sufficiently enlightened, she had not courage to answer such an important question, fearing lest she should contribute to a homicide; but she feared also, and not without reason, that her own life depended on the answer, believing that they would kill her after … they had eaten the woman and her two children.

Her [Mary Teresa's] eyes were opened by the danger to her body, and she began to realize the deplorable state of her soul, which was more to be pitied than that of her body. She felt great horror for the sins of her past life, and her great fault in coming to the hunt without going to confession, and she asked God's forgiveness from the bottom of her heart, promising Him that if He delivered her from this danger, and brought her safely to the village, not only would she confess herself immediately, but would reform her life and do penance. God, who wished to use this woman to make Katharine known, heard her prayer, and after much trial and suffering, there arrived at Laprairie, in mid-winter, five of the twelve [sic] who had gone to the chase. Among them were this woman [Mary Teresa] and her little nephew. She kept part of the promise she had made, taking care to go to confession on her return, but she put off her reform and the promised penance for some time.[223]

Having survived such a harrowing ordeal, it is understandable that Wari Teres might have reached a kind of spiritual impasse. She had made a bargain with God for her survival, but did she feel worthy of that salvation once it had been given? Fortunately, fate was about to bring someone into her life that would free her from that morass. It was a young Mohawk woman who had her own winter hunt horror story, albeit one far less traumatic than that of Wari Teres. Here is how Cholenec describes their meeting:

> The first chapel of the Sault was then under construction. One day Katharine walked around this building merely to see how the work progressed, as did the Christian of whom we speak [Mary Teresa]. But God had planned this unexpected meeting for His glory and the good of these two souls. They greeted and spoke to each other for the first time. Katharine asked where the women would sit in the new church; and the other, in reply, showed her where she thought their place would be. Katharine replied that a chapel of wood was not what God asked most of us, but that He longed rather for our souls, that He might dwell therein and make His temple in them, and that she did not deserve to enter this material chapel, for she had so often driven God from her heart, and merited rather to be put out with the dogs.
>
> These sentiments of profound humility, uttered with tears and with words of grace, touched the other all the more because she did not expect them, and, indeed, were for her words of life, grace, and salvation. Moved by remorse, she soon resolved to carry out the principal part of the promise she had made while on the hunt. She was of a fiery temperament and went to extremes in good or evil; was possessed of great energy, and was also in the prime of her life, that is to say, about twenty-eight or thirty years of age. She gradually became enlightened while listening to Katharine, believing that what she said came from God, and that He had sent this holy girl, of whom so much good was spoken, to help her change her life, as she had promised.
>
> Then she told Katharine her ideas, and they found that both their hearts and their plans were in perfect accord. They became friends during this first interview, and one word leading on to another, they then communicated their most secret thoughts to each other. In order to talk more easily, they seated themselves at the foot of a cross near the bank of the river. They told each other of their past lives, and resolved to unite themselves in

order to do penance. As I was their spiritual director, they spoke to me of this union and asked for my approval, which I gladly gave, seeing that it would be good for both.[224]

Cholenec tells us that the two became inseparable at that point and assisted each other in their devotions. Although Káteri still visited Kanáhstatsi from time to time, she now had a companion who could assist her in her penances: "Several times during the week they went deep into the woods and there chastised their shoulders with rods, as Katharine had been doing by herself for a long time."[225]

The penances would eventually increase in severity, not only for Káteri and Wari Teres, but for the other "Praying Indians" at Kahnawà:ke. Even the priests, who did these things themselves, found the degree to which the Indians did them quite astonishing. That will all be told in due time, once the shock of Wari Teres' hunting trip has worn off!

Akohtsi'a, Káteri's older sister.

23

"I WILL NOT MARRY."

When spring turned to summer, Káteri faced another trial, this time in the form of her sister, who saw wedding bells in her future. She had even picked out a capable young hunter as a potential husband. Quite aware of how vigorously Káteri rejected marriage in the Mohawk Valley, she drew upon her considerable skills as a natural Mohawk orator to convince her younger sister of the reasonableness of her plan:

"It must be admitted, Katharine, my dear sister, that you have a great obligation to Our Lord for having brought both you and us from our miserable country, and for leading you to the Sault where you can work for your salvation in peace of mind, without anything to trouble your devotion. If you are happy to be here, I am not less happy to see you here with us. Increase this happiness by your wise conduct, which will draw on you the esteem and approbation of the whole village. There is just one thing which you can do which will make me entirely pleased with you, and which will make you yourself perfectly happy—that is to think seriously of establishing yourself by a good, sound marriage.

"This is the course followed by all the girls here. You are of a marriageable age, and you need it, even as the others, to withdraw you from the occasions of sin and to supply you with the necessities of life. It is not because it is not a pleasure for your brother-in-law and myself to provide for you, as we have done heretofore, but you know that he is getting old and we have a large family, so that if anything should happen to us and we could not help you, where would you look for aid? Believe me, my dear sister, you should place yourself as soon as possible beyond the possibility of the pains of poverty for the good of both your soul and body, and think seriously of how to avoid them while you are able to do so easily, and with such advantage for yourself and for your whole family who desire it."[226]

Cholenec tells us that Káteri had not anticipated this, but held back her surprise and hurt. Thanking her sister for her good advice, she told her that she needed to think about such an important matter before giving a final answer.

> Our courageous virgin, far from being offended, eluded the first attempt by this clever and unsuspected trick, and immediately sought me to complain a little of her sister, and to tell me of the whole affair. "Katharine," I then said to her, "you are the judge in this matter. It depends on you alone; but think well, for it is a concern of great moment." She replied immediately, and without hesitation, "Ah! my Father, I will not marry. I do not like men and have the greatest aversion to marriage. The thing is impossible." In order to sound and test her more, I dwelt on the strong reasons which her sister had presented to her. She assured me with great firmness that the thought of poverty did not frighten her, that her work would always furnish her with what she needed to eat, and that a few rags would be enough to cover her. Then I sent her back assured that she was doing right.[227]

Once again, the editor of the *Positio* chose to tweak the translation a bit. In Cholenec's original, Káteri did not say, "I do not like men ..." ("Je n'aime pas des hommes ..."). She said, "I hate the men ..." ("Je hais les hommes ..."). Hating men is hardly a Christian virtue, and not something a saint would likely say, but perhaps I'm being far too literal. Chauchetière ignores this incident in his version, but he wasn't there. In 1715, Cholenec wrote another biography of Káteri in which her words on this occasion were as follows:

> "Ah, my father, I am not any longer my own. I have given myself entirely to Jesus Christ, and it is not possible to change masters. The poverty with which I am threatened gives me no uneasiness. So little is needed to supply the necessities of this wretched life, that my labor can furnish it, and I can always find some miserable rags to cover me."[228]

The editor of the *Positio* would make at least one more questionable change to a manuscript, which we will encounter in a later chapter. For now we will continue with the narrative of Father Cholenec and the 17th century *Days of Our Lives*:

> Katharine did not tell me everything in this interview. In her own mind she had already decided her course.... After considering all things well, Katharine and her companion agreed never to marry, the one to dedicate to God her virginity, and the other her perpetual widowhood. They kept this decision a secret, and resolved not to speak of it unless absolutely necessary.
>
> Katharine, however, found she could not help herself on this occasion, because of her sister's pressing insistence. She hesitated to let her know that the affair was already concluded; but it seemed to the other that she had had time enough to make up her mind, so that she asked for her decision with great eagerness. Therefore, this chaste girl, wishing to silence her sister, and to stop her annoying solicitations, told her that she had renounced marriage, and asked to be allowed to live as she was. As for the rest, she said that she had enough clothes for a long time, that she would work in order to feed herself and would not be a burden to her sister, or anyone in the village.
>
> Deeply moved by an answer like this [Katharine's sister] replied: "My sister, how did you form such a strange resolution? Have you thought seriously of what you are doing? Have you ever seen or heard tell of such a thing among the Iroquois girls? Where did you get this strange idea? Can you not see that you expose yourself to the derision of men and the temptations of the devil? Can you expect to accomplish what no girl among us has ever done? Forget these thoughts, my dear sister; do not trust your own strength, but follow the custom of the other girls."
>
> To all this Katharine replied without emotion that she did not fear the jeers of men as long as she did nothing wrong, and that she hoped that God would give her the necessary strength to overcome all the temptations of the devil with which she was threatened, and, since her resolution was already taken, she again begged her not to speak of it any more.[229]

Káteri's sister went to Kanáhstatsi to inform her of Káteri's decision to renounce marriage, and persuaded her to talk her out of it. Kanáhstatsi then spoke to Káteri and urged her to reconsider this unusual decision:

> Because she urged her so insistently, Katharine replied in a voice that rang more than usually firm, that if she thought highly enough of marriage, she would enter that state, but that she wished to hear nothing more of the subject, and that no man would mean anything to her. They separated, and both came immediately to me, Anastasia to complain of Katharine, and Katharine of Anastasia. The younger reached me first, and told me of the suffering caused her by her mother and sister, who urged her to marry, and that she found it impossible to obey them. In order to relieve her of her suffering and to settle the matter, I told her to take three more days to consider the subject, to pray earnestly during that time and recommend her trouble to Our Lord; that I would unite with her in prayer, and that she should adhere closely to whatever God inspired her after the three days; and reminded her that she was her own mistress, and that in an affair of this sort, the decision would always rest with her alone.
>
> Katharine agreed with this plan, but the Holy Ghost influenced her so strongly that she took only a few minutes to deliberate on the choice which she had made a long time before. I was surprised to see her returning, a moment after she had left, to tell me, in an embarrassed manner, that she could not live any longer in a state of indecision. She declared plainly that she had renounced marriage in order to have only Jesus Christ for her Spouse, and that she would consider herself happy to live in poverty and misery for His love. I admit here that, in good faith, I wished to say nothing to Katharine to determine her in this affair, since among the Indians there were so many things opposed to it. I preferred to let God influence His creature directly, not doubting that all would be successfully concluded, if her inspiration came from Him. It was plain to me from her last words that God spoke through the mouth of Katharine, and that He Himself had inspired a decision so heroic. I finally took her part and praised her resolution, and

encouraged her to persevere with the same fervor with which she had begun, assuring her that I would defend her against the others, and that neither I nor the other missionaries would ever abandon her or let her be in want of anything.

I can give assurance that by these few words I drew Katharine's soul from a strange purgatory, putting her in a sort of paradise, because at that moment she truly entered into the joy of the Lord, and she began to feel, in the depths of her soul, a peace, a rest, and a contentment so great that her exterior became quite changed. It is remarkable that this peace never left her until her death, and that from that time forward nothing was able to disturb it—an evident sign that the spirit of God animated her. She thanked me warmly, and if she left me the most contented person in the world, I, for my part, was filled with admiration for so heroic a design, full of veneration for her who had the courage to undertake it, and full of extraordinary joy, seeing that Divine Goodness had prepared in this [the first] Iroquois virgin such a beautiful model of sanctity for the mission, and such a powerful advocate in heaven.[230]

One can easily imagine this drama being acted out on a stage, with Father having one visitor after another in rapid succession:

She had no sooner left me than Anastasia came to make her complaint, saying that Katharine did not wish to marry, even though she was of a marriageable age. I answered her coldly that I was astonished that she wished to torment Katharine about a matter which deserved so much praise, and that she, who had been a Christian for such a long time, had not opened her eyes to the beauty and merit of such a saintly resolution; and that, far from objecting, if she had any faith, she should esteem Katharine all the more, and feel happy and honored herself because God had chosen a young girl from her cabin to raise the banner of virginity among the Indians, and to teach them this sublime virtue which makes men like angels. A more sudden change could not be imagined, and Anastasia seemed to awake as from a profound sleep, blaming herself for her conduct. She took the correct view of Katharine's attitude, and, as she herself was very holy, admired, praised and encouraged her, and looked upon her as already a saint. After this she was always ready to support her in the life she had chosen as the better part. She did more, for she inspired the same sentiments in Katharine's sister, and both regarded her with greater respect and a kind of veneration. They left her in peace, and at entire liberty to do as she pleased in the future. It was thus that Our Lord turned this persecution to the glory and good of His Servant, in order to make known that He was the sole author of this resolution which seemed so strange, and which was new and unprecedented among the Indian girls.[231]

If not marriage to a flesh-and-blood man, what did God have in mind for the young woman? She had rejected an earthly union for a spiritual one with Jesus, but what exactly did this entail? What did it mean to marry the King of Kings and share in his crown of thorns?

24

THE GREAT PENANCES

As a neophyte student of Iroquois history will tell you, stories of ritual torture and cannibalism abound in the *Jesuit Relations* and other 17th century writings. Father Jerome Lalemont once wrote,

> I would make this paper blush, and my listeners would shudder, if I related the horrible treatment inflicted by the Agnieronnons upon some of their captives. This has indeed been mentioned in the other relations; but what we have recently learned is so strange that all that has been said on the subject is nothing. I pass over these matters, not only because my pen has no ink black enough to describe them, but much more from a fear of inspiring horror by recounting certain cruelties never heard of in past ages.[232]

I was once asked during a radio interview to comment on all of these Jesuit horror stories that have dogged us for centuries. "One barbecue goes wrong," I told the interviewer, "and we never hear the end of it."

Many of our people dismiss these accounts as pure propaganda, in spite of archaeological evidence that our ancestors went out for ribs every now and then, but there are others who point to the traditional narratives of the confederation epic that feature a cannibal who is persuaded to change his ways by the reflection of the Peacemaker in the pot of water he was using to boil human flesh. Then there is the Alqonquian word "Mohawk" (and its many variations) that supposedly means "Man Eater." As my brother always says, "All you really have to do is eat one enemy and let the others go. People will leave you alone after that." (As you can imagine, conversations around our table are always this irreverent. Remind us to have you for dinner some time!) These 17th century accounts put forward the notion that our ancestors would take captive warriors and torture them using incredibly barbaric methods. Even women and children took part in this merriment, the women being particularly sadistic and cruel. The point of it all was to test the strength of the captive. If he cried out in pain, he was weak. If he took the torture without flinching and even taunted his torturers to do their worst, he was respected for his courage and strength, and promptly eaten so that everyone would absorb his powerful life force.

The implication is that this bizarre belief system paved the way for Catholicism and the sacrament of Communion. To drink the blood and eat the body of Christ was right up our dark and twisted alley, apparently.

The Jesuit biographers of Káteri Tekahkwí:tha tell us that the *Onkwehón:we Tehatiiahsóntha'*—"Original People Who Make the Sign of the Cross"—felt tremendous shame for their former way of life in the Iroquois villages. "The horror which the new Christians of the Sault had for the life they had led among the Iroquois before their Baptism so aroused them against sin that they did not spare themselves in the practice of great penances," wrote Father Chauchetière.[233]

Father Cholenec expands upon these "great penances" in his own account:

> The Iroquois had become strongly attached to the Church, and these ardent and brave neophytes had conceived such sorrow and shame for the sins of their past lives that even though these had been effaced by Baptism, they still performed great penances for them. Several times a week some of them chastised their bodies until they bled; others, while gathering firewood, wore iron bands around their bodies for entire days. Joseph Togoniron, the famous captain of the Sault, renowned in this country for his bravery under the name of the Great Anie [Mohawk], wore one every Friday and on all the great feasts. Paul Honoguenhag, an appointed ancient, and the first Christian of the Sault, did as much penance; and another, called Etienne, was of such austere virtue that it gave one devotion merely to see him pray. Such were the men. The women, who always go to extremes, did all this and more. Some rolled in the snow, as I saw one young woman do three nights in succession, during the severest weather that I have seen in Canada. Another, in similar cold, which was accompanied by such a heavy snowstorm that it was impossible to see or to keep one's footing, stripped to the waist, held herself erect on the bank of the river, and recited her entire rosary while in this strange posture.

It must be noted that in the Indian language the *Angelic Salutation* is twice as long as in our own. Others went further than this. In mid-winter, having broken the ice with their hatchets, they plunged themselves up to their necks in pools and rivers. Often they had the courage to recite several decades of the beads while enduring this frightful torment. They came out with a shirt of ice around their bodies. One of them did this in the woods on three successive nights, with this result, that, returning to the cabin and not daring to dry herself near the fire for fear of disclosing her penance to the others, as her humility equaled her fervor, she passed the rest of the night on her mat still wearing her coat of ice. On the third night she developed such a violent fever that she thought she was going to die. Anne, the wife of the good Christian Etienne, who equaled her husband in virtue, was not satisfied with plunging herself into the icy river, but she also plunged in her little daughter, Marie, aged three, and pulled her out half dead. When I blamed her later for this action, I asked her what motive had led her to do it. She answered simply and in good faith, that she feared that when the child grew older she would become slack and fall into sin, so she had forced her to do penance in advance.[234]

Cholenec goes on to say that Káteri Tekahkwí:tha suspected that there was something "over and above" these practices that remained hidden from her:

Finally she reached such a high degree of virtue that she discovered part of it and guessed the rest, so that to satisfy her I was obliged to give her a discipline and a little girdle of iron which she used from that time forth to quench her extreme thirst for suffering. If I had left her to herself in this matter, she would soon have surpassed the others, but her strength was not nearly equal to her courage. It was necessary to moderate the latter in order not to exhaust the former, because in spite of all the precautions I took, she managed to evade me at times, as happened that same winter on the Feast of the Purification.

In order in some measure to imitate the holy ceremonies of the Church in the procession customary to that day, and so as

Detail of Káteri statue at St. Patrick's Cathedral in New York City. Photo by Charles Tibble.
Copyright 2008. All rights reserved.

to give Our Lady some proof of the love she bore her, Katharine walked around her field, which was fairly long, and recited her rosary several times, buried up to her waist in the snow.[235]

Chauchetière mentions this "girdle of iron" given to her by Cholenec:

> Her companion says that once while Katharine was carrying a large burden of wood, she wore at the same time a girdle of iron with long spikes, fastened around her, and that she slid on the ice and fell down a hill while coming from her field to the village, and that this fall had pushed the spikes of her girdle well into her flesh. But she only laughed and would not give her burden to her companion, but picked it up and went to her cabin and hid her injury so well that no one suspected it.[236]

It was Kanáhstatsi who first taught Káteri about penance when she first arrived at the Sault.[237] Chauchetière tells us that she put them into practice while on the disastrous winter hunt:

> A savage married to one of Katharine's cousins, observed Katharine one day going to fetch the meat of an animal some one had killed at a distance from the cabin. When they passed by an icy marsh, although it was the middle of winter, Katharine let her companions pass and walked for a long time barefoot on the sharp ice of the pond. This was noticed because they thought that she might be ill and waited for her, but her companions saw that she was barefoot. Katharine, however, without being seen, stopped and put on her shoes, and tried to dissuade them from thinking that she had done anything to mortify herself. They told me also a thing she could not hide from her companion: that, when she went to pray to God near a little brook which she had made her place of prayer, it was her custom to chastise herself harshly with rods. This is all the more credible because of the manner in which she chastised herself in the village. She was not able to pray for long, because she endured such cold there without a fire. She did this especially on feast days, and supplemented it with the devotions she was accustomed to perform at the village.[238]

As we have noted in a previous chapter, Káteri met Wari Teres Tekaien'kwénhtha that following spring, and the two of them became inseparable friends. Wari Teres confided in Káteri that she had also practiced penances:

> She told her how once, when walking in the woods, being oppressed with sorrow at the thought of her sins, she had taken a handful of birch rods and struck herself on the hands. Another time, having climbed up high in a birch tree to obtain some birch bark for some object she was making, she was seized with fear on looking down and seeing many stones. Indeed with reason she thought that if she fell she would fracture her skull. But then a good thought came to her, confirming all the resolutions which she had taken to serve God, for reflecting on her fear, she upbraided herself for having feared death and not the flames of hell. Tears came to her eyes. When she had descended and sat at the foot of the tree, throwing the bark to one side, she gave herself to the salutary thoughts which then possessed her.[239]

This was all Káteri needed to hear.

> Katharine left the cabin, and going into the cemetery which was nearby, gathered a handful of rods. Returning to the cabin she hid them cleverly under the mat on which she was sitting. When the first notes of the bell were heard, Katharine urged everyone who was in the cabin to go to the church, and when the two were alone she closed the door. Katharine first threw herself on her knees and begged her companion not to spare her. The other, on the contrary, wished to be the first, fearing that they would not have enough time. Katharine finally persuaded her companion to do as she asked. After this they said a prayer together, and when their zeal was satisfied, they went to the Sault filled with joy, even though their shoulders were covered with blood. They never found the prayers so short as that day and never were they happier. They did not rest until they had found a suitable place to continue this harsh devotion, and so chose a wooden cabin belonging to a

Frenchman who traded with the Indians, but who lived at Laprairie. This Frenchman left his cabin open, so that this place seemed suitable to them, especially as it was in the middle of the cemetery.[240]

He goes on to describe the way they prepared for confession on Saturdays. They made an Act of Faith in church, then retreated to their place of solitude:

> Then Katharine, who always wished to be the first in suffering, knelt down and received the chastisement. But she always complained that it was not painful enough, and begged her companion to strike harder, even though as I know, the third stroke drew blood. When they stopped, they said the rosary of the Holy Family, and divided it at intervals in each of which they gave themselves five strokes more. Towards the end of their devotions they ceased to count the strokes. It was then that Katharine disclosed the sentiments of her heart in these words: "My Jesus, I must suffer for Thee; I love Thee, but I have offended Thee. It is to satisfy Thy justice that I am here. Vent on me, O God, Thy anger." Sometimes she was unable to speak further, but finished with her eyes bathed in tears, and finally she would say, "I am very affected by the three nails which fastened Our Lord to the cross; they are but a symbol of my sins." When Katharine was thus affected, not less did she affect her companion, who made of Katharine the same supplications that Katherine had made of her.[241]

Finally, we are told of the "sins" that Káteri was so troubled by:

> Most admirable is what this faithful companion of Katharine has affirmed; that in a moment of fervor the holy child told her her sins. She never had anything worse on her conscience than the laxness in which she had lived before her Baptism. This consisted in not having resisted those who had brought her to work on feasts and Sundays; that she had not suffered martyrdom; and that she had often feared death more than sin.[242]

The mortifications recounted here were not only meant to exculpate the sins of Káteri Tekahkwí:tha. Cholenec tells us that she had "tender compassion" for the suffering of Christ:

> She went even further, and wished to share in His pains. Together with all the Saints she carried her cross after Him, and the Divine Master, who guided her, having inspired her with a holy hatred of herself, so much recommended by Jesus Christ and so necessary to salvation, she treated her body with such harshness at the Sault, that it would be difficult anywhere else to find such innocence joined with such austere penance. She tortured her body in all the ways she could invent, by toil, by loss of sleep, by fasting, by cold, by fire, by irons, by pointed girdles, and by harsh disciplines with which she tore her shoulders open several times a week.[243]

These "austere penances" would soon take their toll on the fragile health of the young woman. She was not long for this world, but there was still time for her to reach another level of spiritual development. She was about to consecrate herself not only to Jesus Christ as his spouse, but to the Virgin Mary as her daughter.

25

BRIDE OF CHRIST

As we have already seen, Káteri had to endure the entreaties of her sister and Kanáhstatsi to marry not long after she met Wari Teres. Having dispensed with that pressure, she was now free to become one of the many young women who had devoted themselves entirely to the faith. Father Chauchetière described these women—and the incredible challenges they faced—in his account of the mission for the year 1678:

> We have even seen maidens observing virginity,—at least, they were neither married nor tainted with the vice of the flesh; One even died without having desired to marry, and it was held that she had never done wrong, and had died in that state without baptism. However this may be, there is at least among the iroquois nothing comparable to the brutalities of the flesh which prevail among the outawaks and other savages. This monster, however, upheld by excess in drinks, has ruined everything in the country of the iroquois in these recent years, and has endeavored to ruin everything in this mission through separations of husbands and wives, and through the infirmity—of nature—which is greater in the savage youth than in any other class of men. This monster did not succeed, and has been combated and vanquished by many. We have known of girls bravely refusing clothes, money, and other things of value, which were offered them if they would consent to do wrong. Some have been seen dragged into warehouses, where they were put to a choice, but resisting and threatening to cry out if the men did not desist. Some are known who have during whole years resisted indecent pursuits. Some have been seen striking blows upon the nose, and covering with shame and blood the faces of the incarnate demons who came to tempt them. Some have been known to disfigure themselves by cutting off their hair, which is the principal ornament of the savage girls; and they have been known to carry back to the missionary the presents which had been offered them with evil designs. It is amid such conflicts

that those who had sinned before their baptism have purified their souls, and that those who have been born in the village have sucked modesty with their Christian mothers' milk. There are already several who have carried their virginity to heaven, who were but thirteen, fourteen, fifteen, or twenty years old. Several are still living who, having often refused good offers in marriage, pass the marriageable age, and give to God their bodies and their souls in great poverty, and clothe themselves by alms. This spirit has this year united all those persons, who number thirteen; they have for their object the highest state of perfection. They assemble, and one makes a brief exhortation; or else they tell their faults to one another. They act like the daughters of mercy in france, and have for their office works of charity to their neighbors; they especially take care of the poor and the sick, to whom they carry wood in secret and at evening, and immediately vanish for fear of being perceived. They go to watch the sick, and give them as alms other things which they need. To attain their end, they use mortification and are averse to carnal pleasures, which they treat as the bait of the demon;

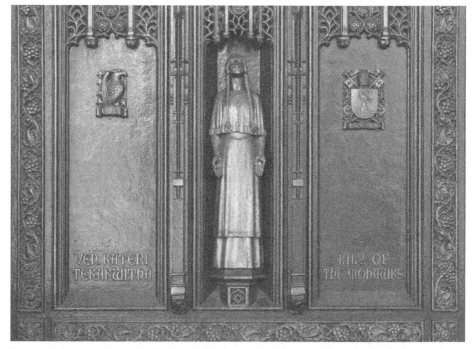

Káteri statue at St. Patrick's Cathedral in New York City. Photo by Charles Tibble.
Copyright 2008. All rights reserved.

and they say, in their excess, that the fathers who wish to make them give up the cingulum [penitential girdle] and discipline are full of mercy, but that they know not how much these women were laden with sins before they had been taught to live aright. Accordingly, they are always seen occupied in carrying wood, or making collars; in planting, spinning, sewing, and making pouches; and in other labors.[244]

Despite the existence of a multitude of women of similar fervor, Káteri and Wari Teres remained somewhat aloof, preferring instead to seek only one other member for their sorority. We turn to Chauchetière's biography to learn who this woman was, because Father Cholenec never mentions her:

Marie Therese Tegaiaguenta thought that it would be better if there were a third, or if they had some other Christian girl with them from whom they could learn all they wished to know. She added that she knew one named Marie Skarichions, who had lived for a long time at Quebec and at the Mission of Our Lady of Lorette, conducted on the same plan as the Mission of the Sault. When Katharine agreed with her companion's suggestion, the three assembled at the foot of the cross, which was planted on the riverside. There the elder companion spoke first, expressed her desire to join them, and proposed that they adopt the rule of life of the Religious she had seen while she was an invalid at Quebec. This meant that they should never separate, that they should dress alike, and if possible, live in the same cabin. Accordingly they chose as their home an island called Heron Island. All this was made part of their deliberations, because they had but little concept of the basic foundations of religious life. Katharine thanked the speaker with tears of joy in her eyes, and begged her to keep nothing from them which would make them more pleasing to God.[245]

Marie Skarichions's name would probably be rendered today as *Wari Skaríhsions*, or "She Undoes Things."[246] Chauchetière goes on to tell us that the women's sense of obedience obliged them to submit their resolution to the priest in charge of the mission:

When they arrived at their decision, one of them went at once to Father Frémin and told him that they had formed an association, yet wished to do nothing unadvised. The priest made light of all these beautiful plans. He told them they were as yet too young in the faith for such a singular project; that Heron Island was so far removed from the village that all the young people who were passing to or from Montreal would be always at their cabin. They themselves saw that what the priest said was reasonable, and forthwith abandoned their idea of a monastery on Heron Island.[247]

Instead, they contented themselves by increasing their austerities to an unbelievable degree, as we learn from Cholenec's account:

Once she asked Anastasia, her instructress, what she considered the severest penance one could do in order to offer the most pleasing sacrifice to Our Lord and to prove one's love for Him. "My child," replied the other, "I know of nothing on earth more terrible than fire." "Neither do I," answered Katharine. She said no more about it then, but in the evening, when everyone had gone to bed, she spent a long time burning her legs with a brand in the same manner that slaves are burned among the Iroquois, wishing in this way to declare herself the slave of her Savior, to whom she then presented herself at the door of the church in the darkness of the night bearing her beautiful marks of the cross. Another time both she and her companion decided that when they were alone they would place a burning coal between the toes, a spot supposed to be the most sensitive to the pain of fire. Katharine later admitted to her companion that she had done it, and remained for a long time in this position. The other was astounded, since, healthy as she was, she had fainted at the thought of suffering the pain of the coal for half a *Hail Mary* alone, and she did not think that Katharine could have done what she did without some sort of miracle.[248]

At this point in the *Positio*, the editor takes an artistic liberty and adds something that does not appear in the original French version of

Cholenec's biography: "The marvel was still greater, however, when the following morning there was no mark of the burn on her foot."[249]

Chauchetière's version ends this way: "The next day she saw Katharine in her cabin and admired her constancy, because she had a large hole in her foot, a thing which she could not have done without feeling great pain."[250]

As summer gave way to fall, Chauchetière informs us that there was yet another crisis to test the faith of the Kahnawa'kehró:non:

> Smallpox went the round of our village at the beginning of autumn. There was, nevertheless, some astonishment, afterward, at the few burials which had taken place; and this blessing of God brought it about that the iroquois no longer said that the faith and baptism occasioned death, for among the iroquois they die by hundreds when smallpox attacks them.[251]

As fall gave way to winter, Father Cholenec tells us, "it was proposed that she should go to the woods for the winter, but she would not hear of it, protesting that she would never again do so."

> As we have already said, she had taken this resolution because of the pain she suffered the winter before in being far from the church and the Holy Sacraments, and in being deprived of all the spiritual aids that she had in the village. I wished to take her on the hunt to restore her health a little, where she would not lack the good nourishment she needed but could not have in the village, where, for staying, she would suffer through need of it, as the winter was long.
>
> Katharine only laughed at this, and a moment later she assumed that devout mien which she had when she came to tell me of her spiritual desires, and gave me this answer, worthy of Tegakoüita, "Ah! my Father, it is true that the body fares well in the woods, but the soul languishes there and dies of hunger, whereas in the village, the body suffers a little from not being so well nourished, but the soul, being close to Our Lord, finds entire satisfaction. Therefore, I abandon this miserable body to hunger and any other misery, that my soul may be content and have its usual nourishment." She therefore

remained in the village for the entire winter, and found what she so eagerly sought, that is, crosses for sustenance, and all the sweetness of heaven for her spirit. These she procured for herself as was her custom. Our Lord, who has promised to sustain those who hunger and thirst after justice, gave her His grace with equal profusion.[252]

Staying home from the hunt was no little hardship, due to the scarcity of food in the village, but it was enough for Káteri to be close to her beloved church, where she would often spend the entire day, "even during the coldest weather in Canada."

> Often, seeing her whole body frozen, I was impelled to make her leave the church and enjoy the warmth of the fire with us; but a moment later she would escape me, saying with a smile that she was not cold, to return to the place where she had left her heart. What have the French to say regarding this, who pass our churches a hundred times a day, without the thought ever occurring to them to enter even once to greet Our Lord on His altar, and who are so bored in church because the Mass they are obliged to hear appears a little long to them?[253]

Káteri had accustomed herself to the scarcity of food by fasting on Wednesdays and Saturdays, and when she did eat, she would often mix her food with ashes to dull the taste.[254] Káteri was not very large to begin with, being no more than four and a half feet tall. (This was determined recently by measuring the length of her femur.)[255] It would have been easy for her to hide any degradation in her physical appearance from those around her.

> One saw Katharine always with her head covered, even in the middle of the summer, while the other Indian women had no other headdress than their hair and were very scantily clothed. When her mother and instructress, to whom I have frequently referred, asked her the reason for a singularity likely to make her ill, and why she did not take the innocent comforts of which the others availed themselves, she replied that she would seem vain- glorious if they saw her with her head lifted and uncovered or

even without a veil. She thus made a virtue of what she probably was forced to do in order to protect her eyes from the glare
of the sun. Thus this soul so attached to God, profited by the
least things, and that which in another might be only an indif-
ferent act, was sanctified by her. So retiring was she that people
began to know her as "the maiden at the Sault who lived like a
Religious." Some Frenchmen of Laprairie had special knowledge
of this, and when they saw her they could not believe their own
eyes, because of her modesty and reserve.[256]

Not that anyone would ever notice, hidden as she was beneath her
blanket, but she changed her mode of dressing as well:

Being a young savage of twenty-two or twenty-three years of
age, she naturally liked to be well dressed. This consisted in
having the hair well greased, parted, and braided in a long
plait which hung down the back; it meant heavy necklaces of
glass beads, pretty cloaks, dresses, moccasins, and pack saddles.
In a word, they were very vain. Katharine thought she could
give up all these things without seeming peculiar, as the rest
would only think that she was not seeking a husband. She
renounced all the red clothing and ornaments of the savages
and only wore a new and simple blue dress on the days when
she received Holy Communion. Though she brought with her
simple clothing a perfect heart which God alone could see, she
could not so conceal her devotion that her companion did not
notice it in moments of their greatest fervor together.[257]

It is mentioned in Cholenec's 1715 biography that Káteri visited
Montréal, something that Chauchetière says was forbidden by Father
Frémin.[258] Father Henri Béchard, accepting it as fact in *Kaia'tanó:ron
Kateri Tekahkwitha* (1994), expanded on the visit with suggestions of
places she may have visited, such as the chapel of Notre-Dame-de-Bon-
Secours and the Hôtel Dieu.[259] Cholenec reminds us that Káteri was
always looking for ways that were pleasing to God:

It was for this reason that while passing some days at Montreal,
where for the first time she saw the nuns, she was so charmed

with their modesty and devotion, that she informed herself most thoroughly with regard to the manner in which these holy sisters lived, and the virtues which they practised. On learning that they were Christian virgins consecrated to God by a vow of perpetual chastity, she gave me no peace until I had granted her permission to make the same sacrifice of herself, not by a simple resolution to guard her virginity, such as she had already made, but by an irrevocable pledge which would oblige her to belong to God beyond recall. I would not, however, give my consent to this step until I had well proved her, and been convinced anew that it was the spirit of God acting in this excellent girl, which had thus inspired her with a design of which there had never been an example among the Indians.[260]

He then goes on to describe her consecration, which took place on March 25, 1679, a day he calls "the happiest and most beautiful of her life ..."[261]

For this great event she chose the day on which we celebrate the festival of the Annunciation of the Most Holy Virgin. The next moment after she had received Our Lord in Holy Communion, she pronounced with admirable fervor the vow she had made of perpetual virginity. She then addressed the Holy Virgin, for whom she had a most tender devotion, praying her to present to her Son the oblation of herself which she had just made; after which she passed some hours at the foot of the altar in holy meditation and in perfect union with God. From that time Katharine seemed to be entirely divorced from this world, and she aspired continually to heaven, where she had fixed all her desires. She seemed even to taste in anticipation the sweetness of that heavenly state; but her body was not sufficiently strong to sustain the weight of her austerities, and the constant effort of her spirit to maintain itself in the presence of God. She was at length seized with a violent illness, from which she never entirely recovered. There always remained an affection of the stomach, accompanied by frequent vomiting, and a slow fever, which undermined her constitution by degrees, and threw her into a weakness which insensibly wasted her away. It was, however, evident that her soul acquired new strength in proportion as her body decayed. The nearer she approached the end of her days, the more clearly she shone forth in all those virtues which she had practised with so much edification.[262]

Cholenec's earlier biography foreshadowed what was to come:

I may say that after she made these two great sacrifices of her soul and body, her soul lived only for Jesus in the Holy Eucharist, and her body lived only so as to die with Him on the Cross, in the midst of sorrow and suffering. I say die on the cross since she truly died on it, having shortened her days by an act worthy of eternal commemoration, although it is rather to be admired than imitated, and with the narration of which I wish to end this matter.[263]

Looking back on this moment from our vantage point three centuries into the future, when Mohawks are more likely to reject a Roman Catholic upbringing in favor of a return to the traditional way of life, it may difficult for us to understand Káteri's whole-hearted acceptance of the teachings of the Jesuit missionaries, even to the point of rejecting an earthly marriage, motherhood, and everything else we associate with the concept. Some might even go so far as to suggest that she had been completely brainwashed into accepting a path in life that, had everyone else taken it, would have ultimately led to our extinction. Perhaps that is what the missionaries intended all along, that their evangelizing was simply a way of burning a field of weeds so that some other plant could grow in its place—that the priests were sent in to do with patient instruction what the Carignan-Salières Regiment could not do with fire. I have no rejoinder for such a harsh opinion, since the Jesuits' own words paint this picture for us, but I do not go so far as to dismiss the very real spiritual experience of Káteri Tekahkwí:tha. Was her understanding of God colored by the racial politics that we associate with missionary work today, or was it something truly universal, a concept so transcendent that embracing it became not only the most desirable thing to do, but the only thing she could do? By dismissing her very real union with the most powerful force in the universe, do we not dismiss our own potential for the same kind of experience?

Detail of Kâteri statue at St. Patrick's Cathedral in New York City. Photo by Charles Tibble.
Copyright 2008. All rights reserved.

26

A Bed of Thorns

Father Chauchetière tells us that although modesty prevented Káteri and Wari Teres from revealing their vows of celibacy and the details of their penances, word had somehow gotten out:

> Two married persons called on Katharine shortly after she had embraced the state of perpetual virginity, a year before she died, with the purpose of learning from her the kind of life a good Christian should lead in this world. Since these two neophytes knew well that Katharine's humility would prevent her from speaking, they sent also for her companion to come to their cabin at the same time they invited Katharine. This man was called Francis Tsonnatouan, and his wife, Margaret. When Katharine and her companion had entered, they closed the door of their cabin to show that what they were asking was a great secret, one that must be kept.
>
> Francis Tsonnatouan (which means *Big Log*), opened the conversation by addressing himself to both Katharine and Therese, saying first that he knew what they were doing and the life they were leading. This he said to lead them to talk, and then told them for his own part he too wanted to be a good Christian, to give himself entirely to God. He spoke at the same time for his wife. Katharine was very surprised at this discourse. After some moments of silence she told her companion to speak.
>
> It would take too long to report everything said on both sides about the things most agreeable to God. I know only that they gave no advice to these two young married people: the wife was only twenty-two years old and the husband scarcely older. They counselled them to go to the priest and propose their good intention to him.[264]

There were also several young women in the village who were drawn to the Káteri and Wari Teres. Chauchetière referred to them as "Kateri's band." Among them were an Onondaga that Father Henri Béchard dubbed "Marie the Penitent," and Marguerite *Gagoüiton*, whose name would probably be rendered today as *Kahkwì:ton*, and translated into English as "It has been Moved." Kahkwì:ton was a young Mohawk woman married to a "senior war captain." She and Marie imitated the severe penances of Káteri and lost a lot of weight because of it.[265]

Although it was not included in the *Positio*, there is a document in the Archives of the Séminaire de Québec written by Father Cholenec in February of 1680, wherein he mentions some of the more notable converts at his mission, one of which is undoubtedly Káteri Tekahkwí:tha:

> There are also here two other women, who live in the same manner, with the same fervor of spirit and the same penances as the two previous ones, and who, as the latter, consecrated themselves entirely to Our Lord and gave him with much courage all they could give him with in this world. So as not to be too long and not to repeat what we have already said, Your Reverence will apply to these last two what I have said of the first two. But the former are in this more admirable and more to be esteemed since they are living in innocence and do for the same love of God what the two others do to satisfy their sins. Of these two young women, who are Mohawks (for the two others of whom I spoke are Onondagas), there is one especially who is small and lame, who is the most fervent, I believe, of all the village, and who, though she is quite infirm and nearly always ill, does surprising things in these matters. And she would beat herself unmercifully, if she were allowed to do so. Something quite important happened to her lately, which Father and I could not marvel enough at.
>
> While scourging herself as usual with admirable ardor (for she exceeds in this particular all the other women, with one exception of Margaret) and that in a very dark spot, she found herself surrounded by a great light, as if it were high noon, lasting as long as the first shower of blows, so to speak, of her scourging, for she scourged herself several times. Insofar as I can judge from what she told me, this light lasted two or three misereres.
>
> We have no cause to believe that there be any illusion in all

this, since this person is quite foreign to guile and very humble. We have, on the contrary, every reason to believe, after having well examined the antecedent, accompanying and consecutive circumstances, that is a grace Our Lord wished to grant to his faithful servant, who is entirely his and who served him with an innocence and a fervor capable of ravishing the angels.[266]

It is a mystery why Cholenec never mentions this "great light" that surrounded Káteri in any of the biographies he later wrote about the young woman. Even more mysterious is why this document was left out of the *Positio* submitted to the Vatican many years later.

For her part, Káteri was still dreaming up new methods to mortify herself, all of which she kept to herself until it was far too late.

About two or three months before her death, this generous girl, desiring to attach herself even more to the cross of her Savior and to testify, by some heroic act, the eagerness she had to participate in His sufferings, in spite of her continual infirmities, and as if she had done nothing until then, decided, in imitation of the Venerable Aloysius Gonzaga, of whom I had spoken to her by chance, to gather a large bundle of big, pointed thorns, which she brought home with her and hid in the lodge. At night, when everyone was asleep, she strewed these thorns upon her mat and then lay down on it, having only her blanket over her body. She had the strength not only to roll herself all night long upon the thorns, but to do this for the three following nights also, the pain being unimaginable, as she afterwards confessed to me. It left her so worn out and emaciated that her face resembled that of a dead person.

Not knowing the real cause of this, we attributed the change in her to her ordinary infirmities, which appeared to us to increase visibly every day. Her companion, however, suspected some secret cause of this change, and was so shrewd that Katharine confessed the truth to her, adding that she thought to continue doing this until her death. "Yes," answered her companion, "but do you know that you offend God by undertaking this sort of excess without the permission of your confessor?" This was enough for Katharine. The shadow of the sin was capable of making her disclose this rare act, which, without this apprehension, she would have kept secret her whole life. She sought me immediately and approached me with these words: "Oh! Father, I have sinned." Then she told me the whole affair, and although in my heart I admired her, I pretended to be displeased and reprimanded her for her imprudence, and in order to prevent her from renewing it, I commanded her to throw these thorns into the fire, which she did with great submission.[267]

Chauchetière adds the following:

Some say that this caused her death; others say that her death was due to the fact that her companion, having been sent with some other Indian girls over the ice to Laprairie to fetch something, Katharine accompanied her, and that she caught cold. This, it was said, was the beginning of her illness.[268]

This same priest, elsewhere in his text, reflected upon her many trials: "It is thus that God conducted Katherine by a very thorny road. The actual thorns of which she made use of for penance, were only a symbol of the interior thorns that were meant to try her soul."[269]

Cholenec provides us with the details of her final illness:

We have observed several times that she had always been infirm, and that besides this, about a year before her death a great illness left her with a slow fever and a severe pain in her stomach, accompanied by frequent vomitings, caused no doubt by continual work, night-watches, fasting, and excessive austerities. These, however, she continued without ceasing until death; as a final proof of which I would recall the agonizing bed of thorns by which this generous girl lessened her remaining health. The fever made all this worse, finally obliging her to keep to her bed, and at the end of two months it took her from us.[270]

She spent these final days "in the exercise of all those excellent virtues which she had practiced so much during her lifetime ..."

The priest who was then in charge of the sick and who visited her every day, could not admire her enough. He always found her with a smiling face, which clearly showed the peace of her soul and the pleasure she found in her pains. One must not be astonished at this, for this holy girl, having suffered on the cross with her Savior and Spouse, was happy to follow His example by dying on it.

Moreover, as all the men were at the hunt, and the women who remained in the village were occupied from morning until night in the woods or in the fields, they left their sick alone all day with a plate of sagamite and a little water within their reach. In this abandoned state Katharine passed all the time of her last illness, but what was ordinarily a cause of pain and annoyance for the other sick, was for her an occasion of new merit and even new consolation. As she knew how to profit by all things, and had for a long time accustomed herself to hold intercourse with God, she made use of this solitude to attach herself more to Him and to become more inflamed with His love.[271]

Chauchetière tells us of the visits of the priests to her deathbed:

She never wished him to leave her cabin. Sometimes he brought to her cabin the little children of whom he had charge in order to divert her, as well as to comfort and teach her. In order to enter more fully into the instructions, Katharine tried to raise herself, feeble as she was, to see the pictures of the Old and New Testament which the priest then explained. The thanks which Katharine gave him and the entreaties she made to induce him to return soon were marks of the hunger and thirst she had after justice. She was so ill at that time that a few days later she died, but she had in mind only her salvation, of which she thought night and day.[272]

Even in her weakened state, Káteri asked to do one more penance when Holy Week began, but the priests would not allow her to fast as she wished.

God accepted her good intention and instead of granting what she asked, she was told that she must think of something else and that she did not have long to live. Who could express the joy that this news gave her, and especially when she was told that the Body of Our Lord would be brought to her![273]

Normally, the sick would be brought to the church for the Viaticum, but an exception was made for Káteri, and the Blessed Sacrament was brought to her on Tuesday evening, April 16, 1680.

> Katharine gathered all her strength to make well this last Holy Communion. She begged her companion not to leave her in this last moment and told her of her poverty, which was so great that she had nothing to cover her decently. Her companion lent her a gown. This extraordinary ceremony of seeing the Blessed Sacrament carried to a sick person attracted the attention of the whole village.[274]

Most of the people had not yet returned from the winter hunt, but those that were home flocked to her lodge to see the dying saint. While she had always been too modest to exhort others, Káteri felt a renewed fervor and began to speak openly to those around her, urging them on in matters of faith.[275]

Cholenec reveals that even in her final hours, he marveled at her purity, but was nevertheless compelled to question her on it:

> I say, and shall always say, that it is a miracle of grace which cannot be understood, how Katharine passed more than twenty years in the midst of the corruption of her country and two years and a half at the Sault, virgin in body and soul, without ever, during all that time, having felt the least thing contrary to this virtue, either in body or soul. This, I say, appears unbelievable, but is nevertheless true. She had already told me so of her own accord, but wishing to assure ourselves still more concerning so marvelous a thing, I questioned her on it the evening before her death, after having given her the Viaticum, and although she had difficulty in speaking, she made an effort and answered me in a firm tone of voice, "No, no," with a gesture that showed the pain she felt in still being questioned at her death concerning a sin that she had held in horror all her life.[276]

Something else happened that night that concerned young Marguerite Kahkwì:ton. This incident was mentioned by Cholenec as being an indication that something truly remarkable was taking place at the mission:

> It is a laudable custom here for two persons of the Holy Family [Confraternity] to take turns in watching during the night whenever the sick are in danger of death. There was question as to who should do this for Katharine, and on Tuesday night, which was the last of her life, I named two of the most fervent members, the younger of whom was also the youngest of the Holy Family [Confraternity], for she was only in her twenty-second year. She sought me after evening prayers to ask my permission to go to the woods to do some penance in order to obtain a happy death for her with whom she was going to watch, for she loved, and was loved by Katharine, being one of those, as we shall mention later, who had associated themselves with her for some time.
>
> This charity was surprising in an Indian maiden, for she passed a full quarter of an hour in performing penance until she bled, on behalf of her friend; but it is still more surprising that the very instant Katharine learned about it, dying on her mat though she was, and having with her only the other person who was to watch with her that night, she turned on her side, begging her to seek the girl and make her come immediately. The woman obeyed, and found the other on the way from the woods to her lodge, where she was going in order to tighten the instrument of her mortification. "Katharine wants you," she told her, "so I came to seek you."
>
> Both entered Katharine's lodge, and Katharine whispered to the younger to let the other watcher rest first, because she wished to speak to her [the younger] in private. The other watcher had in fact already fallen asleep, and Katharine bade the young Indian, who had displayed such charity for her, approach. She encouraged and exhorted her to persevere in the service of God, assuring her that she was very pleasing to Our Lord, and promised her that she would pray for her when in heaven. When this [younger] woman, who had no less humility than fervor, replied that Katharine did not know her well, and that she was a miserable sinner, Katharine took her

by the arm, and, pressing it, said: "I know what I am saying, my sister; I also know where you come from and what you have done. Go, take courage; be assured that you are pleasing in the sight of God, and that I shall help you when I am with Him." This the woman came to tell me the following day, with new veneration for Katharine and new courage to follow her example, as she is still doing at the Sault.[277]

It is Cholenec who tells us how Káteri spent this last night: "She passed the remainder of that day and the following night in sweet and fervent communion with Our Lord, Our Lady, and her crucifix."[278]

Exterior of St. Patrick's Cathedral in New York City, location of Káteri statue. Photo by Charles Tibble. Copyright 2008. All rights reserved.

27

"I WILL LOVE YOU
IN HEAVEN ..."

We now come to the chapter which I have dreaded writing since I began this project—the death of the Lily of the Mohawks. To my great relief, I have the words of those who were there to fill these pages. All I really have to do is arrange the pertinent passages in a chronological order, since the original sources tend to jump back and forth through time according to the thematic way they are written. Still, I cannot help but feel like I a relative who is asked to deliver a eulogy, so close has the subject of this book become to me during the years of research.

We begin with the words of Father Pierre Cholenec, who wrote a letter on May 1, 1680, about two weeks after her death, that mentions the saintly girl:

> ...To say in passing a few words about the Mission. Things there are going very well. And it seems to me, through the grace of God, that never has there appeared such fervor and holiness as during this last feast of Easter, when it seemed that the village was quite changed. What particularly occasioned this, was the death of our [Katharine], about whom I have already spoken to Your Reverence in the last relation. This fortunate maiden and spouse of Jesus Christ left us, on Wednesday of Holy Week, to go celebrate in heaven with Him the triumph of the cross, which she had so greatly loved, and to which she had attached not only her heart or her affections, but also her chaste and virginal body by this life of mortification about which I spoke to Your Reverence. She died as she lived, that is to say as a saint. Such she was regarded here by all the village before and after her death. They assisted at her funeral with great sentiments of veneration, of esteem, of joy and piety, by which, I have already said the village seemed changed and quite steeped in devotion and fervor. Among other marvels, about which we shall speak in their place, as soon as she died, her features suddenly changed

and appeared so joyful and devout that everybody was left extremely astonished and quite ravished in admiration. So much so that we could not tire of looking at them, because this sight, far from causing the least fright, as it happens with regard to the dead, inspired joy and devotion.[279]

Cholenec wrote a more detailed biographical document in 1682, which we find in the *Positio:*

On Wednesday at three o'clock in the afternoon the bell was rung to gather together the savages, who desired passionately to witness the death of this great Servant of God. As if she had only waited this signal she went immediately into her last agony, which was very gentle and which lasted a half hour. She spent the last moments of her life in fervent acts of love, of faith, of hope, and the like, having on each side of her two missionary Fathers and around her all the savages praying. She lost consciousness a little while before she died, and without a struggle this blessed soul left her virginal body to go to her beloved Spouse. She left the whole settlement edified by the examples of virtue which she had given, and in universal regret for the loss it suffered. Her death was accompanied by some circumstances which made me believe that it was similar to that of the saints.

The first circumstance is the change that occurred in her body after her soul had left it. Her face was badly disfigured during her life on account of her continual illnesses, but it changed suddenly a quarter of an hour after her death and it appeared instantly so beautiful and so smiling that the savages who came running to see this wonder were quite carried away by it, as well as the French, who having come into her cabin without knowing she was dead, thought at first she was resting quietly, so great was the sweetness and beauty in her face. But they were much surprised to learn that she was dead and they threw themselves immediately at her feet, not so much to pray to God for her as to recommend themselves to her prayers.[280]

Father Claude Chauchetière, another eyewitness to these events, provides this account:

Wednesday morning Katharine began to sink and her companion thinking she was about to yield up her spirit, remained in attendance on her without being able to leave her. But Katharine assured her she could go to work in the field, and promised to send for her when it was time. It happened as Katharine had promised: she sent for her companion about ten o'clock in the morning. Marie Therese Tegaiaguenta reached the cabin a short while before Extreme Unction was administered. After she had received all the Sacraments, she conversed with her companion. Meanwhile she was constantly sinking. Finally having difficulty in speaking and not being able to raise her voice, and seeing her comrade bathed in tears, she bade her a last farewell.

"I am leaving you," said Katharine. "I am about to die. Always remember what we have done together since we knew each other; if you change I will accuse you before the tribunal of God. Take courage, despise the discourse of those who have no faith, when they wish to persuade you to marry; listen only to the priests. If you cannot serve God here go to the Lorette Mission. Never give up mortification. I will love you in heaven, I will pray for you, I will assist you."

The priest who was kneeling near to say the last prayers for the dying, heard a little of what Katharine said. He kept his eyes fixed on her face to observe what was happening and even encouraged both. Katharine's face was turned toward heaven. Her companion embraced her with one hand, supporting her chin with the other, and listening with attention to the last words of the dying Katharine.

This blessed daughter in saying to her companion, "I will love you in heaven," lost her voice, when phlegm began to choke her. For a long time her eyes had been closed to created things; now she could not speak, but to the very last breath she could hear well. It was remarked that several times when some act was suggested to her, she took new strength, but when she was exhorted to love of God the expression of her face seemed to change. Everyone wished to share in the devotion which her dying countenance inspired. It appeared more like the face of one in contemplation than the face of one dying. Thus she remained until her last breath. Her respiration diminished constantly from about nine o'clock till ten and finally became barely perceptible, though her expression remained unchanged. One of the priests, kneeling at her right side, noticed only a slight contraction of the nerve at the side of her mouth, and so she died as if she were falling asleep. For some time no one was sure she was dead.

When all were assured of her death they delivered her eulogy in the cabin to encourage everyone to imitate her. What her Father confessor said, added to what they had seen, caused everyone to regard her body as a precious relic. The simplicity of the savages made them do on this occasion more than was required, such as kissing her hands, keeping as relics whatever belonged to her, passing the evening and the rest of the night near her, regarding her countenance, which changed gradually in less than a quarter of an hour. It aroused devotion, for when her soul was separated from her body, it appeared more beautiful than it had been when living. This gave joy to all and fortified each one in the faith he had embraced. It was new evidence of the truth with which God favored the savages to make them delight in their faith.[281]

Cholenec was profoundly impressed that Káteri seemed to have "some knowledge concerning the day and even hour of her death, such as could only have come from Heaven." This we find in his 1696 biography:

After giving her the Holy Viaticum on Tuesday morning, we hastened to give her Extreme Unction. She told us that there was no hurry and that the time had not yet come for it. At her word we deferred the administration of the Sacrament until Wednesday morning. We had reason to believe that she would die before noon on that day, but she knew that this was not so. Her beloved companion and some other women of the Holy Family [Confraternity], who for approximately a year had formed a small devotional society with Katharine, which is still called by the name *Katharine's Sisters*, greatly desired to be present when she died. But as they were obliged to seek wood for the following feast days, they were doubtful and did not know whether to go or to remain. They thought the best solution was to ask Katharine herself, not doubting that she had enough power with Heaven to have her death deferred in their behalf. I spoke to her for them, and she answered that they might go to the woods, and would return in time for her death.

At her word they went, nor did she fail them. Until three o'clock in the afternoon she remained in the same condition. After their return, she waited until they had entered the lodge, and I saw this marvel with my own eyes. The last one had no sooner arrived than she entered into her agony while they all knelt around her. Thus they had the consolation of witnessing her death, as they desired and she had promised them.[282]

Cholenec goes on to describe "a marvel of which I was likewise an eye-witness, together with the aforesaid Father and our Indians."

Due to the smallpox, Katharine's face had been disfigured since the age of four, and her infirmities and mortifications had contributed to disfigure her even more, but this face, so marked and swarthy, suddenly changed about a quarter of an hour after her death, and became in a moment so beautiful and so white that I observed it immediately (for I was praying beside her) and cried out, so great was my astonishment. I had them call the Father who was working at the repository for Holy Thursday. He came, as did the Indians, on hearing of this wonder, which we were able to contemplate until her burial. I admit openly that the first thought that came to me was that Katharine at that moment might have entered into heaven, reflecting in her chaste body a small ray of the glory of which her soul had taken possession.[283]

This is how Cholenec described her death in his 1715 biography:

On Wednesday morning she received Extreme Unction with the same feelings of devotion, and at three hours after midday, after having pronounced the holy names of Jesus and Mary, a slight spasm came on, with which she entirely lost the power of speech. As she preserved a perfect consciousness even to her last breath, I perceived that she was striving to perform inwardly all the acts which I suggested to her. After a short half hour of agony, she peacefully expired, as if she were only falling into a sweet sleep.

Thus died Katharine Tegahkouita in the twenty-fourth year of her age, having filled the mission with the odor of her sanctity and the character of holiness which she left behind her. Her countenance, which had been extremely attenuated by her sickness and constant austerities, appeared so changed and pleasant some moments after her death, that the Indians who were present were not able to restrain the expression of their astonishment, and declared that a beam of that glory she had gone to possess was being reflected back on her body.[284]

This change in the appearance of Káteri's appearance shortly after her death, along with the "odor of sanctity"—literally, the smell of flowers or some other sweet scent—stands out in the literature. It would not be long before other chroniclers would begin to embellish this aspect of the story, as happened when Father Pierre-François-Xavier de Charlevoix included a brief account of her life in *Histoire et description générale de la Nouvelle France* (1744):

Her countenance, extremely attenuated by austerity and by her last illness, suddenly changed as soon as she ceased to live. It was assuming a rosy tint that she had never had; nor were her features the same. Nothing could be more beautiful, but with that beauty which love of virtue inspires.[285]

In modern times, it is common for biographers of Káteri Tekahkwí:tha to go even further. Here is what Father Francis Xavier Weiser, S. J., said in *Kateri Tekakwitha* (1972):

The ravages of sickness, the lines of bitter suffering disappeared. Her countenance became fresh, radiant, and incredibly beautiful. Even the pockmarks that had disfigured her from childhood on, could no longer be seen. The face changed color until it showed the attractive hue of a healthy Indian child. The touch of a smile, gentle and charming, as no one had observed on her before, played around her lips.[286]

Margaret R. Bunson, author of *Kateri Tekakwitha: Mystic of the Wilderness* (1992), described her appearance as follows: "Her skin lightened, becoming radiant and white, and the scars vanished from her face, showing the beautiful bone lines and the lovely angles of her heritage."[287]

Lillian M. Fisher goes even further in *Kateri Tekakwitha: The Lily of the Mohawks* (1996): "After a little while, her face became instantly beautiful. The scars from small pox she had worn all her life suddenly disappeared and her skin became flawless."[288]

Cholenec and Chauchetière never actually said that she had smallpox pockmarks to begin with, only that she was disfigured, marked, and swarthy, so it is not surprising that they did not say that her pockmarks were suddenly healed. Perhaps this is another technicality not worth fussing over, but it is interesting to note how "legendary" the life of a saint can become with time.

We resume our narrative with Chauchetière's account of her eulogy:

> When all were assured of her death they delivered her eulogy in the cabin to encourage everyone to imitate her. What her Father confessor said, added to what they had seen, caused everyone to regard her body as a precious relic. The simplicity of the savages made them do on this occasion more than was required, such as kissing her hands, keeping as relics whatever belonged to her, passing the evening and the rest of the night near her, regarding her countenance, which changed gradually in less than a quarter of an hour. It aroused devotion, for when her soul was separated from her body, it appeared more beautiful than it had been when living. This gave joy to all and fortified each one in the faith he had embraced. It was new evidence of the truth with which God favored the savages to make them delight in their faith.[289]

It was Cholenec who delivered this eulogy, as he states in his 1696 biography of Káteri: "I eulogized her at evening prayers and made known to the Indians the treasure they had possessed and lost before they came to know her."[290] Elsewhere in this document, he relates another interesting anecdote which took place the following morning:

> Two French settlers of Prairie de la Madeleine came to the Sault on Thursday morning to assist at the service. They passed

Katharine's lodge, and seeing her laid out upon her mat with such a beautiful and shining countenance, said to one another: "There is a young woman who sleeps peacefully." Learning a moment later that it was Katharine, they retraced their steps to the lodge and knelt at her feet to recommend themselves to her prayers. Having satisfied their devotion, they wished to show the veneration they had for her by making at once a coffin for the interment of such a precious body.[291]

Chauchetière adds to this:

It was not the custom of the savages to make great preparations for a funeral. They greased the hair and the face of their dead and gave them new sandals. Sometimes they only covered them. At the Sault they made Katharine a decent bier. A Frenchman who was in the village wished to make her a coffin through devotion to her. They placed the body in it as usual, but could not cover her face, such was the pleasure they took in looking upon it. Each one read therein what was said of her: that hers was a face of chastity and virginity. They had never learned from their catechisms as much as they learned here. For this reason her face was left uncovered until they placed her in the grave.

Her obsequies were an occasion of both sorrow and rejoicing. The Indians mourned losing her so soon, but they rejoiced to have her as the guardian angel of the Sault.[292]

Cholenec gives this brief description of her funeral:

Her virginal body was buried the following day at three o'clock in the afternoon, not with sorrow, but with the public joy which was inspired in the entire village by her holy life; a joy increased by having in Katharine a powerful advocate near God, and in her precious remains, which they have always venerated, the support, the bulwark, and the guiding spirit of the mission.[293]

The selection of her burial site would also bring with it something of a mystery, which was not apparent to the missionaries at the time:

It is also recounted that some time before her last illness, she was digging a grave in the cemetery together with some other women, in order to bury one of her small nephews. The conversation having turned to this final resting ground wherein each should have a place, they laughingly asked Katharine where hers was. "There it is," she said, pointing to a certain spot. After her death Father Chauchetière did all he could to persuade me to have her buried in the church, but to avoid such an unusual thing, I had a grave made in the cemetery in the exact place she had designated, though I did not know of her prediction until several years later.[294]

With the Lily of the Mohawks laid to rest, her people resumed their observance of Holy Week. Cholenec tells that her death had inspired those in mourning to emulate her sanctity, which became touchingly evident the following day:

There was no delay in seeing the effect, for the next day, on Good Friday, all hearts were so touched at the sight of the cross which Katharine had so loved and which the priest showed them after his sermon on the Passion, that I think that never was seen so piteous a spectacle, or rather, one so devout and touching, for suddenly everyone began to burst forth with such loud cries and sobs that it was necessary to let them weep for quite a long time. The Father then wishing to intone the *Vexilla*, could only pronounce the two first words, because at once the cries and the sobs began again, stronger than before, throughout the church, so that he was obliged to yield a second time to the violence of their grief. The fruit of all this was that they no longer talked of anything but of being converted and of giving themselves entirely to God. That same day and the next and for eight days running, such excessive penances were performed in the settlement that it would be difficult for greater to be done by the most austere penitents in the world.[295]

The shrine that commemorates the first burial site of Káteri in modern-day Ville Sainte-Catherine, Quebec. Photo by the author.

Granite cenotaph donated by Reverend Clarence Walworth of Albany in 1900. The legend reads, Onkweonweke Katsiio Teiotsitsianekaron, which means "The Fairest Flower that ever Bloomed among True Men."

Father Claude Chauchetière was compelled to paint this image of Káteri after having a vision of her not long after her death. Photo by the author, courtesy the St. François Xavier Church in Kahnawà:ke.

28

APPARITIONS AND MIRACLES

In his 2005 book, *Mohawk Saint: Catherine Tekakwitha and the Jesuits*, author Allan Greer wrote that Father Claude Chauchetière was "transformed completely" by his encounter with Káteri: "Something in the dying woman's serenity began to affect the distracted and self-absorbed Jesuit, lifting him up from the depths of gloomy doubt."[296]

Greer took the time to probe the psyche of one of her priests, something that no writer ever bothered to do to any great extent, but it's hard to get excited about how Chauchetière was able to sort through his identity crisis. What concerns me is how he and his fellow priests apparently felt no sense of personal responsibility for the death of a young woman in the prime of her life, a woman who spent the last weeks of her life wasting away in a dismal solitude, convinced by their teachings that this was indeed "what is most agreeable to God." There is no mention in any of the biographies that medical attention was ever sought for her, even though such medical assistance, as primitive as it may have been, was certainly available in nearby Laprairie or Montréal. We read in their own words that a bowl of sagamite and some water was left for her to eat and drink while everyone else went about their daily chores, yet she desired to fast even in the last days of her final illness, convinced as she was that she still needed to practice some form of penance to prepare for Holy Week. Earlier in the texts, we read that a priest gently admonished her for sleeping on thorns—something that undoubtedly hastened her death—but are then told that he secretly admired her for doing so. Before that, they admitted that they provided her and her fellow converts with a "girdle of iron" to wear. If such a thing were to occur in modern times, there would be criminal charges laid against them, and their church would be closed down and dismissed as a cult.

Instead of entertaining a moment of remorse, the priests grappled with the possibility that Káteri Tekahkwí:tha was a saint, something they never hoped to find (or cultivate) among the Indians of the North American wilderness. What troubled them was that there had been accusations made against her not only of adultery but incest, and even though she acquitted herself well against these baseless accusations, there was a twinge of doubt in their minds, and a nagging suspicion that maybe she wasn't as holy and pure as she seemed—that the "lily" was just another "thorn" after all. It would take something truly miraculous to shake those doubts and convince them that they had been in the presence of holiness.

This came in the form of apparitions and healings that began soon after the death of Káteri. These were faithfully documented by the priests, although they did not immediately proclaim them to the world at large. As Father Cholenec noted about the apparitions,

> I admit that I have had difficulty in deciding whether to speak of it, for there are only too many people in the world who set themselves up to believe nothing, especially in matters of this kind. They no sooner hear apparitions mentioned than they protest against them and pretend these revelations are so many illusions and hallucinations, because in truth there have been some that were found to have existed in the imagination rather than in reality. Such persons would prefer thus to believe concerning a poor Indian, as if the hand of God has been shortened, and He were not the Giver of all graces and could not give them to whomsoever He pleased.
>
> The apparitions I am referring to here are so important and clear in detail that I do not see how they could be reasonably called in question. Though the incredulous will always remain so, God will be no less glorified in His Servant, and virtuous people will find in these marvels new motives to love and bless Him, on seeing how liberal He is in rewarding the services rendered to Him, even by the poor Indians.[297]

Cholenec goes on to describe an apparition that was witnessed by Father Chauchetière. It is odd that Chauchetière did not include this incident in his own biography of Káteri, even though his introduction clearly states that the apparitions were to form a major part of the work. Perhaps some later archivist or clergyman who had possession of his manuscript was one of those disbelievers Cholenec mentioned, and took it upon himself to eliminate these pages.

The sixth day after Katharine's death, that is to say, the

Monday after Easter, a person of virtue and worthy of belief [Father Claude Chauchetière] was praying at four o'clock in the morning, when Katharine appeared to him surrounded by glory, with majestic bearing and shining face lifted toward heaven as if in ecstasy. This marvelous vision was accompanied by three circumstances that made it seem more remarkable. In the first place, the vision lasted for two whole hours, during which this person could contemplate her at leisure and did so with a joy and pleasure difficult to express, Katharine wishing by so marked a favor to acknowledge the great service she had received from him during her lifetime. Moreover this same apparition was accompanied by several prophecies, and by as many symbols which might be seen on both sides of Katharine in her ecstasy. Some of these prophecies have already been fulfilled, while others have not yet come to pass. For instance, on her right a church was seen turned over on its side, while on the left there was an Indian tied to a stake and badly burned. These events occurred in the month of April, 1680, and in 1683.[298]

Cholenec, in his 1696 biography, states that this vision appeared to Chauchetière six days after the death of Káteri. He then goes on to state that Kanáhstatsi had a vision two days later. However, he wrote in 1682 that she had this vision four days after her death, which would have been two days before the one described by Chauchetière—a minor discrepancy in an otherwise meticulous collection of personal accounts. It is from Cholenec's earlier account that we find the following:

"One night," says this woman, "after the public prayers, when everyone had gone to bed, I prayed privately for a little while; and then I also went to bed. But scarcely had I fallen asleep when I was awakened by a voice which called me, saying: 'My mother, rise up and look.' I recognized the voice of Katharine. Immediately I sat up and turning toward the side whence she was calling me, I saw her standing beside me, her body so surrounded by light that I beheld only her face, which was of an extraordinary beauty. 'My mother,' she added, 'Look well at this cross which I am carrying. Look, look, how beautiful it is. Oh, how I loved it on earth; oh, how I love it still in Paradise! How much I wish that all of our cabin should love it and rely upon it as I did!' That is what she said to me, and at that instant she disappeared, leaving me so full of joy, and of such sweet consolation that it has lasted until now. Moreover, the cross she held was so beautiful and gave forth such brilliant light that I have never seen anything so lovely and so charming."

This is what this woman told us; and she is, furthermore, very wise and of great good sense. We believe that Katharine wished by this loving visit to recompense all the care she had from this woman, on whom she looked as her mother.[299]

Káteri also appeared on two different occasions to her companion, Wari Teres. For whatever reason, the editor of the *Positio* chose to exclude the first of these from Cholenec's account, so we turn to his original to learn what occurred:

Around that time, Mary Theresa had reported an apparition. She said, "One morning, before dawn, somebody came to knock on the outside of my lodge near the place where I was lying. This person said, 'Are you asleep?' I replied, No! This voice said, 'Good-bye! I have come to say good-bye. I am going to Heaven.' I had recognized the voice of Katharine and went out at once to see her, but she was not there. I had heard the voice of Katharine far in front saying, 'Good-bye!' But I had seen nothing. Katharine said, 'Go and tell the Father that I am going to Heaven.'"

Another day, Mary Theresa had another apparition. She said, "I was angry with my sister and the following night when I was in the lodge, someone came and sat on the mat near me. I saw the person covered in a blanket as Katharine had done in her life and heard her say, 'You do not remember the good resolutions you made?'" The person reprimanded her for what she had done, gave her some advice for her conduct, and said many other things to her. Then, someone sleeping next to her awoke, and Katharine said no more and left. Mary Theresa heard her walk while leaving as if she were still alive. Immediately, Mary Theresa repented her error.[300]

Chauchetière would continue to see visions of the departed maiden, as Cholenec reveals in his 1696 biography:

> In the following year, 1681, on the first of September, and in 1682, on the twenty-first of April, this same person had a similar vision under the same circumstances, with this one difference, that in the first apparition he had seen Katharine as a rising sun, and had heard these words: *Adhuc vini [sic]in dies,* whereas in the two following he saw her as a sun in mid-heaven with these words: *Inspice et fac secundum exemplar* (Exod. 25: 20), God thus making it known that He wished pictures to be painted of Katharine. For a long time we had refrained from doing so, but when they were painted later on they contributed a great deal toward making Katharine known, for, being placed on the heads of the sick, they brought about marvelous cures.[301]

Cholenec provided more details of these visions in a 1715 letter, although there are discrepancies between the various years he claimed these visions occurred:

> The year following Katharine again appeared to the Father, resplendent in all her person. The Father felt an interior inspiration to show her painted image to the people. Finally, three years later he saw her again, like the midday sun, and so brilliant with surrounding light that his eyes could hardly bear it. Now he was bidden to paint her as he saw her. He made the painting as best he could. Other pictures were made also, and though these were badly done on paper, the Canadians value them so highly that there are hardly enough to supply the requests for them. People are very grateful for them and carefully keep them in their homes.[302]

Chauchetière, in the introduction to his biography of Káteri, explained that he had begun to document in writing what he had seen while at the mission, but then felt something more was required:

> I decided to take a second course that seemed to me an idea of Katharine herself, who, in a vision enlightened me to paint

pictures for the instruction of the savages, and to use them for exhorting those whom she wanted to draw after her to heaven, and at the same time to write journals which could serve for my own use. I therefore commenced this work with incredible difficulty, wishing at times to give it all up; but having abandoned it, I would get strange scruples which would not allow me to live in peace or find any rest; so that I had to obey Katharine's request. The first work which I undertook was a picture of the pains of hell designed by a German, one which had been sent to me by M. de Bellemont. This picture was very effective among the savages, and the missionaries themselves asked me to copy it. The fact that it was generally approved gave me courage to attempt a portrait of Katharine which was the one painting I wished to make, in order to accomplish what I had been so strongly inspired to do for my own consolation and that of others. I undertook it after her death, since there was no one but myself to do it. I painted some which many possess in the form of leaflets, but these were too small and not suitable to be seen at a distance, if exposed in a large place, and if they were placed in the lodges they would immediately become smoke-stained. I decided to work on that great picture that portrays the life and customs of Katharine and which at present is still in the church of the Sault for the instruction of the savages.[303]

It is widely believed that a painting hanging in the rectory of the Mission of St. François Xavier in Kahnawà:ke is the work of Chauchetière, and therefore is the painting mentioned in the texts. Elements of Káteri's attire, such as her 17th century trade shirt and moccasins, seem to support this, but the presence of what appears to be a stone church with two rows of windows on the banks of the river is incongruous to her time period, at least as far as Kahnawà:ke is concerned. This painting is similar to an engraving that appeared in *Histoire de l'Amérique septentrionale* (1722) by Bacqueville de La Potherie.[304] A similar engraving was published in the *Kateri* bulletin in 1951; it was apparently part of a treasured collection of pictures of saints in the Abbey of Ligugé in France.[305]

Cholenec mentions another individual who was blessed with an apparition, but it is unclear if he is referring to Kanáhstatsi, Wari Teres, or someone else entirely:

> The last year of her life, when she was obliged to keep almost entirely to her cabin on account of her infirmity, a certain person undertook to see her every day so as to converse with her of God, and explain to her our mysteries. In gratitude, she obtained for this person many graces after her death, even appearing to her several times. She prophesied things to her, and led her to the highest perfection with such grace and heavenly consolation that this person would be lost in contemplation for five and six hours at a time.[306]

Finally, we come to the miraculous healings attributed to her, which are far too many to recount here. The *Positio* includes many detailed accounts of the earliest ones, and the *Kateri* bulletin published in Kahnawà:ke has done an impressive job of documenting the more recent. We will allow Cholenec, writing in 1715, to summarize them as only he could:

> She began to be famous for miracles about six months after her death, and in a short time she scattered very many of them all over the Canadian scene. Earth taken from her grave was as prompt a remedy for whatever illness as it was common. The French from every part of the colony flocked hither to give thanks for favors from Katharine and to venerate her relics kept in our church. Her mere pictures, just the invocation of her name, only the promise of a pilgrimage to her relics, water drunk from her cup, her clothing, her utensils, the touching of anything she used, all are effectual for persons suffering from whatever disease you will. Furthermore, letters from France tell of her aid to many there who besought her.
>
> At length, I refrain from adding more. I would go on endlessly and many volumes would be necessary if I wished to put in writing everything that has come to us from all sides about our Katharine, and is still coming. I shall say but this: Among the miracles related as having been performed by Katharine, I consider the greatest of them all to be Katharine herself, truly the Wonder Worker of the New World.[307]

To add one last bit of pathos to the epitaph of the Lily of the Mohawks, we return to what Cholenec wrote in 1682 regarding her miracles:

> She does not act in the same way toward the sick children for whom prayers are said to her. Experience shows that the earth from her tomb which cures persons of an advanced age, seems rather to draw these little ones to heaven. Furthermore, her tomb is surrounded by children who have died since she was buried there, as if this first Iroquois virgin whom we believe to be in glory, took pleasure in having her chaste body surrounded by these little innocents as by so many lilies.[308]

Is this the ghost of Káteri? A visitor to the shrine in Fonda took this photo inside the chapel around 1952. When it was developed, this ghostly image of an Indian woman appeared to be coming from the altar. This image was found online and is probably impossible to verify.

29

LIFE AFTER KÁTERI

While Káteri Tekahkwí:tha's reputation as a miracle worker spread throughout New France, life went on at Kahnawà:ke. Once their normal period of mourning was over, Káteri's people resumed their planting, hunting, fishing, and the countless other chores that had to be done. There was nothing heartless in their doing so: In the harsh existence of the 17th century North American wilderness, you simply had no choice but to get on with the business of living.

Certainly, the work of the missionaries was enhanced by her shining example. Their writings assure as that she continued to serve as a beacon for the faith, but they also disclose that there continued to be threats to the very existence of the mission and the work they hoped to do there.

Father Chauchetière's annual narrative of the mission and other letters that he wrote help us to reconstruct the years that followed her death.

Father Frémin had left on an extended voyage to France in 1679. Chauchetière informs us that the priests who were left in charge managed to keep the liquor trade at Laprairie from debauching Kahnawà:ke. This is how he began his entry for the year 1680:

> God, who takes pleasure in mingling joys and sorrows in the life of man banished all sorrows from the mission this year. The assaults which had been made upon it for three years then ceased; but the absence of father fremin continually kept our minds in suspense. A great loss and a great profit was also incurred this year. The earth lost and heaven gained. The mission gave to paradise a treasure which had been sent to it two years before, to wit, the blessed soul of *Catherine Tegakwita, who died on the 17th of april.* The esteem in which she was held during her life, the help which many have had from her since her death, the honors which they have continued to render her, and various other circumstances which adorned her life— have made her very well known throughout this country. She served the mission by her good example; but we can say that she served it more after her death, for her lifeless body serves

here as argument to the savages that the faith is worthy of credence, and her prayers continually aid this mission. We may say that she now enters into participation of all the good which is done in it, and which has been done here since her death.[309]

Later in his account, he includes this peculiar statement about Káteri's imitators:

The demon, who saw the glorious success of this mission, used another kind of battery. Transfiguring himself as an angel of light, he urged on the devotion of some persons who wished to imitate Catherine, or to do severe penance for their sins. He drove them even into excess,—in order, no doubt, to render christianity hateful even at the start; or in order to impose upon the girls and women of this mission, whose discretion has never equaled that of Catherine, whom they tried to imitate.[310]

He then lists the many harsh penances that they practiced. The reader has been made quite familiar with these acts in previous chapters, so I need not repeat them here. He does state, however, that "the Holy Ghost soon intervened in this matter, enlightening all these persons, and regulated their conduct without diminishing their fervor."[311] He leaves to our imagination the form the Holy Ghost took when this intervention occurred.

Chauchetière noted a weather-related incident that undoubtedly reminded him of the vision he had witnessed in the days after Káteri's death:

About the middle of the summer, our chapel was threatened with fire from heaven,—which, after several frightful lightnings at broad noonday, and several heavy peals of thunder, struck at a few paces from the main door, and fell upon two oaks, which it stripped. A man who was about to enter the chapel saw all the stones that were on the ground roll about him, but he received no hurt.[312]

This was just a preview of a calamity that was yet to come, as we will see later in this chapter.

In the fall of 1680, the community celebrated the return of Father

Frémin, "who brought from france various furnishings suitable for adorning the chapel."[313] One of these items was an ornate monstrance to display the Eucharistic Host. This gilded vessel with emanating solarrays is preserved in the Mission's museum along with many other treasures.

The happiness of Father Frémin's return spilled over into the year 1681:

Guilded monstrance brought back from France by Father Frémin not long after the death of Káteri in 1680. Photo by the author, courtesy the St. François Xavier Church in Kahnawà:ke.

The two smaller crucifixes were brought back from France by Father Frémin. The larger one dates to the 18th century. Photo by the author, courtesy the St. François Xavier Church in Kahnawà:ke.

Who could relate the Joy which each one felt at seeing the Reverend Father fremin again in his mission? But an extraordinary prodigy which appeared in the sky once more disturbed people's minds. This was the great comet which appeared in autumn. The rumor of war kept all Canada in suspense. Five days after the apparition of the comet, God blessed the mission; for it was then that a sick man who had been given up was cured the next day, after he had invoked the name of Catherine of the Sault. This prodigy of the earth did not yet appear sufficient to outweigh that of the sky. The people then commended themselves chiefly to the Saints of the country; and also, at that place of the Sault, addressed themselves to Catherine.[314]

The comet mentioned above is commonly referred to as the Great Comet of 1680 and also as Kirch's Comet, after astronomer Gottfried Kirch, who discovered it by telescope. This comet was bright enough to be seen during the day and had an extremely long tail.[315]

Chauchetière's account for 1682 is rather sparse, so we turn next to a letter he wrote in the same year that is found in the *Jesuit Relations*:

> We have here a large farm, on which we keep oxen, cows, and poultry, and gather corn for our subsistence. It is sometimes necessary to take charge of all temporal as well as spiritual matters, now that Father Fremin has gone down in an Infirm condition to Quebec, as well as Father Cholenec. Some savages get their land Plowed, and harvest french wheat Instead of indian corn. It is impossible to describe their Joy when They can harvest 20 or 30 minots of french wheat, and are able to eat bread from time to time. But, as this sort of grain costs them too much labor, their usual occupation is to Plow the soil in order to plant indian corn in it. The men hunt, in order to obtain a provision of meat; The women go to the forests, to obtain supplies of wood. If the savages were fed, they would work much more than they do. Our village grows larger every year, while the Lorette mission, where father chaumont is, steadily diminishes. That of the mountain does not decrease, neither does it Increase much; but ours grows continually. We think that in two or three years all the Agniez will be in this Place. More than eighty have settled here recently. We have a chapel 25 feet Wide, and nearly 60 feet Long. We have three Bells, with which we produce a very agreeable Carillon; and the savages will soon have another bell, weighing two hundred livres, to complete the harmony.... There are sixty Cabins—that is to say, from one hundred and twenty to 150 families, as there are at least two in each Cabin.[316]

Later on in his letter, he describes their continuing battle against that demon alcohol:

> We have here no other demon to Contend against than liquor and drunkenness, which make a hell of all the Iroquois villages, wherein life is a continual suffering. The french are the

cause of its giving us much trouble here; for, in order to strip the Savages to their Very Shirts, they follow them everywhere, to make them drink and become intoxicated.

It is admirable to see how some of our Christian savages distinguish themselves in repressing this evil. They spill the liquor; they Break the bottles, with incredible courage, exposing themselves to insults and to Blows, of which some still bear the marks. And, in spite of all this, They do not lose Courage. I Know three or four who would endure martyrdom to prevent anything being done to offend God. They are no longer guided by the french, whom they had Hitherto considered good Christians, but who They now see very plainly are not such.[317]

We also learn that "War is blazing in The country of the *Outaouaks.*"

The Iroquois, especially Those of Onneiout, continue to bear ill will against the Outagamis and the Ilinois. For that reason, they have not forborne to take many captives from the Ilinois, a nation allied to us, after having slain a very large Number of them. In The year 1681, they killed or carried into Captivity a thousand of those people. Among The Captives of this year, 1682, is an Englishman whom They will no doubt burn. All this makes us hope that God will Continue to preserve Canada from Their Cruelty. They bear us malice in earnest, and we were in danger of having A war with them. For four years, we have heard nothing but threats; but God ever preserves us, working miracles of his providence in our favor—As He did Last autumn, when we expected to be attacked by them; but The storm burst elsewhere.[318]

There was a more literal storm brewing in the future of the mission, described by Father Cholenec as "a terrible storm, the likes of which perhaps has never been told, the earth was seen to tremble and the sky to be aglow."[319] The destruction caused by this storm was particularly relevant to the story of Káteri Tekahkwí:tha. It served as an omen of even greater tribulations yet to come.

30

A Prophecy Fulfilled

In a previous chapter, it was revealed that Father Chauchetière had a vision of the Lily of the Mohawks shortly after her death in which he was shown two images: the destruction of the wooden chapel and the burning of an Indian at the stake. I will now relate how these prophecies were fulfilled.

The first of these took place in 1683, and is documented by Chauchetière in his annual narrative of the mission. Although he was personally involved in this, he writes about himself in the third person:

> At last, all the monsters of hell, being powerless to do more, made a last effort in the month of august; and, joining at midnight with a whirlwind, blew down the chapel—a fall remarkable in all its circumstances. All the articles of sacred furniture were preserved whole, except five crosses, which were broken. The statue of the Blessed Virgin, which was at an elevation of eleven feet, was simply overturned. There were three Jesuit fathers in the chapel,—one below, who was ringing the bell, and two above the chapel. All three were saved by a sort of miracle. The one who was below was saved, and carried away from the place where he was, where a great hole was made by the beams, which broke in their fall the joists on which he was kneeling. He found himself in a place of safety,—without fear, without wound, praying and kissing the relics which he wore about his neck. Another of the fathers leaped into the air with the rafters, which formed a sort of cage for him. The last of the three fathers also fell, but was much hurt. He nevertheless extricated himself from beneath the ruins, and soon recovered.[320]

This is how Father Cholenec described the destruction in his biography of Káteri, adding a conversation that took place between the priests upon their extraction from the wreckage. The names of the priests, omitted in the original document by the editor of the *Positio,* have been inserted here in brackets:

The night of the twentieth of August, there was a terrific storm with such lightning and thunder that it could only have been caused by the evil spirit; it hurled the Church of the Sault sixty feet, breaking it into pieces; took it, I say, with such violence at one corner that, though it may seem improbable, it was turned over on the opposite angle and shattered.

Two of the Fathers [Fathers Jean Morain and Nicolas Jean Potier], who were in the church, were lifted into the air with the pieces. Another [Chauchetière], who had come from the house to ring the bell, felt the cord pulled out of his hand and was lifted as the others. All three found themselves on the ground under the debris, whence they were extracted with much difficulty. They thought their bodies would be severely injured by such a violent shock, but they merely had some slight wounds. This they attributed to Katharine's prayers, and when all three of them met, one said: "As for me, I said Holy Mass in honor of Katharine this morning." "And I," said another, "went to her grave this morning to recommend myself to her in a very special manner." "For over a year," added the third [Chauchetière], "I have had an insistent idea that some accident would happen to the mission, so during all that time and even today I went to pray to Katharine at her grave to deliver us from it. Besides, I have not ceased to importune the Superior of the mission to have her bones translated to our church, without knowing why I did so."[321]

The editor of the *Positio* also chose to eliminate two paragraphs in the original which told of how the aggrieved the people of the village were to learn of this disaster:

Father Chauchetière could not restrain his tears by seeing the Natives so afflicted by the loss of their chapel. They said that God had driven them out of the chapel because they did not deserve to enter there. They were inconsolable to see the Fathers wounded and sick, and they said that these Fathers had suffered for them because they did not want to listen to them and live like good Christians. Father Chauchetière was very skilful and seized the opportunity of encouraging them to amend their life with conviction.

They immediately proceeded to rebuild the chapel, and God wanted that there was then in the village an architect who had built five other chapels very well. The senior and most fervent of the chiefs of the Sault, the Great Mohawk, had finished his cabin of bark fifteen days before. He left his cabin, because he had offered it to replace the chapel until another was built. This offer of the Great Mohawk was accepted, and he regarded himself the happiest of his village, because he was blessed to give lodging to Jesus Christ.[322]

Chauchetière described the efforts to rebuild the wooden chapel:

From autumn forward, they labored for the restoration of the chapel. When the workman began, the savages began to work in concert—some by their gifts, others by their prayers; and they exerted themselves with all their might to aid the workmen. When the logs were squared, carting was out of the question; but the savages carried pieces sixty feet long and proportionately thick, and thus accumulated all the timbers where the frame of the building was to be hewn. There was no one who did not work according to his strength. The women and children all carried their pieces of timber; and several went about it with so much fervor that they hurt themselves, and were sick for a long time. But the most admirable of all was the workman who, never having learned, became a master-architect.[323]

This work continued in 1684, but an early spring thaw upset the plans:

When spring had come, we began to erect the chapel, which had been hewn into shape in the woods during the winter. It was our plan to draw the timbers over the snow, and thus to transfer all the pieces to the place where the building was to be erected. The workmen were disappointed, because the snows melted sooner than they expected. We knew not what to do, and could not make up our minds to leave the building until the following year. The village is usually deserted in the months of march and april; there are left in it only some women and children. Those women undertook to transport all the timbers. The posts and beams are clumsy and heavy—for one may imagine that the timbers of a building sixty feet long and twenty-five wide are not light. It was first proposed to these carriers to make a road by land, half a league in length, from the place whence the timbers were to be taken to the one where we were to build. It was necessary to fell and cut great trees, in order to make the passage. When one or two days had been employed at that task, the snow failed, and the labor was lost. They had now but one resort—and one, too, quite difficult and dangerous; this was to throw the timbers into the water, and convey them by means of a little brook which passes at the foot of the place where the village and the chapel now are.[324]

The women of Kahnawà:ke were not to be deterred by the forces of nature, for they were a force of nature unto themselves:

They exposed themselves to the danger of drowning or of freezing. However, the savage women alone, animated with the spirit of devotion and with the desire to have a chapel, did wonders on this occasion. To begin with, they helped to make the road and to cut some trees which had fallen into the brook; it was necessary to go into the water up to the waist, and remain there a whole day. When the road was done, they exhorted one another, and divided themselves into various bands. The little girls and the old women carried the lightest pieces by land; the young women, and those who were not hindered by pregnancy, went along the brook with poles, to guide the timbers through the turns; and the most vigorous, and those who in savage tongue are called "the good christians,"—or, in french, "the devout ones," followed the timbers in the water, having, in a spirit of penance, chosen this severest part of the labor. Their health was much affected thereby; and, above all, they had to make great efforts in order to drag

Atahsà:ta, the "Great Mohawk."

the timbers out of the water. But, as the enterprise was done in order to honor God and in a spirit of christian faith, every one was content with all that might befall her.[325]

To return to the chronology of our narrative, Chauchetière noted that the remains of Káteri were moved to the new wooden chapel in 1684:

> So many persons were seen to commend themselves to the deceased catherine Tegakwita; so many good savages were seen to offer this devotion and found themselves in such necessity this year to address themselves to her, that we believed it was but paying a just tribute to her virtue to remove her from the cemetery—where a little monument had been erected to her, a year before—into the new church. All opinions were unanimous upon that. This transfer, however, was accomplished by night, in the presence of the most devout. Some savages have since been seen to go to pray at the place where she lies, who had begun to go to visit her on the very day when she was buried.[326]

The Great Mohawk who had loaned his own dwelling as a temporary church, contributed some of the finishing touches to the new chapel:

> The captain of the anies has himself made a present to the chapel, worth four beavers,—or 240 livres, in the money of orange,—that is, a candlestick with eight branches, similar to the one which is in the orange meeting-house. It is of bronze, and was made in holland. This captain, going to war, wished to leave a monument of his piety, after having given up his cabin, one year previously, to the service of God.
>
> The chapel being finished, we placed therein the gifts which the savages made for it, or caused to be made—their robes, striped taffeta from china which some have left for it, and an altar-screen. They have decorated a beam which is above the altar with their collars,—which they put about the heads of the warriors, like a crown,—with their porcelain bracelets, with shields which the women wear to adorn their hair, and with belts, which are the savages' pearls. Several

masses have been said by way of thanksgiving for the favors which God has vouchsafed to Catherine of the Sault.[327]

The reconstruction of the church served to reaffirm the loyalties of the Kahnawa'kehró:non to New France:

During the whole summer in canada, one heard nothing but commotions and rumors of war; these, coming to the ears of the savages, served only to make known their fidelity. Who would ever have supposed that the faith and religion had so thoroughly united them with the french as to cause them to take arms against the iroquois and their own nation? They did so, however, as we know; and we owe this obligation to the captains, who knew so well how to direct the matter that men and women preferred to perish rather than lose their faith. The matter was proposed to them in open council, in three ways, giving them the choice. It was said, first, that they might withdraw to their own country if they wished; secondly, that if they remained they might remain in their own village; thirdly, that they could, after all, go with the french. The first statement did not please them at all, and they said that to withdraw from The french and lose the christian faith was the same thing. As for the second, they said that the french would distrust them too much. The 3rd proposal pleased them; and they said that, having but one and the same faith with the french, they wished also to run the same risks together. Accordingly, they set out, and had the approbation of the whole army in their entire conduct—whether they were sent as ambassadors among the iroquois, or our people applied to them for provisions from their chase, or advice were asked from them, as from people expert in war and who had been in close conflict.[328]

This was the year that the governor of New France, Antoine-Lefebvre, Sieur de la Barre, launched an ill-advised and poorly-equipped expedition to punish the Seneca for an attack they had made on Fort St. Louis. Envoys from Kahnawà:ke were sent to the Mohawk, Oneida, and Onondaga ahead of time to warn them that the quarrel was with the Senecas alone. Kahnawà:ke warriors joined the expedition once it was underway. The invaders got as far as Fort Frontenac on the St. Lawrence River before sickness overcame them, and they were forced to make peace with an Iroquois delegation before heading back home, their tails tucked between their legs. The governor was recalled soon after.[329]

The involvement of the Christian Iroquois in the failed attack did not go unnoticed by the delegates of the Confederacy. As their final word in the above-mentioned council, they told the governor, "Prevent the Christians of the Saut and of the Mountain from coming any more among us to seduce our people to Montreal; let them cease to dismember our Country as they do every year."[330]

By 1685, the division between the Iroquois Confederacy and their Kahnawà:ke kin had become a chasm, with the former having renounced the latter, and the latter fortifying their village against the former:

> At the beginning of this year was finished the palisade which they were making about the village,—always acting as people who do not fear to die, being assured that the iroquois, their former relatives, bear ill will against them only because they are christians. Those iroquois had renounced them at the council of war that was held at la famine, which is a place beyond Catarakwi. They had declaimed against them, had jeered at them, and finally uttered various threats against them, which eventually ended only in causing them to lose their places in the council, because they left it in order to come to finish the palisade. This was a second indication of their good faith, for the benefit which they were rendering to the french was great. They went incessantly to scout in the woods, where the iroquois were likely to pass in order to make a descent upon us; and this greatly vexes the iroquois. The palisade, which is pentagonal, then had five bastions, in one of which was a great iron cannon for eight-pound balls. This task is not small, as the village has become very large during these past few years.[331]

In 1687, Jacques-René de Brisay de Denonville, Marquis de Denonville, the new governor, launched another expedition against the Iroquois. The Great Mohawk and Hot Ashes were among those who accompanied him. Denonville lured 50 Iroquois chiefs to Fort Frontenace for a peace council, but instead of capitulating to them as his predecessor had done, he captured them and shipped them to France to serve as galley slaves. He then advanced on the Senecas to ravage their country. It had only been two decades since a French army had done the same thing to the Mohawks, an irony that seems to have been lost on the Great Mohawk.

Hot Ashes, the Oneida leader who was instrumental in Káteri Tekahkwí:tha's departure from the Mohawk Valley, was killed in an ambush during this campaign, but not before giving his last words to a Jesuit priest: "Father, I am dying. God wills it so, and I praise him for it with all my heart. I do not regret life, since Jesus Christ so lovingly gave his up for me."[332]

The Great Mohawk, for his part, has been honored with a monument in the town of Victor, New York, not far from the site of a Seneca town destroyed by the French army.

The Confederacy retaliated by launching an attack on New France in the summer of 1689, destroying the town of Lachine. Although their village had been heavily fortified, the people of Kahnawà:ke were forced to seek shelter within the walls of Montréal.

The Great Mohawk would eventually join another French expedition that destroyed the town of Schenectady in the winter of 1690. In the spring, he led a small group of warriors who captured an Iroquois war party. While camped at Lake Champlain, they were surprised by their own Abenaki and Algonquin allies, who mistook them for warriors of the Iroquois Confederacy and attacked them. Louis de Buade de Frontenac, the governor who succeeded Denonville, explained the sad result of this encounter: "This mistake was the more to be regretted as the Great Mohawk, who had been mentioned in connection with the affair at Corlard [Schenectady], was killed there. This is an irreparable loss which has drawn tears from the eyes of the entire country."[333]

The conflict between the two Iroquois factions eventually resulted in the fulfillment of the second of Káteri Tekahkwí:tha's prophecies, the burning of an Indian at the stake. Cholenec had much to say about this, but this was another instance where the editor of the *Positio* chose to omit the details. This is what his original reported:

> The native burning at the stake, which was seen in the apparition, arrived in 1690 at Onondaga. He was Ettiene Teganannokoa, a Huron from the Mission of Sault-Saint-

François-Xavier, who died a glorious death. When in the midst of the flames, he did not cease to encourage his wife to invoke with him the holy name of Jesus. When he was close to death, he revived all his force, and in imitation of his Master, requested the Lord with a loud voice to convert those who had treated him with such inhumanity.

At Onondaga, in the two years which followed, two women of the Mission of Saint-François-Xavier, who came from Onondaga, Frances Gonannhatenha and Marguerite Garangouas, were also captured and burned from hatred of the Faith and the Mission.

The French who were slaves of the Iroquois escaped continuously. They were witness of these events and they could not tell us these things without crying and drawing tears from the eyes of those who listened to them. One cannot doubt that Catherine had prophesied it a long time before and had obtained for these natives the invincible courage, of which was proven during their torture.[334]

In 1694, Chauchetière was teachings mathematics in Ville-Marie, having been reassigned from his post at St. François Xavier. He wrote a letter to his brother in which he described the torture and death of these two women two years before. We can omit the gory details, but it is hard to ignore his concluding statement: "I was for a long time the confessor of both these women; and I can say that this so happy ending was the reward of a good life."[335]

The late Evelyn Cook was the model for this statue of Kátéri that adorns Kateri Tsiionterihwaienstahkhwa. It is one of the most popular of all her statues. It was created by sculptor Emile Brunet and installed in 1954. Photo by the author.

31

GENEVIEVE OF CANADA

In his sermon on the Mount of Olives, Jesus Christ told the gathered crowd, "And ye shall hear of wars and rumors of wars: see that ye be not troubled: for all these things must come to pass, but the end is not yet."[336] The world Káteri Tekahkwí:tha left behind was one that must have seemed a lot like the "end times" predicted by the Lord. Her time at the Sault was a brief respite from this conflict, but in her absence, the drums of war began to thunder across the valley of the St. Lawrence. Prayers would be offered to Káteri not just for deliverance from sickness, but from total destruction by the enemies of New France.

Marquis de Denonville, his wife, and the Bishop-elect, Monseigneur de la Croix de Chevrière de Saint-Vallier made a pilgrimage to Káteri Tekahkwí:tha's grave in 1685. Father Cholenec noted this visit in his biography of Káteri: "During his first visit to the Sault, our Bishop, wishing to pray on her grave, brought with him the Marquis de Denserville and Madame la Marquise. He eulogized her in two words, calling her the *Genevieve of Canada*."[337]

Cholenec's 20th century counterpart, Father Henri Béchard, explained the significance of this appellation:

> This was quite a comparison. Saint Genevieve, a young maiden of angelic purity, had consecrated herself to God forever through the solemn vow of virginity which she made before Saint Germain at the age of fifteen. She is believed to be the first saint of France, or at least the first one to be recognized as such. She persuaded the Parisians not to flee before Attila the invader, and a little later, saved them from famine. The saint performed many miracles, was the object of widespread devotion for centuries and was invoked as the patron saint of Paris.[338]

Cholenec called Káteri's "greatest marvel" her protection of the Mission of St. François Xavier:

A grace that without doubt will be called the greatest of her marvels to anyone who weighs it well, together with all its circumstances, a singular grace and wonderful miracle, is the preservation of the mission, which we can attribute only to her prayers and her precious remains which we possess. For is it not a very surprising thing that a handful of people, such as our Indians of the Sault, compared to the five Iroquois nations, nevertheless cope with their many enemies who are infuriated against them, who fight and kill them, and even take them as slaves at the very doors of their village? It is true that in this long war we have lost all our veteran braves and the greater part of our warriors, but for a hundred we have lost, seven hundred of their bravest men were killed either by our Indians alone, or by them and the French fighting together.

We have seen as many as fifteen hundred of these fierce Iroquois approach to burn the entire border of Lachine and pass along the length of our territories near enough to our fields to destroy them, had they wished to do so, without losing a single ear of corn. During the seven or eight years that the war has been raging, there has scarcely been a year that they have not raised armies to come and devastate the Sault, either in the springtime during the sowing season, or in the summer during the harvest. Each year they depart to return, declaring that the last days of the Sault have arrived, but all these plans come to nothing and the mission still exists. In the three years that I have been here, only one poor old woman was killed during these sowing seasons and harvests.[339]

The Jesuit considered it something of a miracle that the Iroquois Confederacy never launched an all-out attack on Kahnawà:ke, which they could have easily done at any time during this conflict, but it was hardly a miracle when you consider the strong family ties that existed between the two groups. No matter how bad things got between their respective European allies, there were still people going back and forth on a regular basis, a situation that would last for at least another century.

Consider this account of Count Frontenac's attack on the Mohawk villages in 1693, which was eerily similar to the one carried out in 1666:

Count de Frontenac being desirous to take advantage of the season of their retreat in order to strike a heavy blow on them, dispatched from Montreal in the month of January a force of six hundred and twenty-five men, consisting of one hundred soldiers, two hundred Indians, and the remainder the most active young men of the country, under the command of Sieurs de Mantet, Courtemanche and de Lanoue, Canadian officers, accompanied by Sieur de L'Invilliers and twenty other officers, with orders to proceed against and destroy the Mohawks, and afterwards to commit as great ravages as possible around Orange. This party provided with every thing necessary for so long and fatiguing a march on snow shoes through woods and over frozen rivers, dragging their provisions after them, were guided so correctly by our Indians that they arrived near the three Mohawk villages, within fifteen leagues of Orange without being discovered. At nightfall, on arriving, our Indians in company with some Frenchmen went to reconnoitre two of the Villages, situate a quarter of a league the one from the other. On approaching these, they heard the enemy sing which obliged them to wait until the Indians should retire in order to surprise them whilst sleeping. The main body, in the meantime, advanced in two divisions, so as to be able to make a simultaneous attack on both Villages. Our scouts did not delay reporting that the enemy made no more noise. The Villages, which were surrounded by strong pallisades and closed with gates, were approached; our Indians scaled the inclosure in order to open the gates. A crowd entered and became masters of all the cabins without resistance. The small Village, after having been burnt with all its contents, was abandoned at day break, and the Indians and their families brought prisoners to the large Village where the commanders left a portion of their force to guard them. Early next morning our party set off for the third Village, distant seven or eight leagues, where they arrived in the evening, and surprised it on the following night in the same manner as they had the others; set it on fire and brought the prisoners to the principal Village.[340]

The first village burned by the French and their Indian allies in this campaign was the Caughnawaga archaeological site located at the Káteri

shrine in Fonda, New York. As I noted in an earlier chapter, it is adver-
tised as one of the villages where she lived, but wasn't established until
well after she left the Mohawk Valley.

> The Count's orders were not to give nay quarter to the men
> who would be found under arms, and to bring away the
> Women and children for the purpose of augmenting our
> Indian villages. But this order was not strictly executed,
> because they surrendered at discretion and expressed them-
> selves pleased at having this opportunity to come and live with
> our Indians, to whom they were closely related; so that, of
> about eighty fighting men found in those three villages, only
> eighteen or twenty were killed, and the others, with the
> women and children, were made prisoners to the number of
> two hundred and eighty persons.
>
> This expedition having succeeded as much as could possibly
> be desired, and our Frenchmen having perceived that a young
> Englishman, a prisoner of our Indians whom they brought with
> them on this march, had made his escape during the night on
> which the two Villages were taken, and that he would
> undoubtedly notify the English of their design, judged it unsafe
> to remain any longer in the enemy's country, as the smallest
> delay might prevent their retreat, having to travel over the
> lakes and rivers on which the ice was beginning to rot.
> Therefore, after they had sojourned only one day at the prin-
> cipal Village, they burnt it, and set out with all the prisoners.
> On the first and second days of their homeward march, several
> Mohawks, who, whilst hunting in the neighborhood, had
> learned the destruction of their Villages, came to join them,
> expressing their desire to follow their wives and children.[341]

It is this last sentence that speaks volumes about these Mohawk family
ties. In the aftermath of an invasion that saw their villages destroyed for
the second time, several Mohawks set aside their "savage fury" to trail
after their wives and children who had been taken prisoner. It was noted
in this account that many of the Mohawks who surrendered were happy
for the chance to move to Kahnawà:ke, where they had many kin. They
may have only said this to keep themselves from being killed, but it was

well-known that the French were cautious about using their Christian Iroquois in campaigns against the Iroquois Confederacy because of these strong family connections.

Cholenec gives us another example of Káteri's protection, which one might also attribute to these strong family bonds:

> In the early spring of 1695, one of our renegades came from the Mohawks to seek his mother and sister, saying that the Iroquois had plotted our ruin for the following summer, and that all here must perish. That summer, however, our warriors left us to conduct a convoy to Fort Frontenac, and only the old men remained with the women. All summer long we were busy moving our village, everyone was carting, carrying, transferring from the old village to the new, without a single Iroquois coming into sight, though they knew very well what was going on. Moreover, twenty would have been enough to disturb us in that confusion. On one occasion one of their bands came to the old village, which they surrounded without daring to approach within gunshot. All they succeeded in doing near the Mission of Lachine was to kill two men, and to take three or four women. Farther on they laid a snare for five or six approaching canoes. Thinking that they had captured them all, they attacked and rained a shower of bullets upon them. These canoes were filled with more than thirty women, among them being those most prominent at the mission and in *Katharine's Band.* They had come to land at the little stream where the first village and Katharine's grave were. Without losing their heads in this fierce and unexpected attack, one of the oldest and bravest women began to recite the litanies of Our Lady, while they all withdrew in plain view, not only without any of them being touched, but without a single bullet piercing their canoe, although the savages shot constantly with their guns, and several, from rage, threw themselves into the water in order to lay hold of the canoes. This miracle in all its details is truly inconceivable, but it may be explained by the fact that it happened within sight of Katharine's grave. Katharine blinded our enemies and inspired this confidence and presence of mind among the women, that they might be saved from their enemy.[342]

Cholenec provides us with two other examples that attribute to saintly intervention what can just as easily be laid at the doorstep of human kindness:

> Katharine inspired courage in another group of women who were met by some of a band that came into the vicinity from the Mohawk territory. The Mohawks, seeing themselves discovered, wished to return, and came upon this second band of women, their own relations, and wished to take them with them. It was impossible for the Mohawks to prevail upon them to come. The women protested that they would rather die than give up their Faith and that the men could kill them as their slaves. This astounded the raiders greatly, but, not wishing to avenge themselves on women, they decided to bring them back themselves to the village, and to make a kind of truce with our Indians.
>
> Indeed, when the Count de Frontenac, at the head of two thousand men, both French and Indian, had gone that summer to burn the villages of the Onondagas and Oneidas and to lay waste their fields of corn, these savages, enraged against ours, should more than ever have come to avenge themselves on us during the harvest. Nevertheless, we harvested in perfect security, although all our warriors had gone to the territory of the Mohawks and the English. The women were in the fields from morning till evening with their children, at half a league from the village. Some slept in the fields as in time of peace, and not one of our enemies appeared. We regarded these things as so many marvels of our Guardian Angel, our powerful protectress and patron, the brave Katharine Tegakoüita, who has for so long preserved her beloved Mission at the Sault, and we hope will preserve and augment it more and more in spite of the opposition of our enemies, visible and invisible, the Iroquois and the devil.[343]

It is not my intent to deny Káteri Tekahkwí:tha a single miracle. There is no doubt in my mind that she was watching over her people, and still does to this day. I question only the motives of her biographers in refusing even one moment of humanity to the non-Christian

Mohawk. Cholenec never mentioned that the French burned the Mohawk villages to the ground in 1693. For that matter, he never mentioned that the French burned down the Mohawk villages in 1666, when Kateri Tekahkwí:tha was only ten years old. Even with these devastating attacks in the back of their minds, Mohawk warriors repeatedly spared the lives of their Kahnawà:ke kin. Not only that, a great many of these Mohawks chose to establish themselves in the heart of New France and became "Original People Who Make the Sign of the Cross." By 1700, the northern exodus of Mohawks prompted this observation from Robert Livingston, Secretary of Indian Affairs for the colony of New-York:

> That the Maqua's nation are grown weak & much lessened by the late war, but more since the peace by the French daily drawing them from us to Canada so that near two thirds of s[d] nation are now actually at Canada with their familyes, who are kindly received, being cloathed from head to foot, are secured in a Fort guarded with souldiers, & have Priests to instruct them.[344]

Cholenec ignores this migration, preferring to keep the Mohawks in the role of villain—in league, as he says, with the devil. He wasn't just writing hagiography, but wartime propaganda.

Blessed Kateri Tekahkwí:tha, the Genevieve of Canada and the Wonder Worker of the New World, undoubtedly deserved these honors and accolades, just as she deserves to have her sainthood recognized by the Roman Catholic Church. I believe that she will eventually attain this recognition based on her own merits, and not by comparison to her Mohawk kin and their thorough demonization at the hands of her Jesuit biographers. She was indeed "a lily among thorns," but the thorns came in many different forms, and not all of them were Mohawk.

With that in mind, Robert Livingston will have the last word in this Jesuit-dominated history: "It's strange to think what authority these priests have over their Indian proselites; they carry a chain in their pocket & correct the Indians upon the cômission of any fault, wch they bear very patiently"[345]

Káteri Tekahkwí:tha has inspired countless artists and sculptors throughout the world. Photo collage by the author.

32

The Mohawk Repatriation of Káteri Tekahkwí:tha

More than three centuries have passed since the events of this book took place. The Mohawk Valley village sites where Káteri grew up now have homesteads, pastures, and cornfields on them. The village she moved to as a young woman is now a suburban neighborhood on Montréal's south shore, with a simple roadside shrine as the only reminder that this was the hallowed ground where history was made.

The people of Kahnawà:ke never did return to that site, but established a new village about a mile upstream, dubbed *Kahnawá:kon*, or "In the Rapids," due to its location adjacent to the Lachine Rapids. They stayed there six years, then moved about another mile and a half upstream to where the Suzanne River emptied into the St. Lawrence, calling this site *Kanatakwén:ke*, or "Near the Rapids."[346] In 1716, they relocated about three miles west to what is now modern Kahnawà:ke, the first homes established just east of the stone church. Every time they moved, they took with them the remains of Káteri Tekahkwí:tha and the great Huron wampum belt that adorned the rafters above the altar of the church.

This wampum belt, with its six rectangles and a cross at the center, would become something of a prophecy in itself, as Kahnawà:ke became the "Great Council Fire" of a new confederacy, the Seven Nations of Canada, in the 18th century. Seven Nations warriors fought as allies of the French under the Marquis de Montcalm during the French and Indian War, often against their own kin in the Iroquois Confederacy. They would find themselves divided by the American Revolution and the War of 1812, and by the end of the 19th century, Tsiá:ta Nihononhwentsá:ke was beginning to fade. Periodic revivals of traditionalism further diminished the collective memory of the alliance. In fact, it isn't hard to find Mohawk nationalists who totally reject that such a thing ever existed. Wampum being the symbols to end all symbols, the belt itself has vanished, the victim of the self-conscious nationalism of the 1970's. This is how the *Kateri* bulletin noted the theft in 1977:

Three or four years have passed since three teenagers entered the Mission Church of St. Francis Xavier, slipped through the sacristy, and reached the adjacent museum. There they borrowed a precious relic belonging to the Catholic Indians of Caughnawaga: the wampum belt that the Lorette Hurons had offered to their ancestors in 1677.

. . .

One of these days, perhaps on a dark and snowy afternoon, three teenagers may find their way back to the church with the borrowed wampum belt.[347]

In spite of this diplomatic plea, the belt was never returned. It was rumored that the belt had been stolen because there was fear that since it was a "Seven Nations" belt, it was a threat to the growing traditionalist movement, the logic being that Canada might assume for itself membership in this alliance, and thereby negate the treaty rights that the Iroquois Confederacy claimed. The belt predated the Seven Nations of Canada by about 75 years, so there is little chance of that ever happening, but the fine points of history are often lost in the highly-charged political environments of the modern Mohawk communities.

Meanwhile, Káteri Tekahkwí:tha's following has spread throughout the world, driven at first by the dissemination of the biographies written by the Jesuits, and later by the movement to have her canonized as a saint in the Roman Catholic Church. Káteri's own people have been her strongest advocates, attending in great members her beatification ceremony at the Vatican in 1980, as well as faithfully participating in the annual Tekakwitha Conference held throughout North America. Shrines, statues, and chapels have sprung up in various places to honor the Lily of the Mohawks. Káteri has taken on not only a pan-Indian appearance, but a New Age mysticism that bears little resemblance to the Mohawk ascetic she really was.

Thus, there are now two parallel streams that seem unlikely to ever converge, but which derive from a common source. Having wandered around the outskirts of both of these movements, I have come to appreciate how familiar their adherents would seem to the people of Káteri's era, and how much each would benefit from taking a fresh look at her actual time and place, and by confronting the documentation that exists about her life. Naturally, they would have to read between the lines of

Káteri's tomb at St. François Xavier Church in Kahnawà:ke. Photo by the author.

what was written, and acknowledge the fact that her biographers had a political and religious agenda which colored everything they wrote. This is also true of some of the more recent Jesuit biographers, such as Father Francis Xavier Weiser and Father Henri Béchard, whose otherwise excellent writings fail to bring Káteri's Mohawk kin—and the pressures they faced—from out of the shadows.

The story of Káteri Tekahkwí:tha has always been told from this devotional perspective, which is a different stream of thought than the one in which anthropologists and historians normally dip their paddles. In the introduction to this book, I mentioned there has long been a "western Iroquois" bias among scholars, due to the fact that the Onondaga and Seneca in New York State were considered the last bastions of Iroquois traditionalism, while the Mohawk were noted more for moving to Canada and adopting Christianity. A new generation of scholars has begun to focus some overdue attention on the "eastern Iroquois" and our so-called "conversion." They now understand that we were not cultural buckets that could be dumped out and filled with something else, as the following survey of their research reveals.

In his 1982 study of Catholicism at Kahnawà:ke, David Blanchard argued that 17th century Mohawks accepted elements of Christianity according to their existing world view:

> The drama of culture-contact at Kahnawake presents us with a case where both the natives and the Jesuits [representing the European society] evaluated and manipulated the culture of the other to secure the best end for themselves. The Mohawk were

Tomb of Blessed Káteri Tekahkwí:tha. Photo by the author, courtesy the St. François Xavier Church in Kahnawà:ke.

not witless followers of the Jesuits. They used the Jesuits to gain advantageous trade concessions from the French and had to give something up in return. What did they give? To the Jesuit's way of thinking, the Mohawk gave up their traditional religion and beliefs. In fact, the Mohawk modified their religious practices and developed a syncretistic system of ritual that yielded the desired effect, yet was compatible with Catholicism.[348]

In 1985, Daniel Richter took a deeper look at the factionalism that arose over Jesuit missionary activity among the Iroquois.[349] His insights into the traditionalist perspective were a far cry from the cartoon-like villainy attributed to them by Jesuit scribes. He would revisit this Iroquois vs. Iroquois conflict in a 1992 book, *The Ordeal of the Longhouse: The Peoples of the Iroquois League in the Era of European Colonization*.[350] In 2001, he examined the "chasm" between traditional Iroquoian beliefs and the teachings of the Jesuits:

The chasm between European and Indian religions at first glance could not appear greater. But, as the missionary's comment indicates, the gap may not have yawned so wide as we might think. The same inclusiveness that was so alien to missionaries made it perfectly possible for Native Americans to incorporate elements of Christianity into their spiritual world. Our Father, his Son, and their Holy Spirit joined the diverse other-than-human persons who already populated the universe, and perhaps were even more powerful than any of them.[351]

Richter recognized that it wasn't just religion that influenced how the Jesuit missionaries were perceived, but the realities of intertribal warfare:

No doubt, many people reacted sullenly to French shamans—sorcerers?—who preached alien values of an enemy power. But others—clan chiefs, would-be headmen raised up by the general ferment, military leaders more concerned with Indian than with European foes—saw opportunities for new trading partners, new sources of firearms, new alliances that might reinvigorate the community's spiritual and temporal power.[352]

As for Káteri Tekahkwí:tha, Richter speculated that her Algonquin heritage and her orphaned status may have weakened her kinship ties to the Mohawk community—making her adoptive parents eager to marry her off:

It does not take much of a stretch of our imaginations to under-stand why a young woman trapped in such circumstances might find something attractive in the preaching of French missionar-ies. Nor is it hard to imagine that, when the person now named Kateri left the Mohawk country to resettle at Kahnawake, she found there the kinship, the social acceptance, and the spiritual power she had never before had—under the tutelage of priests who supported her efforts and held her up as a model of piety, among the sisterhood of women who joined her in her chastity and penance, and within a broader community that identified itself as both Indian and Catholic.[353]

Richter accepts the notion that Káteri had something of a marginal existence before her baptism, yet her biographers note that she was a skillful artisan who made not only decorative and utilitarian items, but

Káteri painting on display at the Káteri Sanctuary at the St. François Xavier Church. Photo by the author.

the wampum belts used in diplomacy. She was also the adopted daughter of a leading chief. This hardly sounds like someone with little value or standing in a Mohawk community.

In 1992, John Steckley examined the Jesuit use of Iroquoian imagery to promote Christianity. He stressed the Jesuit strategy of using Indian languages and incorporating "as many Native cultural concepts with as little distortion as possible."[354] These ranged from warfare and torture to matrilineal lineages and familial relationships:

> The warrior complex was used to demonstrate the power of the Christian spirit world, making it an ally to be sought, but an even greater enemy to be feared. The matrilineal lineage, on the other hand, served mainly as the model of closeness shared by Christians, especially in Heaven.[355]

One example Steckley used was the fire Iroquoian peoples employed as a test of courage of their prisoners:

> The Jesuits did not want the Huron and Iroquois to think that the tortures of hell could be endured by the courageous, or that those who proved themselves unflinching in hell would ultimately be admired. They stressed that the fire in hell and the kind of fire used to torture prisoners on earth were quite different, and they emphasized that there could be no admiration for bravery in hell. One way in which the Jesuits stressed the differences between the two kinds of fire was to claim that the

fire in hell was much more piercing and thorough, burning everywhere at once, easily penetrating any object, no matter how damp or thick.[356]

In 1993, K. I. Koppedrayer examined the role of Káteri Tekahkwí:tha's Jesuit biographers in "creating" her, or at least, the popular image we have of her:

> In many ways, the writing of Kateri's biography was an autobiographical exercise for Fathers Chauchetière and Cholenec. Not only did they record moments in her life in which they directly figured, but also they echo, in the trials they show her facing, the challenges and difficulties they themselves faced in the New World. Only the names and faces are different. Just as Kateri had to respond to different voices of authority, so also did her Jesuit fathers. They co-opted her native voice to argue their presence in the New World.[357]

Nancy Shoemaker, emphasizing Blanchard's "syncretism" of Iroquois tradition and Catholicism, wrote in 1995 that the penances practiced by Kahnawa'kehró:non became pronounced in 1678, right around the time of a smallpox outbreak. She suggested that these penances may have been seen as an effective ritual to counter European disease. Furthermore, they served as a "prophylactic" to prevent torture and death at the hands of one's enemies. To Shoemaker, all of this "made sense within an Iroquois cultural framework."

> Certain Christian rituals fit easily into traditional Iroquois beliefs, while the new ritual practices, like penance, offered spiritual power lacking in traditional Iroquois rituals. Whereas the Jesuits emphasized the importance of Christian ritual in determining one's place in the afterlife, Tekakwitha and other Christian Iroquois had new and pressing needs for empowering rituals to control the increasingly uncertain, earthly present.[358]

Shoemaker's explanation for the Iroquois adoption of penance is pure speculation. There is no evidence to suggest that self-torture would have been construed in any way as medicinal, preventive or otherwise. What seems more likely is that they adopted it as a test of their devotion, which would not be that far removed from its original purpose as a test of courage and fortitude.

William B. Hart, writing in 1999, examined the cult of the Virgin Mary among 17th century Huron and Iroquois Christians:

> For many Huron converts, Mary bridged Christianity and the Huron religion through parallel myths of virgin birth, or at least birth by mysterious means. Both Mary and the daughter of Sky Woman in the Huron and Iroquois creation myths were mysteriously impregnated by sacred beings, and, therefore, were virgins when they gave birth to divine sons. In the various versions of Iroquois and Huron creation myths, a woman identified as 'the daughter' or 'the child' of Sky Woman—the goddess who plunged to earth from the Sky World above, and who, thus, represents the catalyst for Indian life on earth—gave birth to twin sons, the first divine humans to occupy the earth. Like Mary, the twins' mother was a virgin, having been miraculously impregnated by a mysterious suitor who placed two arrows across her body after she had fainted. Devotees to the Iroquois religion identified her good son, Teharonghyawago, as the Creator, who, like Christ, taught mankind ethical (as well as practical) ways of living. Shortly after being born, the evil twin, Tawiskaron, killed his mother, thereby conveniently preserving her virginity.[359]

Hart goes on to quote Major John Norton's 1816 journal, wherein he states that even non-Christian Iroquois recognized the interchangeability of Mary and Sky Woman's daughter:

> I, one day asked one of these old men, who in his youth had had much conversation with the Roman Catholic Priests, if he remembered the name of the Mother of Teharonghyawago. He answered, "not in our language, but in that of the Europeans, she is called Maria."[360]

If we already had the concept of a union between a human woman and a spirit in our culture, then Christianity and its "fatherless boy" must have sounded a lot like one of our own legends. This would explain not only the ease of its acceptance, but Káteri taking Jesus as her "divine spouse." Whether she was conscious of it or not, she was the 17th century equivalent of Sky Woman's daughter and the Peacemaker's mother—a human female united with a powerful spirit.

Finally, we come to Allan Greer, whose book about Káteri has been mentioned earlier in this work. Greer has written extensively on the multicultural world of New France, and has authored several articles about Káteri prior to *Mohawk Saint*. His book is a natural progression of the scholarship I have outlined above, but it gives only minimal attention to what all of this history means to Káteri's people today.[361]

Greer describes a visit to Kahnawà:ke that he made a few years after the "Oka Crisis" of 1990. "When I first visited Kahnawake in 1993," he writes, "I had difficulty finding anyone interested in talking about Catherine Tekakwitha." He was waved through a Warrior Society guard post as he entered the reserve and attended Sunday Mass at the St. François Xavier Church:

> It seemed to me that the faithful band of believers dedicated to the cause of their local saint was rather small and, on average, of advanced years. Most villagers I spoke with outside the church were somewhat dismissive of the Mohawk saint, inclined to treat her story as a myth generated by centuries of religious and cultural imperialism.[362]

Greer mentions that around the time of the Oka Crisis, "There had been talk then of destroying Kahnawake's Tekakwitha shrine as a symbol of spiritual conquest and oppression." It is unfortunate that he encountered only the extreme end of the spectrum during his visit, because I have met several advocates of Káteri Tekahkwí:tha in Kahnawà:ke, such as Cathy Rice, a volunteer at the St. François Xavier Church; Albert and Elaine Lazare, the hard-working staff at the Kateri Center; Kateri Deer and Norma Canoe, two sisters who faithfully attend the various events; and Deacon Ron Boyer, the new Canadian Vice Postulator for Káteri's cause. He would find a similar following for Káteri in Ahkwesáhsne, were there are both Káteri and Tekahkwí:tha prayer circles.

The negativity Greer encountered toward Káteri reminds me of the cold reception many residential school students received when they

St. François Xavier Church in Kahnawà:ke. Photo by the author.

returned home, unable to speak their native language. When another culture took one of our women, turned her into an icon, and placed her on a pedestal, many of her own people turned their back on her. By allowing her to be so thoroughly misappropriated, their eyes became blind to her symbolism and significance in our own cosmological tableau.

Even if we don't embrace Káteri Tekahkwí:tha as a manifestation of Sky World on earth, we should at the very least recognize her as a Kanien'kehá:ka woman whose time and place in history is crucial for us to understand. Like a wampum belt held by some non-native museum, or a prisoner held by an enemy, the time has come for the Mohawk repatriation of Káteri Tekahkwí:tha. She has been someone else's symbol long enough.

We could begin this repatriation process, appropriately enough, by demanding that her physical remains be brought back together and given a proper burial. This is happening with human remains held by museums throughout America, so why shouldn't the same happen for Káteri? Today her relics are scattered throughout the United States, Canada and probably Europe because they are said to have healing powers. I don't doubt this to be true, as my own mother has experienced the powerful presence of a Káteri relic, but the time has come to end what is ultimately a ghoulish, medieval practice. If it truly is Káteri's spirit interceding on our behalf, surely she isn't limited to acting only through her physical remains! If returning them to the soil of Mother Earth is out of the question, then at the very least these relics should be interred with the rest of her remains in the marble sarcophagus at the St. François Xavier Church, never to be disturbed again.[363]

By treating her remains with the respect that we would afford any of our other Mohawk ancestors, we would be taking care of some unfinished business that we weren't even aware we had. We would, in a sense, reconnect ourselves to Káteri Tekahkwí:tha in a much more personal and profound way than ever before, which in my mind is just as worthwhile a goal as her canonization as a Roman Catholic saint. We need more than ever to know the Mohawk woman behind the icon and come to grips with what took place in her brief but eventful life.

Is it even possible to chip away at the 300 year old plaster statue and see the human being within? Daniel Richter didn't think so:

> Can we search beneath the myth to recover any glimpses of *her* personality, of the contradictions and paradoxes she may have struggled with as she embraced an alien faith? Kateri left no written words of her own. It is likely that she never learned to read or write in either Mohawk or French, and the only statements Cholenec and Chauchetière attributed to her reflect such predictable pieties as her resolution to "have no other spouse but Jesus Christ." All written sources trace back to the hagiography of Cholenec and Chauchetière.... The truth about the historical individual behind the religious narrative is probably irrecoverable.[364]

As a Mohawk attempting a biography using these same materials, I have struggled with this limitation from the beginning. It has been a dark cloud hanging over the project. Unlike Chauchetière, I had no visions of Káteri to light my way through the shadows. The closest I came was an inner voice urging me to make a reproduction of the missing Huron wampum belt, which I accomplished long before I began the research that would reveal to me that it was given to Kahnawà:ke the same year she arrived there. This extraordinary creation adorned her Holiest of Holies—the chapel where she spent countless hours in fervent prayer—and I can't help but feel it was her voice that compelled me to make it.

It would be impossible for me to *not* have an indelible connection to Káteri Tekahkwí:tha. I have a very visual imagination and could easily place myself in every scene. I have followed Father Lamberville through the longhouse for his first encounter with her. I have stood on the shores of Lake Champlain and watched her rescuers paddle by with her in the middle of their canoe. I have lingered near the wooden chapel when she first met Wari Teres. I have flinched with each blow she struck upon herself in the dark of night. I have watched in silence as she knelt in church, embraced an unseen spirit, and forsook earthly comforts for an eternal union. And finally, I have looked over the shoulders of the mourners and watched in awe when her face was transfigured in the moments after her death. But the moment with the deepest resonance for me was when I placed myself in the moccasins of her uncle as he went looking for her during her "escape." The Jesuits allow him no human emotion, no compassion at all for the daughter—not niece—that he was letting slip away.

In a sense, he still exists to us today. He is the Longhouse activist who wants nothing to do with the myth built up around one of our women. He is the parent who sees his child swept up in a modern fad, movement, or religion that takes his child away from his home and into a world beyond his control. Ultimately, he is any parent whose child has grown up and left the nest. He is all of us.

God help him.

Words of Pope John Paul II
at the time of Káteri Tekahkwí:tha's Beatification
St. Peter's Basillica
June 22, 1980

This wonderful crown of new beauty, God's bountiful gift to His Church, is completed by the sweet, frail yet strong figure of a young woman who died when she was only twenty-four years old: Káteri Tekahkwí:tha, the "Lily of the Mohawks," the first to renew the marvels of sanctity of Saint Scholastica, Saint Gertrude, Saint Catherine of Siena, Saint Angela Merici and Saint Rose of Lima, preceding along the path of love, her great spiritual sister, Therese of the Child Jesus.

She spent her short life partly in what is now the State of New York and partly in Canada. She is a kind, gentle and hardworking person, spending her time working, praying and meditating. At the age of twenty she received Baptism. Even when following her tribe in the hunting seasons, she continued her devotions, before a rough cross carved by herself in the forest. When her family urged her to marry, she replied very serenely and calmly that she had Jesus as her only spouse. This decision, in view of the social conditions of women in the Indian tribes of that time, exposed Káteri to the risk of living as an outcast and in poverty. It is a bold, unusual and prophetic gesture: on 25 March, 1679, at the age of twenty-three, with the consent of her spiritual director, Káteri took a vow of perpetual virginity, as far as we know the first time that this was done among the North American Indians.

The last months of her life were an ever clearer manifestation of her solid faith, straightforward humility, calm resignation and radiant joy, even in the midst of terrible sufferings. Her last words, simple and sublime, whispered at the moment of death, sum up, like a noble hymn, a life of purest charity: "Jesus, I love you."

Mohawks lead a contingent of North American Indians attend Beatification ceremony of Blessed Káteri Tekahkwí:tha at St. Peter's Basilica, the Vatican, Rome.
Copyright L'Osservatore Romano Citta' Del Vaticano, Servizio Fotografico, Arturo Mari.

Pope John Paul II greets one of Káteri's followers after the ceremony. Photographer unknown.

Chief Delisle of Kahnawake delivers the Ohén:ton Karihwatéhkwen, or "Words that Come Before All Else," to Pope John Paul II.
Copyright L'Osservatore Romano Citta' Del Vaticano, Servizio Fotografico, Arturo Mari.

Pope John Paul II and officials of the Roman Catholic Church pose with followers of Káteri Tekahkwí:tha after she is beatified on June 22, 1980.
Copyright L'Osservatore Romano Citta' Del Vaticano, Servizio Fotografico, Arturo Mari.

Prayer for the Canonization of Blessed Káteri Tekahkwí:tha

O God who, among the many marvels of Your Grace in the New World,
did cause to blossom on the banks of the Mohawk and of the St. Lawrence,
the pure and tender Lily, Káteri Tekahkwí:tha,
grant we beseech You, the favor we beg through her intercession;
that this Young Lover of Jesus and of His Cross
may soon be counted among her Saints by Holy Mother Church,
and that our hearts may be enkindled with a stronger desire
to imitate her innocence and faith.
Through the same Christ our Lord.
Amen.

REFERENCES

1. Fenton, W. N., *The Great Law and the Longhouse: A Political History of the Iroquois Confederacy*, University of Oklahoma Press, Norman, 1998, p. 3.

2. Parker, A. C., "The Code of Handsome Lake, the Seneca Prophet," *New York State Museum Bulletin* 163, State University of New York, Albany, 1913, p. 14, as reprinted in Parker, A. C., *Parker on the Iroquois*, Syracuse University Press, Syracuse, 1968.

3. This name was spelled in an old Mohawk-language prayer book as *Tsiatak Nihononwentsiake*. It roughly translates as "seven lands" or "seven nations." It has been standardized here according to the Kahnawà:ke dialect.

4. Myers, M. "The Creation Story: The Sky World," *Traditional Teachings*, North American Indian Travelling College, Akwesasne, 1984, p. 4.

5. Shenandoah, J. and George, D. M., *Skywoman: Legends of the Iroquois*, Clear Light Publishers, Santa Fe, 1998, p. 7-39. Names in this chapter (except those in quotations) have been standardized by Teyowisonte (Thomas Deer).

6. Parker, A. C. "The Constitution of the Five Nations or The Iroquois Book of the Great Law," *New York State Museum Bulletin* 184, State University of New York, Albany, 1916, (Iroqrafts reprint, 1991), p. 65.

7. Parker, Ibid., p. 66.

8. Gibson, J. A., *Concerning the League: The Iroquois League Tradition as Dictated in Onondaga by John Arthur Gibson*, Memoir 9, Algonquin and Iroquoian Linguistics, Winnipeg, 1992, p. xix-xx. Rotinonhsión:ni is translated literally as "They Built the Extended House." It is also spelled *Rotinonhsón:ni*. The official letterhead of the Mohawk Nation Council of Chiefs uses *Haudenosaunee*, a more phonetic way of spelling the Onondaga form of the word.

9. Blanchard, D., *7 Generations: A History of the Kanienkehaka*, Kahnawake Survival School, Kahnawake, 1980, p. 483-486.

10. George-Kanentiio, D., *Iroquois Culture & Commentary*, Clear Light Publishers, Santa Fe, 2000, p. 34.

11. Robinson, D. D., *Saint George, the Serpent and the Senecas*, 1994. Found online at http://www.crookedlakereview.com/articles/67_100/71feb1994/71robinson.html.

12. According to the Nativetech website, "The word "Wampum" comes from the Narragansett word for 'white shell beads.' Wampum beads are made in two colors: white ("Wòmpi") beads ("Wompam") from the Whelk shell ("Meteaûhock"), and purple-black ("Súki") beads ("Suckáuhock") from the growth rings of the Quahog shell ("Suckauanaûsuck")." Found online at http://www.nativetech.org/wampum/wamphist.htm. Wikipedia gives the source of white wampum as the North Atlantic channeled whelk (*Busycotypus canaliculatus*) shell. Found online at http://en.wikipedia.org/wiki/Wampum.

13. Michelson, G., "Iroquoian Terms for Wampum," International Journal of American Linguistics, vol. 57, no. 1, 1991, p. 108-106. According to Teyowisonte, Michelson consulted speakers in Kahnawà:ke and Ahkwesáhsne for his research into modern linguistic terms. Another excellent resource on wampum is Reverend William M. Beauchamp's "Wampum and Shell Articles

Used by the New York Indians," *New York State Museum Bulletin* 41, vol. 8, University of the State of New York, Albany, 1901.

[14]   According to one of my Mohawk language consultants, *oión:wa* is another way of saying wampum belt. Wampum strings are sometimes called *Ahserí:ie*, but this just means "string." The translation of kaión:ni is found in Cuoq, J. A., *Lexique de la Langue Iroquoise avec Notes et Appendices*, J. Chapleau & Fils, Montréal, 1882, p. 160-161.

[15]   Tehanetorens, *Wampum Belts of the Iroquois*, (Reprint), Book Publishing Company, Summertown, 1999, p. 12.

[16]   Clark, N. T., "The Thacher Wampum Belts of the New York State Museum," *New York State Museum Bulletin* 279, The University of the State of New York, Albany, 1929, p. 53.

[17]   It is common for people to translate this term as "Knife Makers" but this is not exactly so, according to my trusty Kanien'kéha linguists. On'serón:ni is short for *Ron'serón:ni* meaning "They Make Hatchets/Tomahawks," which refers to the French. The noun root for hatchet is {-a'ser-}. *?:sera'* means hatchet.

[18]   Pendergast, J. F., and Trigger, B. G., *Cartier's Hochelaga and the Dawson Site*, McGill-Queens University Press, Montréal/London, 1972, p. 334.

[19]   Ibid, p. 39. A site excavated by Sir John William Dawson near McGill University in Montréal was proclaimed to be Cartier's Hochelaga, but Pendergast and Trigger failed to confirm this as fact. "The Dawson site appears most likely to have been a small Iroquoian village that existed early in the sixteenth century and its identity with Hochelaga is far from proven," Trigger concluded. St. Lawrence Iroquoian artifacts from the Dawson site are on permanent display at the McCord Museum in Montréal.

[20]   Howell, S., "Pointe a Calliere Rediscovers the Lost Iroquoian People," *The Montreal Gazette*, Montréal, November 17, 2006.

[21]   Lighthall, W. D., "Hochelaga and Mohawks: A Link in Iroquois History," *Transactions of the Royal Society of Canada*, 2nd series, vol. 5, sec. 2, 1899. Lighthall's monograph represents the state of scholarly thinking in the late 19th century about the Mohawk connection to Hochelaga.

[22]   Horn, K., *Mohawk Nation News*, November 9, 2006.

[23]   Deer, T., The Wampum Chronicles Messageboard, November 15, 2006. (No longer online.)

[24]   Rice, B., *Evidence of What Happened to the Saint Lawrence Iroquoians from the Oral Traditions of the Rotinonshonni and Anishnabé*, unpublished manuscript, 2007.

[25]   Ibid.

[26]   Ibid.

[27]   For more on the St. Lawrence Iroquoians, see: Pendergast, J. F., "The Confusing Identities Attributed to Stadacona nd Hochelaga," *Journal of Canadian Studies*, Trent University, Peterborough, Winter, 1998, p 149-167; Pendergast, J. F., "The Ottawa River Algonquin Bands in a St. Lawrence Iroquoian Context," *Canadian Journal of Archaeology*, no. 23, Canadian Archaeological Association, 1999, p. 63-136; Englebrecht, W., "The Case of the Disappearing Iroquoians: Early Contact Period Superpower Politics," *Northeast Anthropology*, no. 50,

Institute for Archaeological Studies, State University of New York at Albany, Albany, 1995, p. 35-59.

28 Champlain, S. de., *Voyages of Samuel de Champlain*, vol. 2, 1604-1610, Slafter, E. F., ed., Prince Society, Boston, 1878. Slafter's endnotes give this name as *Caniaderiguaronte*. Teyowisonte, who provided me with the standardized Mohawk rendering of this name, suggests that the literal translation is probably more like "there is a hole of water." *Kaniá:tare Kahnhokà:ronte* is also given for Lake Champlain.

29 Champlain, S. de., *Voyages of Samuel de Champlain*, vol. 1, Otis, C. P., trans., Prince Society, Boston, 1880, p. 236. Found online at Project Gutenburg, www.gutenburg.com/etext/6643.

30 Ibid., p. 238.

31 Champlain, S. de., *Voyages of Samuel de Champlain*, vol. 2, Otis, C. P., trans., Prince Society, Boston, 1878, p. 215. Found online at Project Gutenburg, www.gutenburg.com/etext/6749.

32 Ibid., p. 217.

33 Ibid., p. 217-218.

34 Ibid., p. 218-219.

35 Ibid., p. 219.

36 Ibid., p. 220.

37 Ibid., p. 220-221.

38 Ibid., p. 221-222.

39 Parkman, F., *The Parkman Reader: From the Works of Francis Parkman*, Morisen, S. E., ed., Little, Brown and Company, Boston & Toronto, 1955, p. 150. Text of Parkman's *Pioneers of France in the New World* found online at Project Gutenburg, www.gutenburg.com/etext/3721.

40 Fenton, Ibid., p. 243.

41 Dennis, M., *Cultivating a Landscape of Peace: Iroquois-European Encounters in Seventeenth Century America*, Cornell University Press, Ithica, 1993, p. 69.

42 Klinck, C. F., and Talman, J. J., *The Journal of Major John Norton, 1816*, The Champlain Society, Toronto, 1970, p. 198-199.

43 Ibid., footnote, p. 199.

44 Rice, B., *The Great Epic: The Rotinonshonni Through the Eyes of Teharonhia:wako and Sawiskera*, PhD dissertation. Found online at www.wampumchronicles.com/sawiskera1.html. Rice's depiction of the event has the Mohawk chiefs approaching Champlain's allies with wampum strings held out in a peaceful greeting.

45 Clark, Ibid., p. 57.

46 Ron'sharón:ni means "They Are Knife Makers" and refers to the Dutch. The noun root for knife is {-a'shar-}. *?:share'* means knife.

47 This is given as *Te-non-an-at-che* in Hislop, C., *The Mohawk*, Rinehart & Company, Inc., New York/Toronto, 1948, p. 3.

48 Beauchamp, W. M., "A History of the New York Iroquois, Now Commonly Called the Six Nations," *New York State Museum Bulletin 78*, Archaeology 9, New York State Education Department, Albany, 1905, p. 149.

49 Hunt, G. T., *The Wars of the Iroquois: A Study in International Trade Relations*,

University of Wisconsin Press, Madison, 1940, p. 26.

50   Gehring, C. T, and Starna, W. A., "Dutch and Indians in the Hudson Valley: The Early Period," *The Hudson Valley Regional Review*, Hudson River Valley Institute, Marist College, Poughkeepsie, September, 1992, p. 15.

51   Van Laer, A. J. F., trans. and ed., *Van Rensselaer Bowier Manuscripts*, New York State Library, University of the State of New York, Albany, 1908, p. 302. Gehring and Starna mention the same document in their HVRR article but quote from a more recent translation. The questions are numbered in the Van Laer publication, but numbering is omitted here.

52   Ibid., p. 303-304.

53   *Minutes of the Provincial Council of Pennsylvania*, Harrisburg, 1851, vol. 4, p. 707.

54   Michelson, Ibid., p. 113. Translation by my Mohawk informants.

55   *Minutes*, Ibid., p. 707.

56   Michelson, Ibid., p. 113. It is common today to hear Mohawks use the term "Kaswentha" when talking about the Two Row, but it is not of Mohawk origin and is a term borrowed from either the Seneca or the Onondaga.

57   Hill, R. "Oral Memory of the Haudenosaunee: Views of the Two Row Wampum," *Northeast Indian Quarterly*, Cornell University, Ithaca, Spring, 1990, p. 26-27.

58   Muller, K. V., "The Two 'Mystery' Belts of Grand River: A Biography of the Two Row Wampum and the Friendship Belt," *The American Indian Quarterly*, vol. 31, no.1, University of Nebraska Press, 2007, p. 129-164. Muller was able to find the Two Row metaphor cited in various speeches, but not specifically associated with the belt itself.

59   Petition of the Iroquois of St. Regis to Her Majesty the Queen, June 21st, 1892. National Archives Canada, RG-10, vol. 2330, file 63,812-2. This document appears to be an attachment to a letter dated May 21, 1900, along with a list of chiefs dated October 24, 1895. All three are typed and stamped with the number 224462.

60   Jennings, F., Fenton, W. N., Druke, M. A., and Miller, D. R., eds., *The History and Culture of Iroquois Diplomacy: An Interdisciplinary Guide to the Treaties of the Six Nations and Their League*, Syracuse University Press, Syracuse, 1985, p. 158.

61   Lenig, W., "Patterns of Material Culture During the Early Years of New Netherland Trade," *Northeast Anthropology*, no. 58, Institute for Archaeological Studies, State University of New York at Albany, Albany, 1999, p. 55.

62   Snow, D. R., Gehring, C. T., and Starna, W. A., eds., *In Mohawk Country: Early Narratives about a Native People*, Syracuse University Press, Syracuse, 1996, p. 3.

63   Ibid., p. 8.

64   Ibid.

65   Ibid., p. 9.

66   Richter, D. K., *The Ordeal of the Longhouse: The Peoples of the Iroquois League in the Era of European Colonization*, University of North Carolina Press, Chapel Hill and London, 1992, p. 60-61.

67   Thwaites, R. G., ed., *The Jesuit Relations and Allied Documents*, vol. 30, The Burrows Brothers, Cleveland, 1896-1900, p. 229.

68   Marshall, J., trans. and ed., *Word from New France: The Selected Letters of Marie*

de l'Incarnation, Oxford University Press, Toronto, 1967, p. 82.

69 Thwaites, R. G., ed., *The Jesuit Relations and Allied Documents*, vol. 58, The Burrows Brothers, Cleveland, 1896-1900, p. 215-217.

70 Thwaites, R. G., ed., *The Jesuit Relations and Allied Documents*, vol. 45, The Burrows Brothers, Cleveland, 1896-1900, p. 205-207. Tribal names in brackets do not appear in the *Jesuit Relations* but are found in Snow, Gehring, and Starna (1996).

71 Thwaites, R. G., ed., *The Jesuit Relations and Allied Documents*, vol. 33, The Burrows Brothers, Cleveland, 1896-1900, p. 125-127.

72 Thwaites, R. G., ed., *The Jesuit Relations and Allied Documents*, vol. 41, The Burrows Brothers, Cleveland, 1896-1900, p. 87-89.

73 Snow, Gehring and Starna, Ibid., p. 110-112.

74 Ibid., p. 112.

75 Ibid., p. 112-113.

76 Personal communication, May 7, 2008.

77 Jordan, K. A., "Seneca Iroquois Settlement Pattern, Community Structure, and Housing, 1677-1779," *Northeast Anthropology*, no. 67, Institute for Archaeological Studies, State University of New York at Albany, Albany, 2004, p. 36.

78 Snow, D. R., *Mohawk Valley Archaeology: The Sites*, Occasional Papers in Archaeology, no. 23, Matson Museum of Anthropology, The Pennsylvania State University, University Park, 1995, p. 471-473.

79 For more on bark longhouses, see: Snow, D. R., "The Architecture of Iroquois Longhouses," *Northeast Anthropology*, no. 53, Institute for Archaeological Studies, State University of New York at Albany, Albany, 1997, p. 61-84; Kapches, M., "The Iroquoian Longhouse: Architectural and Cultural Identity," *Archaeology of the Iroquois: Selected Readings & Research Sources*, Kerber, J. E., ed., Syracuse University Press, Syracuse, 2007, p. 174-188.

80 Snow, Gehring and Starna, Ibid., p. 126.

81 Ibid., p. 126-127.

82 Ibid., p. 127.

83 Ibid., p. 127-128.

84 Ibid., p. 128-129.

85 Ibid., p. 44-45.

86 Ibid., p. 45.

87 Radisson, P. E., *Voyages of Peter Esprit Radisson: being and account of his travels and experiences among the North American Indians from 1652 to 1684*, Scull, G. D., ed., Prince Society, Boston, 1885, p. 115. For legibility, I have taken the liberty of revising the source. The original text is as follows: "Instantly comes a shower of raine wth a storme of winde that was able to perish us by reason of the great quantity of watter that came into our boat. The lake began to vapour and make a show of his neptune's sheep. Seeing we went backwards rather then forwards, we thought ourselves uterly lost. That rogue that was with me sayd, "See thy God that thou sayest he is above. Will you make me believe now that he is good, as the black-coats [the ffather Jesuits] say? They doe lie, and you see the contrary; ffor first you see that the sun burns us often, the raine wetts us,

the wind makes us have shipwrake, the thundering, the lightnings burns and kills, and all come from above, and you say that it's good to be there. For my part I will not goe there. Contrary they say that the reprobats and guilty goeth downe & burne. They are mistaken; all is goode heare. Doe not you see the earth that nourishes all living creatures, the water the fishes, and the yus, and that corne and all other seasonable fruits for our foode, wch things are not soe contrary to us as that from above?" As he said so he coursed vehemently after his owne maner. He tooke his instruments & shewed them to the heavens, saying, "I will not be above; here will [I] stay on earth, where all my friends are, and not wth the french, that are to be burned above wth torments."

88   Grassmann, T., *The Mohawk Indians and Their Valley, Being a Chronological Documentary Record to the End of 1693*, (self-published), 1969.

89   Snow, *Mohawk*, Ibid.

90   Ibid., p. 365.

91   Ibid., p. 367-369.

92   Rumrill, D. A., "An Interpretation and Analysis of the Seventeenth Century Mohawk Nation: Its Chronology and Movements," *The Bulletin and Journal of Archaeology for New York State*, no. 9, New York State Archaeological Association, Spring, 1985, p. 18-21.

93   Van Laer, A. J. F., trans. and ed., *Minutes of the Court of Fort Orange and Beverwyck, 1657-1660*, vol. 2, The University of the State of New York, Albany, 1923, p. 45.

94   Ibid., p. 47-48.

95   Ibid., p. 211-212. Each paragraph of the speech was numbered in the Van Laer publication. I have chosen to omit the numbers for this and the following quote.

96   Ibid., p. 213.

97   Ibid.

98   Ibid., p. 213-214.

99   Ibid., p. 215. I have omitted the paragraph numbering for this and the following quote.

100   Ibid., p. 217.

101   Ibid., p. 217-218.

102   Ibid., p. 218.

103   Ibid., p. 268-269.

104   Greer, A., *Mohawk Saint: Catherine Tekakwitha and the Jesuits*, Oxford University Press, New York City, 2005, p. xi.

105   *The Positio of the Historical Section of the Sacred Congregation of Rites on the Introduction of The Cause for the Beatification and Canonization and on the Virtues of the Servant of God Katharine Tekakwitha, The Lily of the Mohawks*, Fordham University Press, New York City, 1940.

106   Greer, Ibid., p. 208. Greer calls the *Positio* translations "imperfect," and provides his own translations for the original texts throughout his book. As of this writing, Montréal scholar Diego Paoletti is also in the process of translating the Cholenec and Chauchetière biographies, the results of which are posted at his website, The Life of Catherine Tekakwitha. Found online at http://www.thelifeofkateritekakwitha.net.

107 *Positio*, Ibid., p. 241-242.

108 The "French original" I refer to is the text posted at Diego Paoletti's above-mentioned website. I have not consulted Cholenec's actual document but am relying on Mr. Paoletti's transcription.

109 *Positio*, Ibid., p. 242.

110 Ibid., p. 120-121.

111 Kateri Dream Catchers website,
http://www.christiantelegraph.com/issue1695.html.

112 Brandão, J. A., *"Your fyre shall burn no more"*: *Iroquois Policy toward New France and Its Native Allies to 1701*, University of Nebraska Press, Lincôln and London, 1997, p. 148.

113 *Positio*, Ibid., p. 121-122.

114 Ibid., p. 123.

115 Ibid., p. 123-124.

116 Ibid., p. 125.

117 Marshall, Ibid., p. 288.

118 Ibid.

119 Ibid., p. 289.

120 Thwaites, R. G., ed., *The Jesuit Relations and Allied Documents*, vol. 46, The Burrows Brothers, Cleveland, 1896-1900, p. 241.

121 Thwaites, R. G., ed., *The Jesuit Relations and Allied Documents*, vol. 49, The Burrows Brothers, Cleveland, 1896-1900, p. 137-139.

122 Ibid., p. 145.

123 Ibid., p. 147.

124 Colden, C., *The History of the Five Indian Nations Depending on the Province of New-York in America*, Cornell University Press, Ithica and London, 1958, p. 16.

125 O'Callaghan, E. B., ed., *Documents Relative to the Colonial History of the State of New-York*, vol. 3, Weed, Parsons and Company, Albany, 1853-1887, p. 152. For legibility, I have taken the liberty of revising this source. The original text is as follows: "In answer to Yo[r] letter of the 31st of August I shall tell you that Mons[r] de Courcelle, Governor General of this Countrey signifying to mee that hee had a desire to make inroad upon the Maquaes, to put a stopp to their barbarous Insolencies; I gave my consent to further design, That hee might take with him so many Officers and Souldiers as hee thought fit, either of his Maties Companyes, or those of ye Countrey. Whereupon hee advanced within ffifteene or twenty leageus of the Villages of ye Anniés. But fortunately for them his Guides conducting him a wrong way. Hee did not meete with them, till hee came neare the Village which you name in yor Letter, Neither had hee known there was any of them there, untill hee had surpriz'd all the Indyans that were in two small Hutts at some distance from that place. This truth is sufficiently convincing, to justify Monsr de Courcelle, that hee had no intention to infringe the Peace that was then betweene us, for that he thought himselfe in the Maquaes land. The Moderâcon which he used in the said hutts (although the Persons under his command were driven to the uttermost extremity, for want of Provisions) hath sufficiently manifested the consideracôn wee have alwayes had for our allyes (for untill then wee had no Intelligence, that New

Holland was under any other Dominion then that of the States of the United Belgick Provinces) and understanding that hee was upon the Lands belonging to the Dutch, hee tooke great care to hinder his Companyes from falling into the Village, by which meanes he alone the Maquaes that were there saved themselves."

126   Charlevoix, P. F. X., *History and General Description of New France*, vol. 3, Shea, J. G., trans., Francis P. Harper, New York, 1900, p.87.

127   Lowensteyn, P., *The Role of Chief Canaqueese in the Iroquois Wars*. Found online at http://www.lowensteyn.com/iroquois/canaqueese.html.

128   Charlevoix, Ibid., p.87-88.

129   Not all sources agree on the particulars of Agariata's execution. See: Grassmann, T., "Agariata," in *Dictionary of Canadian Biography*, vol. 1, University of Toronto Press, Toronto, 1974, p. 40-41.

130   Thwaites, R. G., ed., *The Jesuit Relations and Allied Documents*, vol. 50, The Burrows Brothers, Cleveland, 1896-1900, p. 199.

131   Ibid., p. 139-141.

132   Marshall, Ibid., p. 256-257.

133   Ibid., p. 317-318.

134   Ibid., p. 319-320.

135   Ibid., p.322-323.

136   Thwaites, Ibid., p. 143.

137   Marshall, Ibid., p. 323.

138   Thwaites, Ibid., p. 143-145.

139   Marshall, Ibid., p. 323-325.

140   Ibid., p. 325

141   Ibid., p. 326.

142   Ibid., p. 327.

143   Ibid., p. 327-328.

144   Rumrill, Ibid., p. 25-26.

145   Ibid., p. 26-27.

146   Ibid., p. 29.

147   Snow, Ibid., p. 416-419.

148   Thwaites, R. G., *The Jesuit Relations and Allied Documents*, vol. 51, The Burrows Brothers, Cleveland, 1896-1900, p. 185-187.

149   Ibid., p. 187-201.

150   Ibid., p. 201-205.

151   Ibid., p. 205-209.

152   Thwaites, R. G., *The Jesuit Relations and Allied Documents*, vol. 53, The Burrows Brothers, Cleveland, 1896-1900, p. 137.

153   Ibid., p. 149.

154   Ibid., p. 213.

155   Thwaites, R. G., *The Jesuit Relations and Allied Documents*, vol. 63, The Burrows Brothers, Cleveland, 1896-1900, p. 149-151.

156   Thwaites, R. G., ed., *The Jesuit Relations and Allied Documents*, vol. 57, The Burrows Brothers, Cleveland, 1896-1900, p. 69-71.

157   *Positio*, Ibid., p. 122-123.

158   Ibid., p. 135.

159   Ibid., p. 345.

160   Ibid., p. 135-136.

161   Ibid., p. 78-79.

162   Ibid., p. 137-138. The Mohawk form of Katharine is Káteri, which is pro-
      nounced phonetically as either Guh-deh-REE (Kahnawà:ke) or Guh-deh-LEE
      (Ahkwesáhsne). Tekahkwí:tha is pronounced Deh-gah-GWEE-tah in both
      dialects.

163   Béchard, H., *The Original Caughnawaga Indians*, International Publishers,
      Montreal, 1976, p. 83. Another form of Atahsà:ta would be *Atahsénhtha*, or
      "He Befalls."

164   Thwaites, Ibid., vol. 63, p. 177-179.

165   *Positio*, Ibid., p. 247.

166   Ibid., p. 139-140.

167   Ibid., p. 351.

168   The version of Cholenec's full biography published in the *Positio* leaves this
      incident out, but the French text posted on Diego Paoletti's website as well as
      his English translation includes the incident in much the same language as the
      Cholenec text I have quoted in my narrative.

169   Ibid., p. 140-141.

170   Ibid., p. 79-80.

171   Ibid., p. 142.

172   Found online at Wikipedia, the Free Encyclopedia,
      http://en.wikipedia.org/wiki/Fleur-de-lis.

173   Thwaites, Ibid., vol. 46, p. 241.

174   Ibid.

175   *Positio*, Ibid., p. 247-248.

176   Ibid., p. 80.

177   Ibid., p. 151-152.

178   Leder, L. H., ed., *The Livingston Indian Records, 1666-1723*, The Pennsylvania
      Historical Association, Gettysburgh, 1956, p. 45-46. For legibility, I have taken
      the liberty of revising the source. The original text is as follows: "They Say
      with a presnte wee are glad yᵗ yᵉ Kinges Governoʳˢ of MaryLand and Virginia
      have sent you hither to Speak with the Maquess as Alsoo yᵗ yᵉ Goveʳ: Genˡˡ:
      hath bein pleased to destinat & appoynt this place to Speak wᵗʰ all Nations in
      peace finding this fitt place for yᵉ Same, ffor wᶜʰ we doe return his honnʳ hartie
      Thankes, Especially yᵗ his honnoʳ hath bein pleased to Grant you yᵉ Priviledge
      for to Speak wᵗʰ us heir Seing that the Govʳ: Genˡˡ: & wee are one, and one
      hart and one head, for the Covenant that is betwixt ye Govʳ: Genˡˡ: and us is
      Inviolable yea so strong yᵗ if yᵉ very Thunder should break upon yᵉ Covenant
      Chayn it wold not break it in Sunder, wee are Lykwyes glad that we have hared
      you Speak and now we shall ansr. yt in case any of or Indians Should Injur any
      Christians or Indians in yoʳ parts or yoʳ Christians or Indians doe any damnage
      to oʳ Indians wee desyre yᵗ on both Syds the mattoʳ May be Composed, and
      that wᶜʰ is past to be burred in oblivion. They Say further that yᵉ Seneks war

upon thar Jorney to com hither wth six hunderd Men Bot ffor fear Turned back agane Bot wee ware not affrayed to Com heir doe give that upon ane drest Elk Skin and one Beaver."

179 *Positio*, Ibid., p. 152-153.

180 Ibid., p. 153.

181 Ibid., p. 248.

182 Walworth, E. H., *The Life and Times of Kateri Tekakwitha, The Lily of the Mohawks*, Peter Paul & Brother, Buffalo, 1891, p. 186.

183 Paoletti, Ibid., *The voyage of Catherine Tekakwitha to the Mission of Saint Francis Xavier at the Sault, autumn1677 (between the end of September to October)*, The Life of Catherine Tekakwitha website.

184 Broadhead, J. R., *History of the State of New York, First Period, 1609-1664*, Harper & Brothers, New York, 1853, p. 422. My language informants sometimes differ slightly in their standardizations. Teyowisonte gives the name for Lake George as *Kania'tarókte*.

185 Thwaites, Ibid., vol. 51, p. 181-183.

186 Colden, Ibid., p. 15-17.

187 O'Callaghan, Edmund B., ed., *Documents Relative to the Colonial History of the State of New York*, vol. 7, Weed, Parsons and Company, Albany, 1853-1857, p. 573.

188 Beauchamp, W. M., "Aboriginal Place Names of New York," *New York State Museum Bulletin* 108, State University of New York, Albany, May, 1907, p. 73-74. See also: Day, Gordon M., "The Eastern Boundary of Iroquoia: Abenaki Evidence," *Man in the Northeast*, vol. 1, Institute for Archaeological Studies, State University of New York at Albany, Albany, 1971, p. 11-12.

189 Paoletti, Ibid.

190 Thwaites, R. G., ed., *The Jesuit Relations and Allied Documents*, vol. 60, The Burrows Brothers, Cleveland, 1896-1900, p. 275.

191 Thwaites, Ibid., vol. 63, p. 191.

192 Thwaites, R. G., ed., *The Jesuit Relations and Allied Documents*, vol. 62, The Burrows Brothers, Cleveland, 1896-1900, p. 167.

193 A12012-351, National Air Photo Library, Natural Resources Canada.

194 Devine, E. J., *Historic Caughnawaga*, The Messenger Press, Montreal, 1922.

195 Jury, W., "Caughnawaga's Fourth Site," *Kateri*, vol. 9, no. 1, Kateri Tekakwitha Center, Caughnawaga, 1956, p. 6-9. This village was located on the banks of the Suzanne River where it met the St. Lawrence. The third village, *Kahnawá:kon*, or "In the Rapids," was located halfway between the second and fourth village at the modern-day Récréo-Parc Ste-Catherine.

196 Béchard, Ibid., and Greer, Ibid. Although both books cite the drawings as having come from Archives départementales de la Gironde, H Jésuites, the drawings in Béchard are significantly different from those that appear in Greer.

197 Thwaites, Ibid., vol. 60, p. 275.

198 *Positio*, Ibid., p. 153-154.

199 Ibid., p. 249.

200 Thwaites, Ibid., p. 277-285.

201 Thwaites, Ibid., vol. 63, p. 193-195.

202   *Positio*, Ibid., p. 251.
203   *Positio*, Ibid., p. 249-250.
204   Ibid., p. 169-170.
205   Ibid., p. 194.
206   Ibid., p. 251.
207   Ibid., p. 358.
208   Ibid., p. 255-256.
209   Ibid., p. 291-292.
210   Ibid., p. 256.
211   Ibid., p. 81.
212   Ibid., p. 81-82.
213   Ibid., p. 210.
214   Ibid., p. 177.
215   Ibid., p. 358-359.
216   Ibid., p. 193-194.
217   Ibid., p. 260-261.
218   Ibid., p. 262-263.
219   Ibid., p. 263-264.
220   Ibid., p. 265-266.
221   This quote is taken from Diego Paoletti's translation, available on his website.
222   Béchard, Ibid, p. 159-161.
223   *Positio*, Ibid., p. 267-271.
224   Ibid., p. 271-272.
225   Ibid., p. 273.
226   Ibid., p. 274-275.
227   Ibid., p. 275-276.
228   Ibid., p. 365.
229   Ibid., p. 276-277.
230   Ibid., p. 278-279.
231   Ibid., p. 280.
232   Thwaites, Ibid, vol. 45, p. 211-213.
233   Ibid., p. 183.
234   Ibid., p. 282-283.
235   Ibid., p. 286.
236   Ibid., p. 182.
237   Ibid.
238   Ibid., p. 181.
239   Ibid., p. 178.
240   Ibid., p. 183-184.
241   Ibid., p. 184-185.
242   Ibid., p. 185.
243   Ibid., p. 293.
244   Thwaites, Ibid., vol. 63, p. 201-205.
245   *Positio*, Ibid., p. 175.

246   My language consultant offered this interpretation with the caveat that the Mohawk and Huron languages were too different to know for sure.

247   Ibid., p. 176.

248   Ibid., p. 293-294.

249   Ibid., p. 294.

250   Ibid., p. 182.

251   Thwaites, Ibid., p. 205.

252   *Positio*, Ibid., p. 281-282.

253   Ibid., p. 292.

254   Ibid., p. 182-183.

255   This information was provided by Diego Paoletti to *Lily of the Mohawks*, vol. 19, no. 2, Blessed Kateri Tekakwitha League, Auriesville, NY, 2005, p. 4.

256   Ibid., p. 199-200.

257   Ibid., p. 177-178.

258   Ibid., p. 177.

259   Béchard, H., *Kaia'tanó':ron Kateri Tekahkwitha*, Kateri Center, Kahnawà:ke, 1994, p. 111.

260   *Positio*, Ibid, p. 370-371.

261   Ibid., p. 288.

262   Ibid., p. 371.

263   Ibid., p. 294.

264   Ibid., p. 189-190.

265   Béchard, *Original*, Ibid., p. 57, 181-189, 191-198.

266   Cholenec, P. "Of Two Other Women," *Kateri*, no. 70, Caughnawaga, September 1966, p.8-9.

267   *Positio*, Ibid., p. 294-295.

268   Ibid., p. 187.

269   Ibid., p. 195.

270   Ibid., p. 300.

271   Ibid., p. 301.

272   Ibid., p. 201.

273   Ibid., p. 202.

274   Ibid.

275   Ibid., p. 203.

276   Ibid., p. 298.

277   Ibid., p. 304-305.

278   Ibid., p. 302.

279   Cholenec, P. "Excerpt from a Letter of Father Cholenec...on the Death of a Holy Indian Maiden, Written on the First Day of May, 1680," *Kateri*, no. 64, Caughnawaga, March, 1965, p. 7-10. This source names her as Kateri but the original French, published in Henri Béchard's *L'Héroïque Indienne Kateri Tekakwitha* (1980) gives her name as Catherine.

280   Ibid., p. 84-85.

281   Ibid., p. 204-205.

282   Ibid., p. 305-306.

283 Ibid., p. 306-307.

284 Ibid., p. 376.

285 Ibid., p. 438. The passages quoted here are taken from the *Positio*.

286 Weiser, F. X., *Kateri Tekakwitha*, Kateri Center, Caughnawaga, 1972, p. 160.

287 Bunson, M. R., *Kateri Tekakwitha: Mystic of the Wilderness*, Our Visiting Sister Publishing Division, Huntington, 1992, p. 121.

288 Fisher, L. M., *Kateri Tekakwitha: The Lily of the Mohawks*, Pauline Books & Media, Boston, 1996, p. 119.

289 *Positio*, Ibid., p. 205.

290 Ibid., p. 303.

291 Ibid., p. 307.

292 Ibid., p. 206.

293 Ibid., p. 303.

294 Ibid., p. 306.

295 Ibid., p. 86-87.

296 Greer, Ibid., p. 5.

297 *Positio*, Ibid., p. 311.

298 Ibid., p. 311-312. Cholenec mentioned Chauchetière by name in his original, but as we have seen, the editor of the *Positio* often eliminated names that were mentioned in the texts.

299 Ibid., p. 87-88.

300 This is a new translation of the French text of Pierre Cholenec's manuscript available at Paoletti's website.

301 *Positio*, Ibid., p. 313.

302 Ibid., p. 407.

303 Ibid., p. 115-116.

304 Richter, Ibid., p. 127.

305 "Don't Be Afraid!" *Kateri*, vol. 3, no. 4, Kateri Tekakwitha Center, Caughnawaga, 1951, p. 8-9.

306 *Positio*, Ibid., p. 290-291.

307 Ibid., p. 407-408.

308 Ibid., p. 90.

309 Thwaites, Ibid., vol. 63, p. 215-217.

310 Ibid., p. 217.

311 Ibid., p. 219.

312 Ibid., p. 219-221.

313 Ibid., p. 221.

314 Ibid., p. 223.

315 Found online at http://en.wikipedia.org/wiki/Kirch's_Comet.

316 Thwaites, Ibid., vol. 62, p. 169-173.

317 Ibid., p. 183.

318 Ibid., p. 185.

319 *Positio*, Ibid., p. 406.

320 Thwaites, Ibid., vol. 63, p. 229.

321 *Positio*, Ibid., p. 312-313. The identity of the priests is taken from the English

translation of Cholenec's text at Diego Paoletti's website and confirmed by the french version that he has also made available.

322   I have taken the liberty of revising Paoletti's English translation of this text. The Great Mohawk's gift is also mentioned in Thwaites, vol. 63, p. 231.

323   Thwaites, Ibid., p. 231-233.

324   Ibid., p. 233-235.

325   Ibid., p. 235-237.

326   Ibid., p. 241.

327   Ibid., p. 243.

328   Ibid., p. 241-243.

329   O'Callaghan, E. B., ed., *Documents Relative to the Colonial History of the State of New-York*, vol. 9, Weed, Parsons and Company, Albany, 1853-1857, p.239-243.

330   Ibid., p. 239.

331   Thwaites, Ibid., p. 243.

332   Béchard, *Original*, Ibid., p. 124.

333   O'Callaghan, Ibid., p. 474.

334   Paoletti calls him a Mohawk in his English translation, but the original French version identifies him as a Huron. For this translation, I have restored the French forms of the Christian names mentioned in the original.

335   Thwaites, R. G., *The Jesuit Relations and Allied Documents*, vol. 64, The Burrows Brothers, Cleveland, 1896-1900, p. 129.

336   Matthew 24:6, King James Bible.

337   *Positio*, Ibid., p. 334.

338   Béchard, *Kaia'tanó':ron*, Ibid., p. 174.

339   *Positio*, Ibid., p. 331-332.

340   O'Callaghan, Ibid., p. 550.

341   Ibid., p. 551.

342   *Positio*, Ibid., p. 332-333.

343   Ibid., p. 333-334.

344   O'Callaghan, E. B., ed., *Documents Relative to the Colonial History of the State of New-York*, vol. 4, Weed, Parsons and Company, Albany, 1853-1857, p. 648.

345   Ibid., p. 649.

346   Teyowisonte informs me that Kanatakwén:ke actually translates as "Opening in the Village" or "Near the Village."

347   "Tercentenary of a Belt," *Kateri*, no. 11 (vol. 29, no. 4), Kateri Center, Caughnawaga, Autumn, 1977, p. 18-19.

348   Blanchard, D., "…To the Other Side of the Sky: Catholicism at Kahnawake, 1667-1700," *Anthropologica*, vol. 24, The Canadian Research Centre for Anthropology, Saint Paul University, Ottawa, 1982, p. 99.

349   Richter, D. K., "Iroquois versus Iroquois: Jesuit Missions and Christianity in Village Politics, 1642-1686," *Ethnohistory*, vol. 32, no. 1, American Society for Ethnohistory, Duke University Press, Durham, Winter, 1985, p. 1-16.

350   Richter, *Ordeal*, Ibid.

351   Richter, D. K., *Facing East from Indian Country: A Native History of Early America*, Harvard University Press, Cambridge, Massachusetts, & London,

2001, p. 85.

352   Ibid., p. 88.

353   Ibid., p. 89.

354   Steckley, J. "The Warrior and the Lineage: Jesuit Use of Iroquoian Images to Communicate Christianity," *Ethnohistory*, vol. 39, no. 4, American Society for Ethnohistory, Duke University Press, Durham, Autumn, 1992, p. 476.

355   Ibid., p. 503.

356   Ibid., p. 489.

357   Koppedrayer, K. I., "The Making of the First Iroquois Virgin: Early Jesuit Biographies of the Blessed Kateri Tekakwitha," *Ethnohistory*, vol. 40, no. 2, American Society for Ethnohistory, Duke University Press, Durham, Spring, 1993, p. 296. Allan Greer would build upon this theme in his 2005 book, *Mohawk Saint*, cited previously.

358   Shoemaker, N., "Kateri Tekakwitha's Tortuous Path to Sainthood," *Negotiators of Change: Historical Perspectives on Native American Women*, Routledge, New York, 1995, p. 66.

359   Hart, W. B., "'The kindness of the blessed Virgin': faith, succor, and the cult of Mary among Christian Hurons and Iroquois in seventeenth century New France," *Spiritual Encounters: Interaction between Christianity and native religions in colonial America*, University of Nebraska Press, Lincoln, 1999, p. 74.

360   Klinck and Talman, Ibid., p. 91.

361   Greer refers to Káteri as Catherine throughout his book and contends that the name Káteri—a Mohawk version of her Christian name—was popularized in 1891 by author E. H. Walworth in an atmosphere of turn-of-the-century primitivism. While this may be true in the non-native world, Mohawks have been using their own versions of Christian names all along, Káteri being one of them. The Mohawk version of John, *Sawatis*, actually derives from *baptist*, as in John the Baptist.

362   Greer, Ibid., p. 200.

363   It will be impossible to repatriate all of her remains. The Kahnawa'kehró:non who established the community of Ahkwesáhsne circa 1754 brought Káteri's skull with them. It was presumably lost in a fire that destroyed the chapel of the Mission of St. Jean-François Régis in 1762. Another relic of Káteri was stolen from a museum exhibit case at the Saint François Xavier Church in Kahnawà:ke in 2007.

364   Richter, Ibid., p. 81-83.

BIBLIOGRAPHY

Archival

National Air Photo Library, Natural Resources Canada, #A12012-351.

National Archives Canada, RG-10, vol. 2330, file 63,812-2, Petition of the Iroquois of St. Regis to Her Majesty the Queen, June 21st, 1892.

Publications

Beauchamp, W. M., "Wampum and Shell Articles Used by the New York Indians," *New York State Museum Bulletin* 41, vol. 8, University of the State of New York, Albany, 1901.

Beauchamp, W. M., "A History of the New York Iroquois, Now Commonly Called the Six Nations," *New York State Museum Bulletin* 78, Archaeology 9, New York State Education Department, Albany, 1905.

Beauchamp, W. M., "Aboriginal Place Names of New York," *New York State Museum Bulletin* 108, State University of New York, Albany, May, 1907.

Béchard, H., *The Original Caughnawaga Indians*, International Publishers, Montreal, 1976.

Béchard, H., *L'Héroïque Indienne Kateri Tekakwitha*, La Corporation des Éditions Fides, Montréal, 1980.

Béchard, H., *Kaia'tanó':ron Kateri Tekahkwitha*, Kateri Center, Kahnawà:ke, 1994.

Blanchard, D., *7 Generations: A History of the Kanienkehaka*, Kahnawake Survival School, Kahnawake, 1980.

Blanchard, D., "...To the Other Side of the Sky: Catholicism at Kahnawake, 1667-1700," *Anthropologica*, vol. 24, The Canadian Research Centre for Anthropology, Saint Paul University, Ottawa, 1982.

Brandão, J. A., *"Your fyre shall burn no more": Iroquois Policy toward New France and Its Native Allies to 1701*, University of Nebraska Press, Lincoln and London, 1997.

Broadhead, J. R., *History of the State of New York, First Period, 1609-1664*, Harper & Brothers, New York, 1853.

Bunson, M. R., *Kateri Tekakwitha: Mystic of the Wilderness*, Our Visiting Sister Publishing Division, Huntington, 1992.

Champlain, S. de., *Voyages of Samuel de Champlain*, vol. 2, 1604-1610, Slafter, E. F., ed., Prince Society, Boston, 1878.

Champlain, S. de., *Voyages of Samuel de Champlain*, 1878-1880, Otis, C. P., trans., Prince Society, Boston, 1880.

Charlevoix, P. F. X., *History and General Description of New France*, vol. 3, Shea, J. G., trans., Francis P. Harper, New York, 1900.

Cholenec, P. "Of Two Other Women," *Kateri*, no. 70, Caughnawaga, September 1966.

Cholenec, P. "Excerpt from a Letter of Father Cholenec…on the Death of a Holy Indian Maiden, Written on the First Day of May, 1680," *Kateri*, no. 64, Caughnawaga, March, 1965.

Clark, N. T., "The Thacher Wampum Belts of the New York State Museum," *New York State Museum Bulletin* 279, The University of the State of New York, Albany, 1929.

Colden, C., *The History of the Five Indian Nations Depending on the Province of New-York in America*, Cornell University Press, Ithica and London, 1958.

Cuoq, J. A., *Lexique de la Langue Iroquoise avec Notes et Appendices*, J. Chapleau & Fils, Montréal, 1882.

Day, Gordon M., "The Eastern Boundary of Iroquoia: Abenaki Evidence," *Man in the Northeast*, vol. 1, Institute for Archaeological Studies, State University of New York at Albany, Albany, 1971.

Dennis, M., *Cultivating a Landscape of Peace: Iroquois-European Encounters in Seventeenth Century America*, Cornell University Press, Ithica, 1993.

Devine, E. J., *Historic Caughnawaga*, The Messenger Press, Montreal, 1922.

Englebrecht, W., "The Case of the Disappearing Iroquoians: Early Contact Period Superpower Politics," *Northeast Anthropology*, no. 50, Institute for Archaeological Studies, State University of New York at Albany, Albany, 1995.

Fenton, W. N., *The Great Law and the Longhouse: A Political History of the Iroquois Confederacy*, University of Oklahoma Press, Norman, 1998.

Fisher, L. M., *Kateri Tekakwitha: The Lily of the Mohawks*, Pauline Books & Media, Boston, 1996.

Shenandoah, J. and George, D. M., *Skywoman: Legends of the Iroquois*, Clear Light Publishers, Santa Fe, 1998.

Gehring, C. T, and Starna, W. A., "Dutch and Indians in the Hudson Valley: The Early Period," *The Hudson Valley Regional Review*, Hudson River Valley Institute, Marist College, Poughkeepsie, September, 1992.

George-Kanentiio, D., *Iroquois Culture & Commentary*, Clear Light Publishers, Santa Fe, 2000.

Gibson, J. A., *Concerning the League: The Iroquois League Tradition as Dictated in Onondaga by John Arthur Gibson*, Memoir 9, Algonquin and Iroquoian Linguistics, Winnipeg, 1992.

Grassmann, T., *The Mohawk Indians and Their Valley, Being a Chronological Documentary Record to the End of 1693*, (self-published), 1969.

Grassmann, T., "Agariata," in *Dictionary of Canadian Biography*, vol. 1, University of Toronto Press, Toronto, 1974, p. 40-41.

Greer, A., *Mohawk Saint: Catherine Tekakwitha and the Jesuits*, Oxford University Press, New York City, 2005.

Hart, W. B., "'The kindness of the blessed Virgin': faith, succor, and the cult of Mary among Christian Hurons and Iroquois in seventeenth century New France," *Spiritual Encounters: Interaction between Christianity and native religions in colonial America*, University of Nebraska Press, Lincoln, 1999.

Hill, R. "Oral Memory of the Haudenosaunee: Views of the Two Row Wampum," *Northeast Indian Quarterly*, Cornell University, Ithaca, Spring, 1990.

Hislop, C., *The Mohawk*, Rinehart & Company, Inc., New York/Toronto, 1948.

Horn, K., *Mohawk Nation News*, November 9, 2006.

Howell, S., "Pointe a Calliere Rediscovers the Lost Iroquoian People," *The Montreal Gazette*, Montréal, November 17, 2006.

Hunt, G. T., *The Wars of the Iroquois: A Study in International Trade Relations*, University of Wisconsin Press, Madison, 1940.

Jennings, F., Fenton, W. N., Druke, M. A., and Miller, D. R., eds., *The History and Culture of Iroquois Diplomacy: An Interdisciplinary Guide to the Treaties of the Six Nations and Their League*, Syracuse University Press, Syracuse, 1985.

Jordan, K. A., "Seneca Iroquois Settlement Pattern, Community Structure, and Housing, 1677-1779," *Northeast Anthropology*, no. 67, Institute for Archaeological Studies, State University of New York at Albany, Albany, 2004.

Jury, W., "Caughnawaga's Fourth Site," *Kateri*, vol. 9, no. 1, Kateri Tekakwitha Center, Caughnawaga, 1956.

Kapches, M., "The Iroquoian Longhouse: Architectural and Cultural Identity," *Archaeology of the Iroquois: Selected Readings & Research Sources*, Kerber, J. E., ed., Syracuse University Press, Syracuse, 2007.

King James Bible.

Klinck, C. F., and Talman, J. J., *The Journal of Major John Norton, 1816*, The Champlain Society, Toronto, 1970.

Koppedrayer, K. I., "The Making of the First Iroquois Virgin: Early Jesuit Biographies of the Blessed Kateri Tekakwitha," *Ethnohistory*, vol. 40, no. 2, American Society for Ethnohistory, Duke University Press, Durham, Spring, 1993.

Leder, L. H., ed., *The Livingston Indian Records, 1666-1723*, The Pennsylvania Historical Association, Gettysburgh, 1956.

Lenig, W., "Patterns of Material Culture During the Early Years of New Netherland Trade," *Northeast Anthropology*, no. 58, Institute for Archaeological Studies, State University of New York at Albany, Albany, 1999.

Lighthall, W. D., "Hochelaga and Mohawks: A Link in Iroquois History," *Transactions of the Royal Society of Canada*, 2nd series, vol. 5, sec. 2, 1899.

Marshall, J., trans. and ed., *Word from New France: The Selected Letters of Marie de l'Incarnation*, Oxford University Press, Toronto, 1967.

Michelson, G., "Iroquoian Terms for Wampum," International Journal of American Linguistics, vol. 57, no. 1, 1991.

Minutes of the Provincial Council of Pennsylvania, Harrisburg, 1851, vol. 4.

Muller, K. V., "The Two 'Mystery' Belts of Grand River: A Biography of the Two Row Wampum and the Friendship Belt," *The American Indian Quarterly*, vol. 31, no.1, University of Nebraska Press, 2007.

Myers, M. "The Creation Story: The Sky World," *Traditional Teachings*, North American Indian Travelling College, Akwesasne, 1984.

O'Callaghan, E. B., ed., *Documents Relative to the Colonial History of the State of New-York*, Weed, Parsons and Company, Albany, 1853-1857.

Parker, A. C., "The Code of Handsome Lake, the Seneca Prophet," *New York State Museum Bulletin* 163, State University of New York, Albany, 1913, as reprinted in

Parker, A. C., *Parker on the Iroquois*, Syracuse University Press, Syracuse, 1968.

Parker, A. C. "The Constitution of the Five Nations or The Iroquois Book of the Great Law," *New York State Museum Bulletin* 184, State University of New York, Albany, 1916, (Iroqrafts reprint, 1991).

Parkman, F., *The Parkman Reader: From the Works of Francis Parkman*, Morisen, S. E., ed., Little, Brown and Company, Boston & Toronto, 1955.

Pendergast, J. F., and Trigger, B. G., *Cartier's Hochelaga and the Dawson Site*, McGill-Queens University Press, Montréal/London, 1972.

Pendergast, J. F., "The Confusing Identities Attributed to Stadacona nd Hochelaga," *Journal of Canadian Studies*, Trent University, Peterborough, Winter, 1998.

Pendergast, J. F., "The Ottawa River Algonquin Bands in a St. Lawrence Iroquoian Context," *Canadian Journal of Archaeology*, no. 23, Canadian Archaeological Association, 1999.

The Positio of the Historical Section of the Sacred Congregation of Rites on the Introduction of The Cause for the Beatification and Canonization and on the Virtues of the Servant of God Katharine Tekakwitha, The Lily of the Mohawks, Fordham University Press, New York City, 1940.

Radisson, P. E., *Voyages of Peter Esprit Radisson: being and account of his travels and experiences among the North American Indians from 1652 to 1684*, Scull, G. D., ed., Prince Society, Boston, 1885.

Rice, B., *Evidence of What Happened to the Saint Lawrence Iroquoians from the Oral Traditions of the Rotinonshonni and Anishnabé*, unpublished manuscript, 2007.

Richter, D. K., "Iroquois versus Iroquois: Jesuit Missions and Christianity in Village Politics, 1642-1686," *Ethnohistory*, vol. 32, no. 1, American Society for Ethnohistory, Duke University Press, Durham, Winter, 1985.

Richter, D. K., *The Ordeal of the Longhouse: The Peoples of the Iroquois League in the Era of European Colonization*, University of North Carolina Press, Chapel Hill and London, 1992.

Richter, D. K., *Facing East from Indian Country: A Native History of Early America*, Harvard University Press, Cambridge, Massachusetts, & London, 2001.

Rumrill, D. A., "An Interpretation and Analysis of the Seventeenth Century Mohawk Nation: Its Chronology and Movements," *The Bulletin and Journal of Archaeology for New York State*, no. 9, New York State Archaeological Association, Spring, 1985.

Shoemaker, N., "Kateri Tekakwitha's Tortuous Path to Sainthood," *Negotiators of Change: Historical Perspectives on Native American Women*, Routledge, New York, 1995.

Snow, D. R., *Mohawk Valley Archaeology: The Sites* and *Mohawk Valley Archaeology: The Collections*, Occasional Papers in Archaeology, no. 23, Matson Museum of Anthropology, The Pennsylvania State University, University Park, 1995.

Snow, D. R., Gehring, C. T., and Starna, W. A., eds., *In Mohawk Country: Early Narratives about a Native People*, Syracuse University Press, Syracuse, 1996.

Snow, D. R., "The Architecture of Iroquois Longhouses," *Northeast Anthropology*, no. 53, Institute for Archaeological Studies, State University of New York at Albany, Albany, 1997.

Steckley, J. "The Warrior and the Lineage: Jesuit Use of Iroquoian Images to Communicate Christianity," *Ethnohistory*, vol. 39, no. 4, American Society for Ethnohistory, Duke University Press, Durham, Autumn, 1992.

Tehanetorens, *Wampum Belts of the Iroquois*, (Reprint), Book Publishing Company, Summertown, 1999.

Thwaites, R. G., ed., *The Jesuit Relations and Allied Documents*, The Burrows Brothers, Cleveland, 1896-1900.

Unknown Author, *Lily of the Mohawks*, vol. 19, no. 2, Blessed Kateri Tekakwitha League, Auriesville, NY, 2005.

Unknown Author, "Tercentenary of a Belt," *Kateri*, no. 11 (vol. 29, no. 4), Kateri Center, Caughnawaga, Autumn, 1977.

Unknown Author, "Don't Be Afraid!" *Kateri*, vol. 3, no. 4, Kateri Tekakwitha Center, Caughnawaga, 1951.

Van Laer, A. J. F., trans. and ed., *Van Rensselaer Bowier Manuscripts*, New York State Library, University of the State of New York, Albany, 1908.

Van Laer, A. J. F., trans. and ed., *Minutes of the Court of Fort Orange and Beverwyck, 1657-1660*, vol. 2, The University of the State of New York, Albany, 1923.

Walworth, E. H., *The Life and Times of Kateri Tekakwitha, The Lily of the Mohawks*, Peter Paul & Brother, Buffalo, 1891.

Weiser, F. X., *Kateri Tekakwitha*, Kateri Center, Caughnawaga, 1972.

Websites

C/1680 V1. Found online at http://en.wikipedia.org/wiki/Kirch's_Comet.

Deer, T., The Wampum Chronicles Messageboard, November 15, 2006. (No longer online.)

"Fleur-de-lis," Wikipedia, http://en.wikipedia.org/wiki/Fleur-de-lis

Kateri Dream Catchers website, http://www.christiantelegraph.com/issue1695.html.

Lowensteyn, P., *The Role of Chief Canaqueese in the Iroquois Wars*, http://www.lowensteyn.com/iroquois/canaqueese.html

Paoletti, D., The Life of Catherine Tekakwitha, http://www.thelifeofkateritekakwitha.net

Rice, B., "*The Great Epic: The Rotinonshonni Through the Eyes of Teharonhia:wako and Sawiskera*," PhD dissertation, The Wampum Chronicles, http://www.wampum-chronicles.com/sawiskera1.html

Robinson, D. D., *Saint George, the Serpent and the Senecas*, 1994, http://www.crookedlakereview.com/articles/67_100/71feb1994/71robinson.html

"Wampum," NativeTech, http://www.nativetech.org/wampum/wamphist.htm

"Wampum," Wikipedia, http://en.wikipedia.org/wiki/Wampum

Appendix

The author is grateful to the New York State Museum for permission to take photographs and create illustrations from artifacts found in the Rumrill collection. Catalogue information is as follows:

Chapter 10

First Illustration:
A2005.13BJ.99.67.1-3/ metal axe and 2 axe eye fragments

Second Illustration:
A2005.13BJ.99.19.5/ metal effigy- lead, possible bird
A2005.13BJ.99.19.3/ metal effigy - lead, reminiscent of a bear and / or the legendary Piasa Bird
A2005.13BJ.99.19.8/ metal effigy - lead, possible turtle
A2005.13BJ.99.19.7/ metal effigy - lead, possible turtle
A2005.13BJ.99.19.1/ metal effigy - lead, in the shape of a cross
A2005.13BJ.99.19.4/ metal effigy - lead, possible Thunderbird
A2005.13BJ.99.19.6/ metal effigy - lead, possible turtle
A2005.13BJ.99.18.1/ medal - lead, reminiscent of Catholic medallion, ovoid, perforation broken
A2005.13.BJ.99.19.2/ metal effigy, lead, in the shape of a cross, broken, perforated

Third Illustration
A2005.13BJ.99.35/ Gun part - small bellied lock plate with main spring firelock upper flint vice jaws.
A2005.13BJ.99.45.1-5/ gun parts - vertical acting firelock sears fragments

Chapter 15

First Illustration:
A2005.13BJ.99.73.1-3/ metal utensils
A2005.13BJ.99.76/ miniature metal cup

Third Illustration:
A2005.13AX.99.019/ glass trade beads
A2005.13BW.99.73/ glass trade beads
A2005.13AU.99.52.1-139/ glass trade beads

Made in the USA
Monee, IL
20 October 2020